The

ESSENTIAL

BAR

BOOK

An A-to-Z GUIDE to
SPIRITS, COCKTAILS,
and WINE
with 115 RECIPES for
THE WORLD'S GREAT
DRINKS

JENNIFER FIEDLER

TEN SPEED PRESS
Berkeley

How to Use This Book

That cocktail renaissance has unleashed a tide of products on the market, both new and revived, is a good thing for discerning drinkers. But the ever-expanding mass of terms, classifications and specialized processes can be dizzying to even the most experienced among us.

This book is designed to help make sense of today's liquor shelves and bar menus, defining everything that savvy imbibers should need to know now. With an emphasis on the historical origins of ingredients, the definitions provided here in an A-to-Z format tackle everything from alcohol types to specialized liqueurs, equipment to instructions. Curious about that bottle of Old Tom Gin you found at your local market? Find the definition under "O," then learn about how it compares to London dry gin by reading the "Gin" entry.

Also included are recipes for 115 essential cocktails, the blocks on which contemporary bar programs are built. Whether you're looking to order confidently at the bar or build out your liquor shelf at home, the terms and recipes provided here should give you everything you need to fluently speak "bartender."

Cocktail Recipes

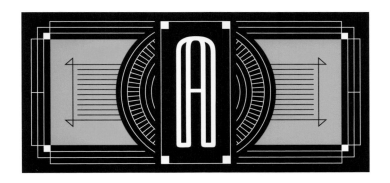

ABSINTHE

(n.) This boldly flavored spirit is flavored with a distinct mix of herbs and botanicals, most often anise, fennel, and wormwood. It is thought to have been created in France or Switzerland as a medicinal elixir and was first commercially produced in 1797 by what would become the Pernod company.

Most often associated with a bright-green color, absinthe is actually made in a variety of shades. Green absinthes are typically French, resulting from an extra maceration that draws chlorophyll from hyssop or other herbs, while Swiss versions are typically white and have less alcohol (note that "white" absinthes are generally clear in color). American absinthes, sometimes made with mint and verbena, tend toward a more natural brown-green color because distillers typically forgo stabilizers that preserve the hue.

With its distinctive flavor, absinthe became a signature component in certain classic cocktails such as the Sazerac and the Death in the Afternoon. It developed a larger-than-life reputation in the late nineteenth century for its supposed hallucinogenic properties, which would later be debunked as bad reactions to its super-high alcohol content. Perhaps

ABSINTHE FRAPPÉ

"AT the first cold sip on your fevered lip, you determine to live through the day." So went the ode "Absinthe Frappé" from the 1904 musical *It Happened in Nordland*. This drink hails from a time when absinthe was a highly popular apéritif (before its ban in 1912) and considered a morning pick-me-up. Simple, icy, and strong, the frappé is a less fussy alternative to the pomp and circumstance of traditional absinthe service.

Serves 1

1 ounce absinthe
¼–½ ounce simple syrup
   (1:1, sugar:water)
2 dashes anisette (optional)
1–2 ounces chilled water

Glassware: absinthe or rocks

Add all ingredients to a cocktail shaker. Add ice and shake until chilled. Pour into an absinthe or rocks glass over crushed or pebble ice. Top with additional ice.

because of its association with illicitness, absinthe (nicknamed "the green fairy" for the vivid color of the French version) was adopted by the Parisian bohemian set in the 1800s, and it became so popular in the mid-nineteenth century that happy hour became known as *l'heure verte* (the green hour). Nevertheless, a long ban in France, the United States, and other countries helped fuel its mystique and gave rise to the absinthe substitutes, which include pastis (France) and Herbsaint (New Orleans).

In 2007, absinthe became legal again in the United States, although it is subject to new regulations, the most important of which is a limit on the presence of thujone, the wormwood extract with the supposed hallucinogenic properties. Ritual vestiges from the nineteenth century still haunt the spirit, such as serving it with water dripping over a sugar cube into the glass, which was perhaps necessary with the crudely made absinthes of the past but isn't now that the quality has improved. If not serving it in a cocktail, though, do consider diluting it with water, as most contain well over 60 percent ABV. Brands to seek out include Vieux Pontarlier, St. George Absinthe Verte, Kübler, and Pernod.

ABSINTHE FOUNTAIN

(n.) This theatrical accessory used to dispense ice-cold water can be used in the preparation of absinthe cocktails, though it is not necessary.

ABSINTHE SPOON

(n.) Used in the ritual of preparing absinthe, this perforated spoon sits atop a glass of absinthe to hold a sugar cube. When ice-cold water is poured over the cube, it dissolves into the glass.

ABV

(n.) An abbreviation for "alcohol by volume." In the United States, producers are required to list the ABV of a product on the front label, expressed as a percentage.

ADONIS

LIGHTER take on the Manhattan made with fino sherry instead of whiskey, this stylish cocktail was swept into the canon in the late 1800s on a wave of sherry fandom. Cocktail genealogists will note that save for using sweet vermouth instead of dry, the Adonis is nearly a perfect mirror image of the Bamboo, another sherry-based cocktail from the same era. As such, the pair make excellent foils for comparing and contrasting different styles of both sherry and vermouth. The drink takes its name from a Broadway musical that debuted in 1884 to great popular acclaim.

Serves 1

2 ounces fino sherry
1 ounce sweet vermouth
2 dashes orange bitters

Garnish: orange peel

Glassware: cocktail or coupe

Add all ingredients to a mixing glass. Add ice and stir until chilled. Strain into a chilled cocktail or coupe glass. Garnish with an orange peel.

Note: *On the fino front, Lustau's La Ina has a stronger, more pungent acetaldehyde note than most finos and tends to hold its own against more brooding flavors. On the vermouth side, the savory complexity of Carpano Antica is a good choice. For a fruitier riff on the drink, try Dolin or Martini & Rossi.*

A

ACHOLADO

(n.) A Peruvian pisco made from several varieties of grape, as opposed to the "puro" style, which is made from a single variety.

ADVOCAAT

(n.) A Dutch liqueur made from brandy, sugar, and eggs. This shelf-stable eggnog-like product is typically thick like pudding, custard yellow, and under 20 percent ABV. Traditionally consumed as a chilled digestif with whipped cream (and eaten with a spoon), advocaat also is frequently used in making desserts such as ice cream or custards. It also makes an appearance in cocktails such as the Snowball. Though commercial versions can be hard to find, it is simple to make at home.

AGAVE

(n.) A cactus-like perennial plant native to the American Southwest and Mexico that yields a starchy heart (the *piña*) used to make tequila and agave nectar.

AGAVE NECTAR

(n.) A sweetener made from the agave plant. To make agave nectar, juice is extracted from the ripe heart of the plant (the *piña*), which is then filtered and heated to make a syrup. The level of heating determines the color and flavor of the product: light agave nectar has little flavor, while dark or amber agave can display a caramel- or vanilla-like flavor. Depending on the processing, agave nectar can be up to three times sweeter than sugar; a general rule of thumb is to substitute agave nectar for sugar at a ratio of two to three.

AGE

1. *(n.)* A quantifiable amount of time between a product's creation and either its on-sale date or its consumption. For spirits, age is generally calculated by the amount of time the product spends in barrels or tanks, so a twenty-one-year-old bourbon

— continued

AIRMAIL

L **ANDING** somewhere between a French 75 made with rum and a Daiquiri topped with Champagne, this rum sparkler made its print debut in *Esquire* magazine's 1949 edition of *Handbook for Hosts*. The warm tones of the honey soften the edges of the rum and Champagne, making this an easy drink to throw back, but consider yourself forewarned about the deceptively high alcohol content. Cocktail historian David Wondrich speculates that the name—a nod to the fastest way to send things—is a reference to how quickly these will transport you to tipsiness.

Serves 1

1½ ounces golden rum
¾ ounce lime juice
Scant ¾ ounce honey syrup
   (2:1, honey:water, see note)
Champagne (or any dry
   sparkling wine)

Garnish: orange or lime peel

Glassware: Collins

Add rum, lime juice and honey syrup to a cocktail shaker. Add ice and shake until chilled. Strain over ice into a Collins glass. Top with Champagne and add a straw. Garnish with a lime or orange twist.

Note: *To make honey syrup, combine 2 parts honey with 1 part hot water in a jar or bowl. Shake or stir to dissolve.*

A

will have been stored in barrels for at least twenty-one years before it reaches the market. For wine, age is counted from the year the grapes were harvested, so a wine made from grapes picked in 2007 will bear the vintage date of 2007 and the bottle will be said to have five years of age in the year 2012.

Many wines and spirits have legal definitions for how long the product must age before sale. For spirits and wine that benefit from aging, the process is thought to mellow the flavors and add complexity. Though a product's age is commonly touted by those who market spirits and wine, age does not always correlate with quality, and many types of alcohol are meant to be consumed soon after production, such as most of the clear or white spirits.

2. *(v.)* The process of storing an alcohol before consumption, either before or after bottling.

AGUARDIENTE

(n.) A generic term for a spirit distilled from a fermented fruit base or sugarcane that is defined differently from country to country. The name is a compound from the Spanish *agua* (water) and *ardiente* (burning), so it should come as no surprise that many of these spirits are high-proof. Different countries have varying definitions for local aguardientes, usually having to do with the base material of the spirit or added flavorings. In Portugal, the spirit is made from wine or pomace and it is frequently used to fortify port. In the Caribbean and some Central and South American countries, it is made from sugarcane and can be bottled with no flavoring (Costa Rica) or flavored with anise (Colombia).

ALCOHOL

(n.) Alcohol meant for consumption is known more scientifically as ethyl alcohol or ethanol, which is a by-product from the fermentation of fruits, grains, or vegetables. The

ALABAZAM

WHILE working at the Criterion Hotel in London, American Leo Engel reportedly came up with this recipe, which he included in his 1878 edition of *American and Other Drinks*. Modern audiences will look at the ingredient list and see a Sidecar with a dash of simple syrup and heavy dose of bitters, which accent the deep, rich flavor of the brandy.

Serves 1

1½ ounces Cognac
½ ounce Cointreau
¼ ounce Angostura bitters
¼ ounce lemon juice
¼ ounce simple syrup
    (1:1, sugar:water)

Glassware: cocktail or coupe

Add all ingredients to a cocktail shaker. Add ice and shake until chilled. Strain into chilled cocktail or coupe glass.

ALASKA

COCKTAIL historians have yet to uncover why this striking cocktail, which dates back at least to the early twentieth century and was included in the *Savoy Cocktail Book*, is named for the forty-ninth state. One of many variations on the Martini, this drink gets its unusual color from the inclusion of yellow Chartreuse, which, when combined with gin, creates an effect of botanicals on botanicals. The yellow version of the Alpine liqueur made by Carthusian monks is softer and more floral than its more famous green cousin, and for that reason, some prefer matching it to Old Tom gin in this drink.

Serves 1

1½ ounces gin
½ ounce yellow Chartreuse
1 dash orange bitters

Glassware: cocktail or coupe

Combine ingredients in a mixing glass and fill with ice. Stir well for 20 seconds and strain into chilled cocktail or coupe glass.

A

chemical reaction works like this: As yeast cells consume sugar—the essential act of fermentation—they produce both ethanol and carbon dioxide. When consumed by mammals, ethanol creates a state of intoxication, and humans have used it as a recreational psychoactive drug for millennia. When used as a beverage, it is frequently mixed with water and flavorings to make it more palatable. Drinking alcohols are generally broken down into three broad categories: wine, beer, and spirits.

ALLOCATION

(n.) A set number of bottles that a winery or distributor will release to a restaurant, consumer, or store; commonly associated with highly desired wines and mailing list subscriptions at cult wineries, which intentionally minimize the number of bottles one outlet is allowed to buy.

AMARO

(n.) A type of bitter Italian liqueur typically consumed as an apéritif or digestif. Part of the potable bitter family, the style emerged in the nineteenth century as a digestive aid. Production usually involves macerating herbs, spices, roots, dried fruits, or citrus in a base spirit, which is then sweetened and either aged or bottled at anywhere between 20 and 60 percent ABV. Many formulas, often containing complicated combinations of herbs and spices, have been kept secret and are passed down through generations. Amari are usually served neat, on the rocks, or mixed with soda with an orange slice, but bartenders are also experimenting with using them in cocktails. Brands to try include Averna, Ramazzotti, and Fernet-Branca.

AMARETTO

(n.) This almond-flavored liqueur is distilled from apricot pits or almonds. The name is thought to be the diminutive of amaro, a type of Italian bitter

AMARETTO SOUR

FOR many people, the name of this drink conjures up bottled cocktail mixers and university bar crowds of a certain variety. Portland bartender Jeffrey Morgenthaler's higher-proof but feathery-light egg white version makes for a sophisticated take on the standard recipe. His version relies on a backbone of strong bourbon, an unusual addition that rounds out the fruit of a high-quality amaretto, a liqueur made from almonds and apricot pits. Egg white blends and buoys the stronger ingredients, creating a more sophisticated cocktail than most of the Amaretto Sours to come before it.

Serves 1

1½ ounces amaretto (preferably Lazzaroni)
¾ ounce bourbon, cask proof (Booker's is a good bet)
1 ounce lemon juice
1 teaspoon simple syrup, rich (2:1, sugar:water)
½ ounce egg white

Garnish: lemon peel and a brandied cherry

Glassware: rocks

Add all ingredients to a cocktail shaker and dry shake. Add ice and shake well. Strain over ice into a rocks glass. Garnish with a lemon peel and a brandied cherry.

A

spirit, as the sugar content of amaretto counters the natural bitterness of the spirit. Although the recipe has roots in Italy—legend points to a birthplace in Saronno, Italy, in 1525—examples are now produced all over the world. The most recognized brand is Disaronno.

While the spirit is often served neat or on the rocks as a digestif, it also makes an appearance in several mixed drinks, perhaps most famously the Amaretto Sour. Amaretto is also frequently used in baked goods and desserts, such as tiramisu, and is added to coffee.

AMBER ALE

(n.) Less a distinct style of beer than a description of its color, an amber ale is typically deep gold to red with a malty profile. Its hop character can vary from light to heavy, depending on the producer, but the beer generally has a citrusy edge. Amber ales are often similar to pale ales, but they have a more pronounced caramel flavor and more body. The darker styles may also be labeled as "red ales."

AMERICAN OAK

(n.) A type of wood commonly used to make casks and barrels. Products aged or fermented in new American oak gain a more pronounced sweet spice and vanilla flavor than those aged in French oak.

AMONTILLADO

(n.) A hybrid style of sherry. Initially it is made like a light, crisp fino sherry, with a layer of flor (yeast) allowed to develop over the aging wine, but the flor is either allowed to die or is killed off by fortifying the wine, which then exposes the wine to oxidation. The resulting amber-colored wine is darker and nuttier than fino sherries but lighter than oloroso, a style made without flor.

AÑADA

(n.) A vintage-dated sherry, a style that is growing increasingly rare.

AMERICANO

DON'T let the name fool you: the Americano's heritage is distinctly Italian. Born from the Milano-Torino, a drink made of equal parts Campari (from Milan) and red vermouth (from Torino) served over ice, the Americano, now topped up with soda water and garnished with an orange twist, is believed by some to have been christened during Prohibition as the favored beverage for American tourists seeking *la dolce vita* in Italy. Though its heavyweight cousin, the Negroni, may have more currency among the cocktail cognoscenti today, this fizzy afternoon-appropriate drink still has some cultural cachet; it was James Bond's favorite beverage before he switched to Martinis.

Serves 1

1½ ounces Campari
1½ ounces sweet vermouth
Soda water

Garnish: orange slice or orange peel

Glassware: Collins or rocks

Add Campari and sweet vermouth to a Collins or rocks glass. Add ice and top with soda. Garnish with an orange slice or orange peel.

Note: *An Americano works well with all walks of sweet vermouth, but we prefer Carpano Antica. In a pinch, Martini & Rossi makes a fine, albeit fruitier substitute.*

A

ANALYZER

(n.) Part of a patent still, this column heats up an alcoholic liquid and turns it into steam so that a concentrated alcoholic matter in the form of vapor will be transferred to the rectifier and recondensed there.

AÑEJO

1. *(n.)* A category of tequila that has been aged in wood barrels between one and three years.

2. *(n.)* A category of mezcal that has been aged in wood barrels for more than twelve months.

ANISETTE

(n.) A clear, sweet anise-flavored liqueur flavored with aniseeds. Like other liquors in the anise-flavored family, anisette turns milky white when combined slowly with cold water. It is usually consumed neat or over ice with water and a lemon slice.

APÉRITIF (APERITIVO)

(n.) An umbrella category relating to the time of consumption rather than a specific drink, an apéritif is an alcoholic beverage consumed before a meal. The tradition stems from eighteenth-century France (apéritif) and Italy (aperitivo), where it was believed that a drink—usually something bitter or bubbly and not terribly alcoholic—would help to stimulate the appetite. The same school of thought brought about the digestif, which closes a meal. Popular choices for apéritifs include sparkling wine, fortified wines (vermouth or sherry), cocktails such as the Americano (made with vermouth, Campari, and soda water), and an Aperol spritz. Of particular fascination among the cocktail cognoscenti in the United States now are a class of European aromatized wines made with quinine, called *quinquinas* (France) and *chinati* (Italy).

A

APEROL

(n.) An Italian apéritif, this bright-orange-red liqueur is often thought of as a less bitter, less alcoholic Campari. First produced in Padua, Italy, in 1919 by the Barbieri company, the proprietary recipe for Aperol is thought to include cinchona, rhubarb, gentian, and bitter orange. Typically consumed as an apéritif, Aperol may be served over ice with seltzer water and an orange slice, or in cocktails such as the Aperol spritz, a mix of prosecco, Aperol, and seltzer water.

ANGEL'S SHARE

(n.) The small amount of spirit or wine that evaporates while the liquid is aging in barrels.

ANGOSTURA BITTERS

(n.) Originally conceived as a medicinal tonic by Dr. J. G. B. Siegert in Venezuela in the early nineteenth century, this proprietary formula for bitters became a staple in cocktail making during the latter part of that century. The recipe for the bitters, now produced on the island of Trinidad, remains a secret, but many guess it has a gentian root base. Note that the Angostura company also produces an orange bitters, which is quite different in flavor.

APPELLATION

(n.) A geographic boundary in which certain wine-making and grape-growing rules must be followed in order for the wine to carry the name of the appellation. Countries set their own regulations for areas, usually having to do with acceptable grape varieties, the interventions performed on the pressed grape juice by the wine maker, and aging. Each country has their own organizational system: France is controlled by the Institut National de l'Origine et de la Qualité, Germany has the Qualitätswein bestimmter Anbaugebiete (QbA) system, and the United States' American Viticultural Area system is regulated by the Alcohol and Tobacco Tax and Trade Bureau.

A

AQUAVIT

(n.) Similar in structure to gin, this Scandinavian spirit is distilled from grains or potatoes and flavored with caraway plus a slate of other herbs and spices, including cinnamon, anise, cardamom, and citrus peel. Although aquavit is often bottled young, when the spirit is clear or light yellow, some versions, usually Norwegian ones, are aged in oak barrels. The best versions are made by distilling the flavoring agents with the alcohol, though some brands, as well as most homemade aquavits, are made by soaking the spices in a neutral spirit. Though the spirit is primarily associated with Scandinavia, some versions are produced in the United States as well.

The spirit is usually consumed neat, either at room temperature or chilled, and often with foods such as crawfish or pickled or smoked herring. Aquavit plays a large role in Scandinavian holidays, especially the Swedish midsummer celebration, when shots are consumed while singing a number of drinking songs. Brands to try include Aalborg, O.P. Anderson, Krogstad, and Linie, which has the quirky distinction of having been sent on a ship across the equator and back.

ARAK

(n.) Also known as "arrack," this anise-flavored spirit is the national drink of Lebanon and can be found throughout the Middle East. Similar in character to ouzo and raki, arak is distilled from a grape base and flavored with aniseed. Arak is commonly served at mealtimes in a ratio of one part arak to three parts cold water, which turns the drink a milky white, and ice is added after the mixing.

ARRAK

(n.) A spirit distilled from palm wine (a lightly alcoholic beverage fermented from coconut palm sap) originating in Sri Lanka but now made throughout South Asia. Higher-end versions will be aged for fifteen or more years in vats made from

halmilla trees and develop a brown caramel color. The best young versions will be clear and made from 100 percent palm sap, while cheaper bottles will stretch their volume with a neutral spirit. In the United States, only bottles of anise-flavored spirit from the Middle East can bear the "arrak" label.

AROMA

(n.) A term used to describe a particular scent or odor of a beverage, it is often used in the evaluation of wines to describe recognized traits that arise from the wine's grape variety, terroir, or winemaking techniques. In the professional wine-tasting arena, aroma differs from the term "bouquet," which is used to describe scents developed in wine after aging, such as honey, leather, or mushrooms.

AROMÁTICO

(n.) A Peruvian pisco made from a single aromatic grape variety. Many grape varieties may be used, including Albilla, Italia, Torontél, or Muscatél.

AROMATIZED WINE

(n.) Wine that has been flavored with botanicals, such as orange peel, wormwood, quinine, or anise. These can be sweet or dry and are generally either served as apéritifs or mixed into cocktails. Many of these wines are also fortified, such as vermouth or *quinquinas*, which generally have an ABV of 14 to 24 percent.

ASTI

1. *(n.)* A sparkling white wine made in Piedmont, Italy, from the Moscato Bianco grape. Though the town of Asti and the surrounding regions may gain more recognition in the wine world for producing ageable red wines such as Barbera d'Asti, the more significant export by volume is a sparkling white wine, Asti (sometimes referred to as Asti Spumante) and its less intensely sparkling cousin, Moscato d'Asti. Made from the aromatic Moscato Bianco grape, a member of the Muscat family, these wines tend to be floral, fruity, low in alcohol (under 9 percent ABV), and

A

slightly sweet, with a residual sugar level of around 3 to 5 percent. They are best consumed young, before the aromatic notes fade.

2. *(n.)* A province and town in southern Piedmont, Italy, famous for producing a pair of sparkling white wines, Asti Spumante and Moscato d'Asti, and red wines such as Barbera d'Asti.

ATOMIZER

(n.) An item of bartending equipment that allows liquids to be sprayed in a fine mist. Most often thought of as a fussy way of adding small amounts of vermouth to Martinis (sometimes you'll see these sold as "Martini misters" or "vermouth atomizers"), the atomizer has found new life with bartenders who are experimenting with adding exotic aromatics to cocktails.

AUSLESE

(n.) A German classification for wines that are made with very ripe grapes; literally, it means "select picking" in German. Richer in body than Spätlese, the next rung down on the hierarchy, these wines are usually sweet but can also be medium-dry or dry. The sweeter styles should be served as a dessert wine, while dry versions can be paired with rich main-course dishes.

AVERNA

(n.) An Italian amaro flavored with herbs, citrus, and roots. Created in 1868 by Salvatore Averna, this liqueur skews slightly bitter and has a dominant orange flavor. Traditionally consumed as an apéritif or digestif, it is also used in cocktails by adventurous bartenders.

AVIATION

NEARLY lost for almost half a century, this pale-purple concoction was restored to its original glory only within the last decade. The drink was first documented in 1911, though—as far as we know—a recipe didn't appear until 1916, in Hugo Ensslin's *Recipes for Mixed Drinks*. The unusual combination of gin, maraschino liqueur, crème de violette, and lemon juice made for a distinctive—if oddly hued—cocktail. The reasons it fell out of favor? A double whammy. First, in the 1930s the recipe bible of the era, the *Savoy Cocktail Book*, dropped crème de violette from the recipe, resulting in a predominantly sour drink, and then crème de violette was discontinued altogether in the 1960s in the United States. Rothman & Winter re-created the liqueur in 2007, making it possible to prepare the original recipe again, to the delight of a new generation of bartenders, who have championed this forgotten drink.

Serves 1

2 ounces gin
¼ ounce maraschino liqueur
½ ounce lemon juice
¼ ounce crème de violette
(or ¼ ounce simple syrup,
1:1, sugar:water)

Garnish: brandied cherry

Glassware: cocktail or coupe

Add all ingredients to a cocktail shaker. Fill shaker with ice and shake until chilled. Strain into a chilled cocktail or coupe glass. Garnish with a brandied cherry.

Note: *The Aviation can be a tricky cocktail to balance depending on the type of gin, quality of citrus, and sweetness of the crème de violette. Don't be shy—test the cocktail before straining and serving to ensure a balanced drink. Adjust with a dash of simple syrup or squeeze of citrus accordingly.*

BACK

(n.) A secondary order at a bar, served in a separate glass, that is meant to complement the first (e.g., "I would like a bourbon neat with a water back"). This component is usually soda or water, though it could be something else, such as the brine from a pickle jar, called a "pickleback," which is typically ordered alongside whiskey. The pair of beverages may be sipped together, consumed one after another, or added to each other at the consumer's discretion.

BACKBAR

(n.) The area behind the bar with shelves for storing glassware, equipment, or extra bottles of liquor.

BAILEYS

(n.) Created in 1974 by Gilbeys of Ireland, this sweet Irish cream liqueur is made from a proprietary blend of Irish whiskey, cream, cocoa extracts, sugar, and additional flavorings. The bottles have a shelf life of two years, as the alcohol helps to preserve the cream. Note that the presence of dairy makes the product coagulate when introduced to acidic

B

ingredients, such as citrus juice or wine. Usually served straight or over ice as an after-dinner drink, Baileys may be mixed into coffee, shooters, or cocktails as well, such as the mudslide or B-52.

BALANCE

(n.) A nebulous term used in evaluating wine, beer, spirits, and cocktails that indicates whether its components work together harmoniously. A balanced wine, for example, would not be overly tannic, alcoholic, or acidic. This concept is difficult to measure empirically, however, and is largely considered a matter of personal preference.

BANANA LIQUEUR

(n.) Also known as "crème de banane," this sweet banana-flavored liqueur, which is usually dyed yellow, is commonly used in tropical-style drinks and in desserts. Brands to try include Bols.

BARLEY WINE

(n.) An intensely flavored beer that is high in alcohol, often reaching an ABV of 8 to 15 percent, on par with most wines. The style's family tree is tangled, with references to barley wine dating to the ancient Greeks, but the first record of a commercial brewery making the style appears in the late nineteenth century with England's Bass & Co. Modern examples tend to dial up the flavor on all fronts, with lots of malt character, high hop bitterness, and plenty of spice, though English versions can be subtler than their Yankee counterparts. This style is usually brewed as a seasonal beer around the winter holidays.

BAROLO CHINATO

(n.) An Italian fortified wine made from Barolo wine and flavored with botanicals and spices, including bark from the cinchona tree. Although it has roots as a medicinal elixir, today the aromatic wine is usually served straight as a digestif or over ice with soda water as an apéritif.

BARBADOS SWIZZLE

COCKTAIL historian David Wondrich dates this cooling classic to the late nineteenth century, when ice—an essential ingredient of the swizzle—became available in the Caribbean. Though the ingredients for this drink are similar for those in the Collins family (save a dash of bitters), what really distinguishes the swizzle is the use of crushed ice, which is blended into the drink using a swizzle stick. This technique results in a frost forming on the glass.

Serves 1

2 ounces dark rum (preferably from Barbados)
½ ounce lime juice
½ ounce simple syrup (1:1, sugar:water)
5–6 dashes Angostura bitters

Glassware: Collins

Add rum, lime juice, and simple syrup to a Collins glass. Add crushed ice and swizzle with a bar spoon or swizzle stick. Add more crushed ice and dash Angostura bitters liberally over top.

BARBARY COAST

THIS Prohibition-era cocktail, which likely takes its name from the eponymous San Francisco red-light district, binds the unlikely bedfellows of gin, Scotch, and crème de cacao with a slug of heavy cream. The creamy result has a bit of a milk-shake aura about it. Since the flavors of all the ingredients get muddied together, choose blended Scotch, which is a more economical choice than single malt.

Serves 1

¾ ounce gin
¾ ounce blended Scotch
¾ ounce crème de cacao
¾ ounce heavy cream

Glassware: cocktail

Pour the ingredients into a cocktail shaker filled with ice. Shake well. Strain into a chilled cocktail glass.

B

BARSPOON

(n.) A bartending tool; usually a long, thin-handled spoon used for stirring, mixing, and layering drinks. A good spoon will assist the drink maker in stirring the drink properly to limit the aeration of the cocktail. Models with a twisted handle provide the user with extra control.

BASE

(n.) A cocktail-making term used to indicate a spirit, wine, or other alcohol around which a recipe will be built. For example, a Whiskey Sour has a base of whiskey.

BATAVIA ARRACK

(n.) Not to be confused with arak (the anise-flavored liquor of the Middle East) or arrak (a Sri Lankan spirit distilled from palm wine), this Indonesian spirit is distilled from sugarcane and red rice and has a smoky rum-like flavor. An essential component in a number of nineteenth-century punches and cocktails, as evidenced by its inclusion in recipes in Jerry Thomas's 1862 *How to Mix Drinks*, Batavia arrack (literally, "Javanese liquor") fell out of favor as rum became more plentiful in the Western world, but it has recently been resurrected stateside as a result of the recent cocktail renaissance and interest in all things pre-Prohibition.

BATTONAGE

(n.) A wine-making technique in which the wine maker stirs the wine when it is aging in the tank or barrel, reagitating the sediment of dormant yeast cells and other particles that have precipitated out of the wine during the maturation process. Some wine makers claim this process adds body and a smooth character to the wine.

BEAUJOLAIS

(n.) A wine-making region in France most famous for producing red wine made from the Gamay grape. Located to the south of Burgundy's core wine-producing regions (the Côte d'Or and the Côte Chalonnaise) and

B

to the north of the Rhône Valley, Beaujolais is technically considered a part of Burgundy, but its idiosyncratic output (based on Gamay) makes it unique.

Beaujolais gained international fame in the mid-1980s for Beaujolais nouveau, a fresh, fruity style of wine made from grapes harvested during that year. A hugely successful marketing campaign that involved releasing the wines on the third Thursday in November inspired Beaujolais nouveau parties around the globe, which grew increasingly lavish, sometimes outfitted with live elephants or hot air balloons. Though the fad has faded somewhat, the style of wine remains popular.

Beaujolais is also home to ten crus (Saint-Amour, Juliénas, Chénas, Moulin-à-Vent, Fleurie, Chiroubles, Morgon, Régnié, Brouilly, and Côte de Brouilly), which have higher quality standards. Wine professionals often recommend these bottles for good value, as they tend to be overlooked by those seeking nouveau.

BEER

(n.) A fermented beverage made from grains, yeast, water, and hops. Archaeological evidence points to early versions of beer being made in Mesopotamia and Egypt some ten to fifteen thousand years ago, a practice that gained traction as civilization transitioned from a nomadic to an agricultural one. Chinese history also points to similar innovation, with evidence of millet- and rice-based brewing dating to 7000 BC. Since the science behind fermentation was not understood, the transformation of grain-soaked water into an alcoholic beverage (and its effect on killing waterborne pathogens) often took on a mystical connotation, with many cultures through the ages—including the Egyptians, Greeks, and Romans—ascribing religious significance to beer. In the Middle Ages, monasteries throughout Europe became known for advancing brewing practices. Early colonists in North America brought brewing traditions from England and Germany, where the tradition of brewing flourished until Prohibition. The rise of the craft beer scene since the 1970s has helped brewing gain momentum again in the United States.

The basic template for making beer works like this: A mixture of grains, primarily malted barley, are soaked in hot water to release the sugars. That liquid (wort) is strained and then cooked for around an hour with hops added at various intervals. When the wort has cooled, yeast is added and the beer undergoes fermentation, which converts the sugars in the liquid to alcohol and carbon dioxide.

Different styles of beer can be made by altering the grain bill (the combination of grains), the types and amount of hops, and the strain of yeast. The grain most commonly used to make beer is barley, which has been malted to better access the sugars present in the grain. Wheat, corn, and millet are also sometimes used. Which grains are used and the degree to which they are roasted will change the flavor profile of the finished beer. The final ABV of the beer is dependent on how much sugar was extracted from the grains and the type of yeast used to ferment the sugars, but in general, most beers range from 3 to 8 percent ABV.

BEER STEIN

(n.) A handled beer mug, often ornately decorated, made out of stoneware, pewter, porcelain, silver, or glass with a hinged lid. The lid is thought to have been added to the design to comply with sixteenth-century German laws that required all beverage containers to be covered to protect drinkers from disease. Steins, which are largely considered decorative, have found new life as collector's items.

BEERENAUSLESE

(n.) A German classification for wines made from hand-selected, high-quality, very ripe berries that have been affected with botrytis, or noble rot; literally, it means "berry select picking" in German. A step up in richness from Auslese, these wines are sweet and often display the

BEE'S KNEES

A **TWIST** on the Gin Sour, this shaken and strained mix of gin, honey, and lemon juice is thought to have bubbled up during Prohibition in the United States, when questionable bootlegged spirits needed masking in the flavor department. The cutesy name is an idiom that developed around the same time meaning "the very best," along with other, less appetizing phrases such as "the flea's eyebrows" and "the cat's whiskers." The recent fascination with old-timey everything has brought the spotlight on this simple, refreshing drink once again.

Serves 1

1½ ounces gin
Scant ¾ ounce lemon juice
¾ ounce honey syrup
    (2:1, honey:water, see note)

Garnish: lemon peel or lemon wheel

Glassware: cocktail or coupe

Add all ingredients to a cocktail shaker. Add ice and shake until chilled. Strain into a chilled cocktail or coupe glass. Garnish with a lemon peel or lemon wheel.

Note: *To make honey syrup, combine 2 parts honey with 1 part hot water in a jar or bowl. Shake or stir to dissolve.*

BELLINI

THIS sparkling brunch standard has roots in Venice, Italy, where bar owner Giuseppe Cipriani is said to have created it in the early twentieth century as a seasonal offering for his continental outpost of the venerable Harry's Bar. Essentially an Italian version of a Kir Royale—a dollop of white peach puree topped with prosecco and an optional dash of raspberry or cherry juice—the drink supposedly takes its name from fifteenth-century artist Giovanni Bellini, who favored using a peachy-pink color reminiscent of the drink's hue.

Serves 1

1½ ounces white peach puree, finely strained
4 ounces prosecco or dry sparkling wine

Glassware: flute

Add finely strained peach puree to a flute. Using a bar spoon rested inside the lip of the glass, gently pour sparkling wine over the bar spoon to avoid foaming.

typical "noble rot" character, which has a sweet honey-apricot flavor with a viscous mouthfeel.

BEHIND THE STICK

(phrase) An idiom that refers to the act of bartending, or working behind the bar counter. Some believe this phrase evolved from the wooden handles used to dispense kegged beer.

BELGIAN ALES

(n.) A large category that encompasses a number of styles of beer that originated in Belgium, including Trappist ales, saisons, lambics, gueuzes, Flanders red ales, and many others.

BÉNÉDICTINE

(n.) A French brandy-based herbal liqueur. Created by Alexandre Le Grand in the late 1870s, reputedly from a recipe used by Benedictine monks in Normandy, the formula has been kept a secret, but the flavor is sweet with thyme and vanilla under-

tones. The most common way to consume it is mixed with brandy in a B&B cocktail, though it also appears in the Singapore Sling.

BENTONITE

(n.) A type of clay used in fining wine. The clay binds to particulates in the wine and then precipitates out of the wine, resulting in a final product with greater clarity.

BIÈRE DE GARDE

(n.) A French style of farmhouse ale traditionally made in the winter or spring and stored in a cold cellar for consumption in the summer. The name translates as "beer that has been stored." There are three substyles—blond, brown, and amber—so the color can range from pale gold to dark brown, and the beer may have some haziness if unfiltered. The profile generally skews sweet and malty with a medium body and mild hop flavor and aroma (though the paler versions may have more). Commercial versions may be found in France

B

BETWEEN THE SHEETS

WITH its cheeky name, it should be no surprise that this Prohibition-era cocktail skews a little promiscuous; it features an unusual mingling of two base spirits, basically borrowing the bones of the Cognac-based Sidecar and adding an extra hit of rum. With that potent mix established, consider your company as you take the drink's name as a prescient warning or jaunty invitation for how a night of tipping these back might end.

Serves 1

¾ ounce Cognac
¾ ounce rum, white or golden
¾ ounce Cointreau or Combier
½ ounce lemon juice

Garnish: orange peel

Glassware: cocktail or coupe

Add all ingredients to a cocktail shaker. Add ice and shake until chilled. Strain into a chilled cocktail or coupe glass. Garnish with an orange peel.

BIJOU

THIS improbable cocktail—a blend of gin, sweet vermouth, and Chartreuse, a green herbal French liqueur—was invented in the United States in the late nineteenth century. Most commonly attributed to bartender Harry Johnson, who included the recipe in his 1900 tome *The Bartenders' Manual*, the drink, it has been theorized, got its name (which means "jewel" in French) from the gem-colored clear, red, and green alcohols combined in the recipe. The original formula calls for either a cherry or an olive for a garnish, but history has come down on the correct side of this debate: today's version uses a cherry.

Serves 1

1 ounce gin
1 ounce sweet vermouth
¾ ounce green Chartreuse
1 dash orange bitters

Garnish: brandied cherry

Glassware: cocktail or coupe

Add all ingredients to a mixing glass. Add ice and stir well. Strain into a chilled cocktail or coupe glass. Garnish with a brandied cherry.

B

and the United States, where is it now made year-round.

BIODYNAMIC

(adj.) A farming and farmed-goods production practice invented by Rudolf Steiner in the 1920s that is gaining in popularity among vintners. Loosely related to organic agriculture, biodynamics include among its central tenets crop diversification and rotation, planting and harvesting according to the celestial calendar, and treating the farm or vineyard as an ecosystem. Though the U.S. government doesn't impose rules for labeling, several independent companies offer a certification process. In general, if a wine states that it is made from biodynamic grapes, only the grapes were subject to the biodynamic rules, whereas if the label says it is a biodynamic wine, the producer must also follow a complex set of regulations in the winery.

BITTER ALE

(n.) A British term for a style of pale ale that became popular in the mid-nineteenth century as alternative to the mild ales and porters popular with the working class. In *Amber, Gold & Black*, author Martyn Cornell points out that bitters were "particularly in vogue with young middle-class and upper middle-class consumers," and by 1855, humor magazine *Punch* was "making jokes about the 'fast young gents' who drank 'bitter beer' living an 'embittered existence.'"

These light-colored ales, made bitter through a heavier hand with hops, come in a variety of permutations, from the well-hopped style of the India pale ale to the higher-in-alcohol extra special bitter (ESB) style. Modern bitters (the term seems to have caught on only in the commonwealth countries) can be found in a range of styles, from pale to amber in color, with varying degrees of alcohol levels, but they generally tend to have a pronounced hop character.

B

BITTERS

1. *(n.)* A high-proof alcohol infused with herbs, roots, and spices. Invented as a medicinal tonic, they were originally meant to aid digestion and cure a variety of ailments, including colds and coughs. Common ingredients include cloves, dried citrus peel, gentian root, quinine, and cardamom. By the eighteenth century, bitters were mixed with spirits in cocktails to make them easier to take, and the public began to consume them recreationally.

Commonly described as a spice or seasoning for cocktails, bitters, which can add depth and complexity to a drink when used judiciously (usually one or two dashes per drink), were an essential component of early cocktails. Largely forgotten after Prohibition, save for Angostura and Peychaud's, bitters have experienced a revival over the past two decades. The cocktail craze of the 2000s and the farm-to-table movement have acted as fuel to the fire, and now it's possible to find artisan-made selections across the country, as well as in-house versions at many of the best bars and restaurants. Some brands that are widely available and worth seeking out are Scrappy's, Bitter Truth, and Bittermens.

2. *(n.)* Potable bitters are liqueurs and spirits distilled with herbs and spices that are meant to be consumed in small quantities. In Europe, these strong, bracing drinks are usually consumed after a meal to encourage digestion. Brands to look out for include Underberg, Fernet-Branca, and Averna. For a more comprehensive discussion, *see:* Amaro.

BLACK AND TAN

(n.) Sometimes called a half and half, this drink is made by layering dark stout on top of a pale ale or lager. The layering effect works because stout is less dense than than most lagers. To properly make a black and tan, fill a pint glass halfway with a pale ale or lager. Place a spoon, with the bottom of the bowl facing up, as close to the liquid as possible, then

pour the stout slowly over the back of the spoon.

BLACK RUM

(n.) These super-dark, rich rums carry strong notes of vanilla, spice, and molasses. The color is achieved by aging in very charred oak barrels or by adding dark molasses or caramel flavorings for a more consistent color. Gosling's Black Seal, a notable example in the category, is the trademarked ingredient in a Dark 'n' Stormy.

BLANCO

(n.) Literally "white" in Spanish, this term designates a tequila or mezcal that has not been aged in wood; also known as *plata*. The clear spirit has a more neutral flavor than those aged in wood, and because of this, it tends to work well in mixed drinks.

BLEND

1.*(n.)* A wine that has been made from two or more grape varieties.

2.*(n.)* A cocktail-making technique that involves mixing ingredients with ice in an electric blender; the drink is then generally referred to as "frozen."

BLENDED WHISKEY

(n.) A whiskey made by blending single-malt whiskeys from different distilleries together, a technique most commonly practiced by larger brands.

BLIND TASTING

(n.) A style of evaluating wine (or other beverages) in which drinkers are given partial or no knowledge about what they are tasting. The practice supposedly allows tasters to evaluate the quality of wine removed from biases about particular producers, regions, or grapes.

BLONDE ALE

(n.) This pale to golden-colored ale is the slightly fruitier, lightly malted cousin of pale lagers, such as pilsners.

BLACK VELVET

THIS genre-bending mix of smooth Irish stout and Champagne is said to have been invented by a London bartender in the mid-nineteenth century for a mourning celebration of Prince Albert, consort of Queen Victoria. Contemporary drinkers, however, might recognize it as a dressier cousin of the popular pub drink the black and tan, a beer drink that layers stout over a pale ale. Layering the ingredients makes a neat party trick: the lighter density of the stout (usually lower in alcohol than Champagne) allows the dark liquid to float on top of the sparkling wine. Or, for something less precious, simply mix the two.

Serves 1

3 ounces Champagne
3 ounces Guinness

Glassware: flute or coupe

In a flute or coupe glass, add Guinness. Top gently with Champagne.

BLOOD AND SAND

THE recipe for this drink first popped up in the *Savoy Cocktail Book* in 1930, with the title thought to be a nod to Rudolph Valentino's 1922 silent film of the same name (itself an adaption of a 1909 Spanish novel) about the rise and fall of a bullfighter. A mix of equal parts Scotch, sweet vermouth, cherry liqueur, and orange juice, shaken and strained into a coupe, makes for one of the rare cocktails based on Scotch. Note: Not all cherry liqueurs are created equal; your best bet for this drink is the Danish liqueur Cherry Heering.

Serves 1

1 ounce blended Scotch
1 ounce cherry liqueur
   (preferably Cherry Heering)
1 ounce sweet vermouth
1 ounce orange juice, freshly
   squeezed

Glassware: cocktail or coupe

Add all ingredients to a cocktail shaker. Add ice and shake. Strain into a chilled cocktail or coupe glass.

Made in varying styles around the world, the beers are generally crisp, clear, and medium-bodied, with moderate hop flavor and an ABV of around 4 to 5 percent. In the United States, blonde ales are often seen as a gateway into craft beers for the pale lager–loving American palate.

BOAL

(n.) A medium-sweet style of classified Madeira wine, made from the Boal grape (Bual in Portuguese). The wine, which is usually served as a digestif, tends to have notes of caramel, coffee, dried fruit, and citrus peel.

BOCK

(n.) A style of lager that is usually medium-bodied, brown in color, and with little hop or fruit flavor. Developed in Einbeck, Germany, in the fourteenth century, the bock style would gain in popularity in Munich three hundred years later. The name is thought to come from a mispronunciation of Einbeck as "ein bock," which means "goat," and because of this, many breweries put a goat on the label for this style of beer.

Subtypes in this category include Maibock, or Helles Bock, which skews lighter in color, and dark-brown Doppelbock, which tends to be maltier. Eisbocks, made by freezing the beer to remove excess water and concentrate the product, have the highest alcohol content in this category and are generally full-bodied, with a deep caramel color.

BODEGA

(n.) A Spanish word for winery.

BOILERMAKER

1. *(n.)* A shot of whiskey served with a chaser of beer. This combination is presumably named for the profession of metalworking and dates to before the 1930s, according to cocktail writer David Wondrich. The two may be consumed one after another, whiskey first, or combined before drinking.

BLOODY MARY

ALONGSIDE the Mimosa, this jazzed-up concoction of tomato juice and vodka reigns as the patron cocktail of brunch and first-class flights. With its origins in the early twentieth century, there's debate as to whether bartender Fernand Petiot brought the recipe to the King Cole Bar in the St. Regis New York from his previous job at Harry's New York Bar in Paris, or Hollywood actor George Jessel invented it, as midcentury Smirnoff ads claimed (most likely the former). Regardless, the simple template is ripe for innovation. Classic embellishments include lemon juice, hot sauce, and Worcestershire, as in the recipe below, but other savory additions, including horserad-ish, celery salt, olives, and wasabi, all make regular appearances. Swapping out vodka for alternate spirits creates the Red Snapper (gin), Bloody Maria (tequila), Bloody Derby (bourbon), and a host of other drinks.

Serves 1

2 ounces vodka
4 ounces tomato juice
½ ounce lemon juice
½ teaspoon Worcestershire
2–4 dashes hot sauce
Salt and pepper to taste

Garnish: celery stalk or lime wedge

Glassware: Collins or highball

Add all ingredients to a mixing glass, and add ice. Roll back and forth between mixing tins and strain into an ice-filled Collins or highball glass. Garnish with a celery stick, lime wedge, or desired garnish.

2. **(n.)** In the United Kingdom, the term refers to a mixed beer drink that combines half a pint of draft mild ale and half a pint of bottled brown ale.

BOISSIERE

(n.) This brand of vermouth comes in both dry (French) and sweet (Italian) versions. Although it was originally made in Chambéry, France, production moved to Torino, Italy, in 1971. The more famous dry bottling is bright and fruity, with notes of elderflower and chamomile, and is often referred to as the classic Martini vermouth.

BOTTLED IN BOND

(phrase) A legal term referring to American spirits (usually whiskey) that have been processed according to regulations set forth in the Bottled-in-Bond Act of 1897, which was created to protect consumers from distillers who adulterated their product with fillers or flavorings. Distillers must comply with a different set of regulations for each spirit category to bear the bottled-in-bond label; whiskey, for example, must be made by one distiller at one distillery during one season, then aged for four years and bottled at 100 proof. The main incentive for compliance is a tax exemption, which allows distillers to postpone payment of excise taxes until the spirit is ready to be bottled for the market, though few distilleries note this on the label anymore.

BOTTOM SHELF

(adj.) A slangy phrase that has come to mean cheap, low-quality alcohol; a reference to where bartenders store less expensive bottles of alcohol behind the bar, because they are used in making mixed drinks more frequently, and therefore need to be more easily accessible.

BOULEVARDIER

(n.) American expat Erskine Gwynne made a splash in Paris in the 1920s both with his literary magazine, *The Boulevardier*, and with this cocktail

B

recipe of the same name, which famed Harry's New York bar owner Harry MacElhone included in his recipe compendium *Barflies and Cocktails*. Contemporary drinkers will recognize the formula as either a riff on the Negroni, with twice the amount of bourbon for gin, or a Manhattan with Campari instead of bitters. The simple formula is a boon to cocktail nerds, as it allows plenty of room for experimentation; try using spicy rye or different amari and vermouths.

BOUQUET

(n.) A wine-tasting term used to evaluate aromas that develop in the bottle from aging. These scents can include things such as honey, leather, truffle, or petrol. This differs from the term "aroma," which is used when evaluating the character of younger wines and spirits.

BOURBON WHISKEY

(n.) This American subset of whiskey is made from distilling a fermented mash that contains at least 51 percent corn and aging the liquor in new charred white oak barrels. Though some are made from 100 percent corn, most producers use around 70 percent, with the remainder of the grain mix filled out by malted barley, rye, or wheat for different flavor profiles. By law, the liquor must be distilled at no more than 160 proof and aged in barrel at no more than 125 proof, with no additives or flavorings other than water allowed.

Bourbon can legally be made in any state in the United States, but its spiritual home is Kentucky, its birthplace. The creation story goes that settlers in the 1700s found it easier to transport liquor than grain over the hilly terrain to sell in markets, and a regional whiskey was born, with the whiskey from Bourbon County gaining a reputation for a distinctive style. Alternate theories posit the spirit takes its name from Bourbon Street in New Orleans, a popular point of sale for the product. Production for the big commercial houses today is centered in the area between Lexington and Louisville, Kentucky, which some of the

BRAMBLE

CREATED by London bartender Dick Bradsell in 1984 while at Fred's Club in Soho, this simple Gin Sour is transformed with a drizzle of crème de mûre, a French blackberry liqueur that adds a tart-sweet character and a rosy-pink color as it precipitates through the iced drink. The ingredients are available year-round, but come high summer, the Bramble tends to take on a new resonance with its cooling properties and the addition of just-picked ripe blackberries.

Serves 1

2 ounces gin
¾ ounce lemon juice
¼ ounce simple syrup
   (1:1, sugar:water)
½ ounce crème de mûre

Garnish: blackberries and
lemon wheel

Glassware: rocks

Add gin, lemon juice, and simple syrup to a cocktail shaker. Add ice and shake until chilled. Strain over crushed ice into a rocks glass. Drizzle crème de mûre over top and garnish with blackberries and lemon wheel.

B

biggest brands, including Jim Beam, Maker's Mark, Wild Turkey, and Heaven Hill, call home.

Clear when distilled, the liquor gains its brown color and many flavor characteristics from time spent aging in barrels made from charred new oak. Producers are allowed to add the word "straight" to their labels if the bourbon is aged for more than two years. At large houses, the barrels are stored in multistory buildings (rick houses) where temperature and humidity differ on each level, influencing the aging process. The master distiller has the option to blend casks from different levels to achieve varying styles. Small-batch bourbon, a marketing term that has no legal definition, can refer to the distiller selecting choice barrels for a select blend or bourbon made in small quantities.

Although bourbon largely fell out of favor in the United States after Prohibition, the spirit has recently seen a comeback, especially in the super-premium category, spurred by the microdistillery boom and the cocktail craze. A few notable produc-

ers in the premium category include Pappy Van Winkle, Eagle Rare, George T. Stagg, Black Maple Hill, and Woodford Reserve.

BRANDIED CHERRIES

(n.) Preserved in sugar and brandy (or other spirits), these cherries make a good alternative to maraschino cherries and can be used as a garnish in cocktails such as the Manhattan and Rob Roy.

BRANDY

(n.) Brandy is a spirit distilled from fermented fruit juice or fruits. Though most commonly associated with the French wine-based distillates of Cognac and Armagnac, the broad category also includes Calvados (apples), grappa (grape pomace), eau de vie (various fruits), Kirschwasser (cherries), and many more. Legally, brandy must be made from fermented fruit juice or a fruit by-product, distilled at less than 190 proof, and bottled at more than 80 proof.

BRANDY ALEXANDER

DATING to before Prohibition, this creamy cocktail is thought to have been invented at Rector's bar in New York by bartender Tony Alexander. The occasion was supposedly a marketing campaign for a railroad company that wanted to advertise itself as a clean mode of transportation, hence the white color of the drink. The classic recipe features gin, crème de cacao, and cream, but contemporary audiences may be more familiar with the brandy version.

Serves 1

1 ounce brandy
1 ounce crème de cacao
1 ounce cream

Glassware: cocktail

Shake all ingredients with ice and strain into a cocktail glass.

BRÀULIO

(n.) An Italian amaro from the Lombardy region that has an herbaceous, piney character and a note of menthol.

BREATHE

(v.) To allow a wine to be exposed to oxygen by opening the bottle, pouring the wine in a glass, or decanting the wine. Wines change when exposed to oxygen, sometimes for the better. When a wine is overly tannic or young, it may benefit from some aeration, which can unlock more aromas and flavors. The greater the surface area of the wine exposed to oxygen, the greater the aeration. Opening the bottle allows the wine to breathe a little, swirling wine around a glass allows for more, while decanting the wine into another vessel creates the most. Some wines benefit from just a small amount of aeration—one to two minutes—while others (usually young red wines) require a day or more.

BRETTANOMYCES

(n.) Colloquially known as "Brett," this strain of yeast sometimes used in beer and wine making can be found either ambiently (on the skins of fruits or on oak barrels, for example) or cultivated. Brettanomyces can produce a range of flavors and aromas in a finished product, including horsey, smoked, Band-Aid, and metallic characteristics. Some consider the presence of Brettanomyces in wine or beer a flaw, labeling it a "spoilage yeast." As such, many wine makers work to keep their wineries sterile to avoid contamination; others, however, find that small amounts of Brett can add character and complexity. Certain beer styles—lambics, gueuzes, farmhouse ales, and Flanders red ales—depend on the yeast for their distinctive flavors.

BRIX

(n.) A scientific measurement of how much sugar is in a grape, which can indicate the level of ripeness. Grape growers use Brix measurements

BRANDY CRUSTA

THE crusta's position as an essential link on the classic cocktail family tree is easy to trace in this recipe. From its ancestor, the Old Fashioned, it takes a dash of bitters on top of the base spirit. But the roots of the Sidecar, the crusta's more famous descendant, are also visible in the choice of bold, rich Cognac, orange liqueur, lemon juice, and a sugared rim.

Serves 1

2 ounces Cognac
1 teaspoon orange curaçao
1–2 teaspoons lemon juice
1 teaspoon simple syrup
1 dash Angostura bitters

Garnish: sugar rim and lemon curl

Glassware: cocktail or coupe

Prepare a cocktail or coupe glass with a sugar rim. Cut a wide, long swath of lemon peel and place inside the rim the glass. Add all ingredients to a cocktail shaker. Shake over ice and strain into prepared glass.

during harvest to help decide when to pick the ripening grapes. Most growers pick grapes when they reach 21 to 25 Brix.

BROWN ALE

(n.) Although the term was used to refer to a style of sweet, low-alcohol, brown-colored ale popular in England in the beginning of the twentieth century, the term has ballooned to encompass a wide variety of styles than can be lumped together by their brown color. Some have nut flavorings (either from roasting the malt in a particular way or adding nut extracts), others are high in alcohol (reaching above 7 percent ABV), and others still are intensely hopped.

BROWN SUGAR

(n.) When raw sugar is processed to white sugar, the molasses is removed; brown sugar is the result of adding some of that molasses back to white sugar, which results in a deeper caramel-like flavor and soft texture. Some companies also add chemicals

and dyes to their products to improve the texture and consistency. Brown sugar is usually sold in two versions: light, which has less molasses, and dark, which has more. When called for in cocktails, brown sugar can add color as well as a hint of molasses flavor.

BRUT

(n.) A classification for Champagne that indicates the wine is very dry and has less than fifteen grams of residual sugar per liter. Extra brut is even drier, at less than six grams per liter, while brut nature, brut zero, and ultra brut, the least sweet of the categories, mean the wine contains less than two grams of residual sugar per liter.

BUCK (MULE)

(n.) Falling under the umbrella of coolers, this family of drinks distinguishes itself by the addition of ginger ale as the fizzy component to a base of liquor and citrus juice. The citrus is often left in the drink, which is

BRONX

CONJURED up at the turn of the twentieth century by Waldorf-Astoria bartender Johnny Solon for a lunchtime customer, this cocktail outfits the Martini for day drinking with the addition of orange juice. In the tradition of the Screwdriver and the Mimosa—other O.J.-based drinks—the sweet-acidic character of the juice tempers the alcohol's bite, making this very easy to tip back.

Serves 1

2 ounces gin
¼ ounce dry vermouth
¼ ounce sweet vermouth
1 ounce orange juice

Garnish: orange peel

Glassware: cocktail or coupe

Add all ingredients to a cocktail shaker. Shake over ice and strain into cocktail or coupe glass. Garnish with an orange peel.

BROOKLYN

I **KE** all siblings, Brooklyn (the borough) has its own identity, but it will always be defined in relation to its more famous relative, Manhattan. And so it should stand to reason that the Brooklyn (the drink) is something of a funhouse mirror image of the Manhattan cocktail: dry vermouth is substituted for sweet, and it gets a slug of the slightly offbeat maraschino liqueur and obscure Amer Picon for good measure.

Serves 1

2 ounces rye whiskey
1 ounce dry vermouth
⅛ ounce maraschino liqueur
¼ ounce Amer Picon, Torani
    Amer, or Amaro Cio Ciaro

Garnish: orange peel

Glassware: cocktail

Add all ingredients to a cocktail shaker. Shake over ice and strain into prepared coupe glass. Garnish with an orange peel.

served in a tall glass. Although the buck is thought to have originated in near parallel with the rickey in the late 1890s, the most famous example of this category is the Moscow Mule, a relatively late addition to the canon, invented in the 1950s.

BUILD IN GLASS

(phrase) A cocktail-making technique in which the unmixed ingredients are poured directly into the serving glass. A cocktail stirrer or straw may be served with the drink so the consumer can blend it.

BUY BACK

(n.) A round of drinks comped by the bartender. Some bar owners give bartenders a discretionary fund or allowance for giving free drinks to customers, usually those who have bought multiple rounds. This practice is thought to encourage customer loyalty.

CACHAÇA

(n.) Invented in the sixteenth century soon after Portuguese colonialists introduced sugarcane to Brazil, cachaça is a liquor distilled from fermented sugarcane juice. Few regulations about the production exist. The cane juice may be distilled in pot stills or column stills and is generally sold unaged. Brazil has fought to keep the product from being labeled "Brazilian rum," opting to use a proprietary name, much like bourbon's establishment as a subset of whiskey.

Slowly gaining in recognition through the 2000s in the United States, this liquor remains wildly popular in its home country and is inextricably tied to the Caipirinha, Brazil's most famous cocktail. The Caipirinha's heavy dose of sugar and lime is thought to have been a way to mask crudely produced cachaça, but recent gains in quality mean more bartenders are experimenting with alternative cocktails that highlight the spirit's character. Brands to check out include Leblon and Mãe de Ouro.

Aged cachaça is also a new frontier. Like rum, this product is not subject to much regulation, but producers are experimenting with versions aged in Brazilian wood or oak that are made for sipping neat.

CAIPIRINHA

A **SPIN** on the Daiquiri, this sweet-sour drink calls for cachaça, a Brazilian take on rum distilled from fermented sugarcane juice. Wildly popular in Brazil, the combination of lime juice, sugar, and cachaça is thought to have originated to mask the taste of crudely produced cachaça. As production techniques have improved, so has the cocktail. Riding the Mojito's recent wave of popularity, the Caipirinha has been gaining traction in the United States, no doubt on account of a new wave of quality cachaça imports finally making their way stateside.

Serves 1

1 lime, quartered
2 teaspoons sugar
2 ounces cachaça

Garnish: lime wedge

Glassware: rocks

In a rocks glass, add lime pieces and sugar, and muddle until well juiced. Add cachaça and ice. Stir to mix and garnish with a lime wedge.

C

CALIFORNIA COMMON

(*n.*) Also known as steam beer, this amber lager is brewed with a strain of lager yeast that allows the beer to be fermented at warmer temperatures. The style was developed in nineteenth-century California, when refrigeration, which would have allowed the cooler temperatures necessary for lagering (the practice of letting beer ferment at cooler temperatures for longer periods of time—*see:* Lager), was scarce. The result is a medium-bodied amber-colored beer with an assertive minty-woodsy hop kick balanced by malt character. Anchor Brewing Company holds the trademark for "steam beer," so other breweries must use the "California Common" label.

CALIMOCHO (KALIMOTXO)

(*n.*) A sweet, bubbly ode to bottom-shelf ingenuity, this mix of equal parts red wine and cola has become a modern Spanish classic, championed by Basque teenagers and American study-abroad students alike. Whether mixed in the bottle just outside the convenience store or carefully portioned into real glasses, this unlikely yet strangely winning combo is the perfect hot summer-night antidote to cocktail and wine seriousness.

CALISAY

(*n.*) An herbaceous Spanish liqueur made with quinine. Traditionally consumed as a digestif, the herbal, spicy drink is also sometimes used in mixed drinks.

CALL DRINK

(*n.*) A drink order in which the desired brand of liquor is specified (e.g., "I would like a Hendrick's Martini.")

CALVADOS

(*n.*) An apple brandy made in the Normandy and Brittany regions of France that is usually consumed either as an apéritif or as an after-dinner drink. Calvados begins as

C

cider, which is made from more than two hundred varieties of apples in the region. The cider is then distilled into an eau de vie, which must be aged for at least two years in oak barrels. The regulations for aging Calvados are similar to those for aging Cognac.

The production of Calvados is regulated by the French *appellation d'origine contrôlée* system, which dictates the methods that each of eleven subregions must follow when making the liquor. The basic Calvados labeling is the least strict, allowing for brandy to come from anywhere within the area and have only a single distillation in a column still. Calvados from the Pays d'Auge region, which is generally considered the highest quality, must be distilled twice in copper pot stills.

Large producers dominate the market, but an emerging cadre of smaller grower-producers is making an impression on Calvados aficionados. Look for bottlings from Christian Drouin, Michel Huard, and Domaine de Montreuil.

CAMPBELTOWN

(n.) A Scotch-producing region on Scotland's Kintyre Peninsula. The region is said to have housed more than thirty-two distilleries in the eighteenth century, when shipping reigned and the region could take advantage of its coastal position, but production has dropped off markedly since then.

CANADIAN WHISKY

(n.) Legally, Canadian whisky must be distilled from fermented grains, aged for three years in wood casks, and bottled at 80 proof or higher. The fermented grain mash—usually made of corn—is often distilled at alcohol levels much higher than bourbon is, which means the flavor from the grains is largely neutralized. Producers are allowed to mix in a small amount of flavoring alcohol, usually distilled from rye, and coloring for additional character. Labeling laws allow bottles to bear the name "Canadian Rye Whisky" regardless of how much rye is used.

C

Though distilling has been a part of Canadian history since the late eighteenth century, Canadian whisky rose to prominence only during Prohibition—as bootleggers funneled the product across the porous Canadian–United States border—and then after, when stores of legally made liquor flooded the then-open U.S. market.

On account of its stripped-down, light character, Canadian whisky generally has a poor reputation among whisky lovers and cocktail aficionados. There are some signs of life, though: in 2010 respected producer Buffalo Trace invested significantly in the product in a bid to bring a higher standard to the category.

CANTEIROS

(n.) An aging process for Madeira in which wines are left to age in casks in heated lofts and attics. The oxidative aging process contributes the "maderized" quality to the wine, which was originally gained when wines would travel long distances stowed on ships.

CARBOY

(n.) A glass or plastic container that holds five to fifteen gallons, commonly used in home brewing or home wine making.

CARPANO ANTICA

(n.) Not as bitter nor as sweet as its cousin Punt e Mes, this smooth red Italian vermouth is supposedly based on the original recipe for the first commercial vermouth by Turin resident Antonio Benedetto Carpano in 1786. The exact formulation is a secret, but fans of the alcohol prize its bold flavor tinged with citrus peel, cocoa, and spices. Use it in cocktails such as the Negroni or Manhattan, or pour it over ice for an apéritif.

CASEIN

(n.) A dairy-based product used to fine wines. The protein in the casein binds to particulates in the wine and then precipitates out of the wine, resulting in greater clarity.

CASINO

SWAP the crème de violette in an Aviation for a few shakes of orange bitters and you'll basically arrive at the Casino, a Prohibition-era cocktail that is decidedly less purple. The two drinks share a core of gin and lemon juice and are accented with the addition of maraschino liqueur, but they diverge both in the aforementioned final ingredient and in that Old Tom gin is sometimes recommended for the Casino, which will helps to sweeten the drink without the Aviation's added liqueur.

Serves 1

2 dashes maraschino liqueur
2 dashes orange bitters
2 dashes lemon juice
1½ ounces Old Tom gin

Garnish: brandied cherry

Glassware: cocktail

Shake all ingredients with ice and strain into a cocktail glass. Add the cherry on top and serve.

C

CASK

(n.) Wooden barrels, or casks, have been used for millennia to transport liquids throughout Asia and Europe, falling out of favor only relatively recently with the advent of modern packing materials. But casks continue to play an integral role in the aging of wine, beer, and brown spirits such as whiskey and Cognac, as time spent in a wooden cask can add distinct color and flavor.

Usually made from oak, new barrels are charred to different degrees, which can impart flavors of vanilla, caramel, and smokiness to the liquid. The wood also imparts some tannins to the spirit, which can add astringency and harshness. Factors affecting the transfer of flavors include the percentage of alcohol of the spirit, the temperature and humidity of the storage room, the amount of char on the barrel, and the type of wood. Barrel size can also play an important component: the larger barrel, the less flavor imparted to the spirit. Old barrels, usually used for three or more years, transfer less flavor and might be almost neutral, meaning they add no flavor. Some spirit makers search out gently used barrels to achieve a specific flavor profile, such as Scotch producers who age their product in sherry barrels for a nuttier finish. Casks, especially new models, tend to be quite expensive, so some producers take a shortcut by adding oak chips or caramel coloring to the liquid in lieu of properly aging, both of which create an inferior product.

The type of wood used to make a cask can affect the flavor of the liquid stored in it, and as such regulations for certain products call for specific types of wood. Bourbon, for example, must be made with new charred white oak casks.

CASK ALE

(n.) Also called "cask-conditioned ale," this is an unfiltered, unpasteurized ale that has been conditioned in a cask and is served straight from the cask without forced carbonation using carbon dioxide or nitrogen. Cask ales can be made in many styles,

from India pale ales to bitter ales; they are distinguished by the production methods for storing and serving the beer.

Cask ale comes from a long tradition of brewing: before the stainless steel keg was commonly used (beginning in the 1950s) and before bottling beer became popular (in the 1700s), draft beer was served from casks. The process for making cask ale works like this: After the primary fermentation, beer is transferred into a cask, where it can continue fermenting and conditioning, sometimes with extra sugars added by the brewer to encourage a more vigorous second fermentation or fining agents to help clarify the beer. The beer will continue to develop and ferment (causing some carbonation) in the cask as it is shipped to bars and pubs. Depending on the style, the beer will age for a few days (for lighter beers) or longer than a year (for stronger beers). To serve, the bartender will use a hand pump (called a beer engine) or a cask tap to pull the beer from the cask without the help of pressurized gas, as with a keg.

Though casks were traditionally made from wood, modern versions are more often made from metal or plastic. Common cask sizes include the pin (5.4 gallons), the firkin (10.8 gallons), and the kilderkin (21.6 gallons).

CASK STRENGTH

(adj.) A spirit that is bottled from a cask undiluted; the term is most often applied to bourbon or whiskey. Most spirits are watered down before being bottled at around 80 proof, or 40 percent ABV. Cask strength or barrel-proof spirits skip this step and are bottled straight from the barrel. The final ABV will depend on how much alcohol has evaporated during the aging process; every barrel or cask is different. Some legal regulations for spirits require the producer to water down their spirits to alcohol levels within given parameters before bottling.

CHAMPAGNE COCKTAIL

SWAP whiskey for Champagne in the Old Fashioned template and you'll get this pedigreed cocktail, which was first mentioned in 1862 in Jerry Thomas's *How to Mix Drinks*. With its low alcohol content and bubbly constitution, this recipe makes a good candidate for day drinking or a nonbitter apéritif. The question as to whether you pony up for the good stuff or choose a down-market sparkling wine depends largely on your opinion of the sacredness of Champagne.

Serves 1

1 sugar cube or 1 barspoon sugar
3 dashes Angostura bitters
Champagne

Garnish: long, curly lemon peel

Glassware: flute

Add sugar cube or sugar to a flute. Dash Angostura bitters over sugar to soak. Slowly top up with Champagne. Garnish with a long, curly peel of lemon.

Note: *A dry sparkling wine like Crémant de Bourgogne is best if you don't have Champagne on hand. Also: The type of bitters used can dramatically alter the drink. While Angostura is classic, playing around is encouraged. Brad Thomas Parsons, author of* Bitters, *adds an element of citrus, employing yuzu or Meyer lemon bitters in combination with a dot of Angostura to maintain "that pretty amber hue."*

C

CAVA

(n.) This Spanish sparkling wine is made in a number of regions, but most come from the Penedès area, which accounts for 95 percent of production. The grapes most commonly used in the wine are three indigenous varieties: Macabeo, Xarello, and Parellada. Rosé Cavas feature grapes such as Garnacha or Pinot Noir. As in Champagne production, producers must carbonate their wine using the *méthode champenoise* technique (called the *método tradicional* in Spain), in which a little yeast and sugar are added to the wine before bottling to spark a secondary fermentation, which will add bubbles. Most Cavas are best when consumed young, within one or two years of release, and their price (usually around $10) makes them an attractive candidate for economical cocktail making.

CENTRIFUGE

(n.) A piece of bartending equipment repurposed from industrial food processing to clarify fresh juices—straining taken to the extreme. The machine spins vials of liquids or solids—anything from citrus juice to pressed olives or rhubarb extremely fast, either inducing an emulsion or separating solids from liquids by density. Introduced behind the bar by the molecular mixology movement of the 2000s, this pricey machine is becoming more common in high-end bars.

CHAPTALIZATION

(n.) A wine-making process in which sugar is added to unfermented grape juice to increase the alcohol in the final product, as the more sugar the yeast consumes, the higher the alcohol content. Chaptalization is often used in cooler growing areas, where the grapes don't develop enough natural sugar to create a sufficiently alcoholic beverage. Certain countries and regions restrict or prohibit the process, as critics of the practice claim that adding sugar adulterates the finished product.

C

CHARTREUSE

(*n.*) Produced since the eighteenth century by Carthusian monks (who probably based their recipe on the work of a sixteenth-century alchemist), this French liqueur originally used for medicinal purposes is one of the earliest-known herbal liqueurs. There are two versions: the 110-proof green, which has more spice and pepper notes, and the 80-proof yellow, which skews sweeter and mellower. The exact recipes are kept secret by the monks, but more than 130 herbs, plants, and botanicals are said to be used to create the vividly hued spirits, which are sweetened with sugar and aged in oak casks for five years. Premium versions, which have been aged for twelve years, bear the VEP label (Vieillissement Exceptionnellement Prolongé) and are worth searching out. Note: When color is not specified in a recipe, default to the basic green version.

CHASER

(*n.*) A mild beverage, usually water or beer, sipped after consuming a shot of hard liquor, or a shot of hard liquor consumed after sipping a mild beverage.

CHÂTEAU

(*n.*) This French word means "castle"; it can also refer to a winery or a wine estate. In the European Union, using "château" on a wine label indicates that the grapes for the wine have come from vineyards controlled or owned by the winery. In the United States, however, the term has no legal definition and is often used to suggest a certain level of fanciness.

CHENIN BLANC

(*n.*) A white wine grape used to make dry, sweet, and fortified wines. The grape hails from France's Loire Valley, where it is best known for producing quality wines in the appellations of Saumur, Vouvray,

Anjou, and Quarts de Chaume. Other production areas of note include California and South Africa, where the grape is known as Steen. Chenin Blanc is fairly versatile. Though it works well in blends, when it is produced in better areas it produces quality single-varietal wines in styles from dry to sweet. Flavor characteristics commonly associated with the grape include melon, peach, and citrus.

CHILL/CHILLING

(v.) The process of cooling a liquid to proper serving temperature, most often used in reference to wine. The ideal serving temperature for wines depends on the type. Sparkling wines and light white wines should be very cold, around 40 to 50 degrees Fahrenheit. Fuller-bodied white wines and light reds show best with a medium chill of around 50 to 60 degrees. Heavier reds and dessert wines benefit from being served slightly cooler than room temperature, at around 60 to 65 degrees. To quickly cool a wine, submerge the bottle in a bath of ice water or place in the freezer for 15 to 30 minutes. Conversely, some wines stored in cool cellars may need to be warmed to the proper temperature before service.

Beers also benefit from being served at the correct temperature. In general, lighter-colored beers such as pilsners and wheat beers should be served cold, at temperatures between 40 and 45 degrees Fahrenheit, while heavier barley wines and imperial stouts and ales work better at warmer temperatures, from 55 to 60 degrees, with medium-bodied and amber ales falling somewhere in between.

CHINA

(n.) Pronounced "KEE-na" in Italian, this style of amaro is made with the bark of the cinchona tree. Ferro-China and China Martini may be the most recognizable brands of this liqueur.

CITRUS

(n.) Citrus fruits, including but not limited to lemons, limes, oranges, and grapefruits, play an essential role

C

in many cocktails. Their distinctive sweet-sour flavor is also essential to many liqueurs and bitters, such as curaçao (laraha citrus), Grand Marnier (bitter orange), Campari (orange), limoncello (lemons), and orange bitters (Seville oranges), plus many more. Their fresh juice often plays an important role in the composition of cocktails, while the zest, peel, or sliced fruit provide the final dressing in the form of garnishes. For information on how best to prepare fresh citrus for cocktails, *see*: Wheel, Wedge, Slice, Zest, Twist, Citrus Reamer, Citrus Squeezer.

CITRUS REAMER

(n.) A handheld tool for extracting juice from citrus fruits. The most common versions are made from wood or plastic and consist of a handle attached to a pointed, multifaceted reamer. The reamer is inserted into the citrus flesh and twisted back and forth to extract the juice. When working with a large amount of citrus, using a juicer is usually quicker.

CITRUS SQUEEZER

(n.) A two-handled tool that, when squeezed, compresses half of a citrus fruit between two small bowls in order to extract the juice. Common versions are made of stainless steel or enameled aluminum.

CLAM JUICE

(n.) The bottled or canned juice of shucked clams, which is occasionally used as a mixer in cocktails.

CLARET

(n.) A nickname for red Bordeaux, used primarily in the United Kingdom. Derived from the Latin word for "clear," the name originally described the French wines of the fourteenth and fifteenth centuries, which were a pale color. The British began using the term to refer exclusively to red Bordeaux in the eighteenth century.

CLOVER CLUB

THIS frothy cocktail was the signature drink for the eponymous gentleman's club that used to meet in Philadelphia's Bellevue-Stratford Hotel in the late 1800s. The first known recipe for the drink, a close relative of the Pink Lady, was published in 1911 in the bar book for the Waldorf-Astoria in New York. The drink largely fell out of favor in the mid-twentieth century—some historians speculate the raw egg white kept would-be admirers at bay—but the cocktail renaissance of the early twenty-first century has put it back in the spotlight. This modern take on the Clover Club is from bartender Julie Reiner's Brooklyn bar of the same name.

Serves 1

3–4 raspberries
Scant ½ ounce simple syrup
  (1:1, sugar:water)
1½ ounces gin (preferably
  Plymouth)
½ ounce dry vermouth
  (preferably Dolin)
Scant ½ ounce lemon juice
¼ ounce egg white

Garnish: 2–3 raspberries

Glassware: cocktail or coupe

Add raspberries to a cocktail shaker and muddle with simple syrup. Add remaining ingredients and dry shake. Add ice and shake again until chilled. Double-strain into a chilled cocktail or coupe glass. Garnish with skewered raspberries.

C

CLASSIC COCKTAIL

(n.) A cocktail developed between 1887 and 1934, after the publication of Jerry Thomas's *How to Mix Drinks* and before the end of Prohibition in the United States, respectively.

CLONE

(n.) A viticultural term for a variant of a grape variety. For example, Pinot Noir has more than one hundred clones, all with slightly different performance characteristics such as higher-yielding vines or early ripening grapes. Wine makers often make a blend out of several different clones.

CLOS

(n.) A French word for a walled vineyard (though the walls may no longer exist).

CLUB SODA

(n.) Carbonated water with added minerals, commonly sodium bicarbonate or salt, club soda was designed to approximate mineral water, which is often naturally fizzy but can carry a hefty price tag. English chemist Joseph Priestley invented the process of carbonation in 1767, when he realized that the carbon dioxide produced during the fermentation of beer could be infused into water. Soon after, Jacob Schweppe, a Swiss watchmaker, figured out how to manufacture carbonated water (which has no added minerals) and club soda. These products would become the cornerstone of the Schweppes Company, which is still in existence today. The added salt or sodium bicarbonate helps to mitigate the sour flavor from the carbonic acid, a by-product of carbon dioxide.

COBBLER

An offshoot of the punch family tree, a cobbler is, at its most basic, a mix of a spirit, sugar, crushed ice, and fruit, all served with a straw. The category is thought to have originated in early nineteenth-century America with the advent of readily available

C

ice, which some theorize is where the drink gets its name (the ice resembles cobblestones). The Sherry Cobbler, one of the most popular cocktails of the late 1800s, is perhaps the most famous member of this category. In his book *Imbibe!*, cocktail expert David Wondrich speculates that the popularity of the then–newly invented straw and this cocktail rose together. Once considered the height of fashion, the drink largely fell out of favor until the recent cocktail revival.

COCKTAIL STIRRER

(n.) A thin rod, usually made of plastic, glass, or metal, used to mix the ingredients of a cocktail, either in the glass in which it is being served or in a mixing glass before it is strained. The drink may be served with or without the stirrer. In some cases the stirrer performs a more decorative role, and many bars place their logo on stirrers for branding purposes.

COCONUT CREAM

(n.) The thick, creamy substance that naturally rises to the top of full-fat coconut milk. The cream may be canned on its own, in which case it will be labeled as "coconut cream," or it may be skimmed off the top of canned coconut milk.

COCONUT MILK

(n.) A white, creamy liquid extracted from grated coconut flesh. The milk comes in a range of thicknesses depending on how much water has been added or how much liquid has been extracted.

COCONUT WATER

(n.) The liquid inside a young green coconut. Coconut water is usually colorless or slightly milky and has a nutty flavor.

C

COGNAC

(n.) This grape brandy is made in the Charente region of France. The Dutch invented Cognac in the seventeenth century after experimenting with different types of French wine as a distillate before deciding the wines from the Cognac region worked best. Growers began to produce grapes specifically for distillation of brandy and the center of production moved to the region. Cognac production thrived in France until phylloxera, a grapevine pest, devastated the vineyards in the late nineteenth century. It took until after World War II for the vineyards to recover, and the spirit gained popularity in Asia and the United States.

Due to intense consolidation in the twentieth century, more than 90 percent of the production is now owned by the four major brands: Hennessy, Rémy Martin, Courvoisier, and Martell. There are, however, some small grower-producers remaining that are worth searching out, most notably Navarre, Dudognon, and Paul Beau.

Only certain grapes may be used to make the base spirit; Ugni Blanc, Folle Blanche, and Colombard are the most common. After pressing, the grape juice ferments by wild yeast and is then double distilled in copper alembic stills. The spirit is aged in oak casks for at least two years, then moved to glass carboys to await blending. Most producers blend the spirit from among several vintages to achieve a consistent house style, though a few make single-vintage examples.

There are several levels of classification, based on the age of the youngest spirit in the bottle: V.S. (very special) indicates two years of age, V.S.O.P. (very superior old pale) has at least four years, and X.O. (extra old) means that the youngest spirit has been aged for at least six years, though it has often been aged much longer.

Although Cognac is typically consumed neat, as a digestif, it also makes an appearance in some important cocktails, such as the Sidecar and the French 75, as well as basic mixed drinks.

C

COINTREAU

(*n.*) A French orange-flavored liqueur. First produced in 1875 by the Cointreau family, this clear spirit is made by distilling a neutral spirit with bitter and sweet dried orange peels and then sweetening the results with sugar. Often consumed neat as an apéritif or digestif, it may also be used in cocktails where triple sec is called for, such as the Margarita or the Sidecar. Essential oils from the orange peels make this liqueur somewhat volatile, so make sure to carefully reseal the bottle to maintain its quality.

COLD COMPOUNDING

(*n.*) A technique for flavoring liquor in which essential oils are added to a neutral spirit to make an approximation of a spirit distilled with botanicals. This is usually done for spirits of lesser quality, as the flavor tends to dissipate quickly.

COLD FILTER

(*v.*) A beer-making technique that improves the clarity of beer. After the initial burst of fermentation, brewers often let beers sit before bottling (*see:* Condition), which allows proteins and other particles to settle, creating a clearer, brighter beer. Chilling a fermented beer encourages these particles to lump together so they may be caught by filters, giving the brewer an opportunity to either bottle the beer sooner or mask brewing problems that lead to haziness. Some styles of beer benefit from being cold filtered, but many brewers claim the process can strip or alter the flavor of beer and should be avoided. Similar techniques are used in making wine (cold stabilization) and spirits (chill filtering).

COLHEITA PORT

(*n.*) A type of tawny port made from a single vintage and aged for at least seven years.

C

COLLINS

(n.) A family of fizzy cocktails (the most famous being the Tom Collins), which swap out different liquors or wines for the base spirit but keep the same, bright lemony profile from the supporting cast of seltzer, lemon juice, and sugar.

COLLINS GLASS

(n.) This tall cylindrical glass holds between 10 and 14 ounces of liquid and is more slender than the highball glass. It takes its name from the Tom Collins cocktail.

COLONY

(n.) This Prohibition-era classic takes its name from the Colony restaurant, an uptown speakeasy that hosted many a tony Manhattanite during the dry days of the early twentieth century. As did many cocktails of the time, this drink has a base of gin, which was easier to produce well (and quickly) than other spirits. An old-school mix of gin and juice, the drink has an herbal flavor that is rounded out by bittersweet grapefruit juice and plain old sweet maraschino liqueur.

COMPLEXITY

(n.) An often-used but poorly defined wine-tasting term. Generally, complexity is viewed as a positive trait, indicating that a wine has many facets, but the term is often mistakenly applied to strongly flavored wines.

CONCRETE VAT OR EGG

(n.) A fermentation vessel for wine, used as an alternative to the more common stainless steel vats. The rounded corners of the egg shape are thought to encourage a more even fermentation, and the thermal properties of concrete allow the wine to maintain a more constant temperature throughout the process as compared to stainless steel tanks, which have comparatively thin walls.

C

CONDITION

(v.) A beer-making technique that can be employed after the first fermentation to settle and clarify the beer and impart desired flavor characteristics. After the initial fermentation slows and most of the sugars have been converted to alcohol, some yeast cells are still interacting with sugars that haven't been processed already. Conditioning—the process of letting the yeast continue to work—may take place in the same fermentation vessel, in a second vessel such as a cask, keg, or carboy, or in the bottle. Depending on the style of beer, this can take a few days or more than a year. If left in the fermentation vessel, the yeast cells that have already precipitated out of the beer can impart negative rubbery or soapy flavors. Some producers therefore elect to move the beer to a second vessel for conditioning (*see:* Cask Ale). Others will bottle the beer with an extra dose of sugar to reignite the fermentation process and carbonate the beer in the bottle; these beers are called "bottle-conditioned" and will contain a small amount of sediment from the yeast settling. Cold conditioning (leaving the beer to rest in a cold environment) can help to further clarify the beer, and many lagers develop their flavors from being cold-conditioned.

COOLER

(n.) A catch-all category for a broad swath of drinks made by mixing a liquor or fortified wine with a carbonated beverage, served over ice and often garnished with a citrus peel. The drink is often named for the base spirit, such as the Campari cooler or a Scotch cooler, or a location where the variation originated, such as the Boston cooler (rum, lemon, and soda) or Narragansett cooler (bourbon, orange juice, and ginger ale).

COOPER

(n.) A producer of wooden vessels used in the alcoholic beverage industry; a cooperage is the collective output of his or her work as well as the place where he or she works. Tradi-

tionally wooden vessels such as casks or barrels were used to store and transport dry goods and liquids around the world. Many styles of wine, spirits, and beer were developed around the flavors that specific cask types imparted. Depending on the type of wood, the size of the vessel, the age of the cask, and how it is treated, a liquid may take on very different characteristics when aged in a cask. For example, French oak tends to impart a lightly spicy and fruity character to a liquid, whereas American oak gives a more powerful tannic and vanilla-like profile. Larger vessels will impart less flavor, as there is less surface area in contact with the liquid, while smaller ones will have a more intense effect. A cooper may char the inside of the cask to impart more spicy and smoky flavors.

Wood casks are used less frequently today because of their expense compared to alternative containers made out of plastic or metal. Some producers turn to oak chips or staves to impart oaky characteristics to their product, but this is generally viewed as an inferior method.

COPITA

(n.) A small stemmed sherry glass that is often used for tasting spirits; sometimes called a "nosing copita."

CORDIAL

1. *(n.)* In the United States, the terms "cordial" and "liqueur" can be used interchangeably to denote a sweetened spirit, though the latter sounds less grandmotherly.

2. *(n.)* Outside the United States, the term describes a fruit-based sugar syrup used as a mixer in both alcoholic and nonalcoholic beverages. Lime cordial, such as Rose's brand, may be the most famous example of this category.

CORDIAL GLASS

(n.) A small glass, usually 1 to 4 ounces, used for serving liqueurs. Classic versions have short stems, though modern designs tend to omit them, which makes them look similar to shot glasses.

CORPSE REVIVER #2

OF the entire family of gruesomely named pre-Prohibition drinks thought to be intended to rouse oneself in the morning, version no. 2 remains the best known. A lighter take on the Sidecar, with gin and Lillet used instead of Cognac, this drink finishes fresh and citrusy, with a hint of herbal complexity from the absinthe. Such a drink is a reasonable choice for eye-opening activities if you keep in mind the instructions from the 1930 *Savoy Cocktail Book*: "Four of these taken in swift succession will unrevive the corpse again."

Serves 1

1 dash absinthe
1 ounce gin
1 ounce Cointreau
1 ounce Lillet
1 ounce lemon juice

Garnish: orange or lemon peel

Glassware: cocktail or coupe

In a chilled cocktail or coupe glass, add a dash of absinthe. Roll around to coat and discard excess. Add remaining ingredients to a cocktail shaker. Add ice and shake until chilled. Strain into prepared cocktail or coupe glass. Garnish with an orange or lemon peel.

CORKAGE

(*n.*) The amount a restaurant or bar charges a customer who wants to have his or her own wine opened on site. Usually it is a per-bottle fee.

CORKED

(*adj.*) Used to describe a wine that is flawed from the presence of 2,4,6-trichloroanisole (TCA), which creates off aromas and flavors that are often described as smelling like cardboard, wet dog, or moldy cork. The most common culprit for contamination is the cork used the seal the bottle, though TCA can also be passed to wine via wine barrels or other wine-making equipment. For this reason, wines bottled with a screw cap or another alternative closure have a much lower incidence of TCA contamination, though the cork industry has exerted much effort in producing TCA-free corks. Sensitivity to TCA in wine varies among individuals; some can detect the presence of TCA in the single digit parts per trillion.

CORKSCREW

(*n.*) A tool with a spiral metal appendage (the "worm") used to remove a cork from a wine bottle. A corkscrew works when the worm is twisted fully into the cork and then pulled upward by a handle, drawing the cork from the bottle. To make opening a bottle easier, many corkscrew models include lever systems, which increase the amount of force exerted on the cork, which makes it easier to remove.

COUPE

(*n.*) This squat bowl-shaped glass was designed in mid-sixteenth-century England for serving sweet warm Champagne, the popular style of the time. Contemporary sparkling wine drinkers have largely abandoned the coupe as the large surface-to-air ratio turns the wine flat faster, but it has been found new life as a festive cocktail glass.

COSMOPOLITAN

BEFORE the "Cosmo" became the must-have liquid accessory of Sarah Jessica Parker acolytes, there was the Cosmopolitan, popularized in 1988 by bartender Toby Cecchini at the Manhattan hotspot the Odeon. Adapting a pink-hued mock Martini that had been floating around Florida and San Francisco, Cecchini retooled the ingredient list with higher-quality mixers, choosing Absolut Citron vodka, lime juice, Cointreau, and cranberry juice. Popular in the Miami and New York club scenes, the drink gained national exposure via *Sex and the City*, and in the late 1990s it would become the go-to order for upwardly mobile urban women. Strip away all the silly cultural associations, however, and what you're left with is a doctored-up Cape Cod—a little sweet, not too alcoholic, and very, very pink.

Serves 1

2 ounces citron vodka
1 ounce Cointreau
1 ounce lime juice
½ ounce cranberry juice

Garnish: lemon twist

Glassware: cocktail or coupe

Add all ingredients to a cocktail shaker. Add ice and shake until chilled. Strain into a chilled cocktail or coupe glass. Garnish with a lemon twist. And only a lemon twist.

Note: *Despite common pop culture associations, the original Cosmopolitan is a rather dry cocktail. The recipe can be tweaked with other orange liqueurs such as Combier, which will result in a slightly sweeter recipe. Ditch the cranberry cocktail for natural, tart cranberry juice.*

C

CRAFT BREWERY

(n.) Generally used to refer to a small, independently owned brewery, this term may be used interchangeably with "microbrewery." The term originally described the small breweries that began opening in the 1970s in England and the United States, differentiating them from the large multinational breweries that dominated the beer market. The notion of "craft" put an emphasis on using quality ingredients and traditional or innovative brewing techniques. As the movement grew, with smaller breweries growing rapidly and being bought out by larger companies, the parameters for what can be described as a craft brewery have become more nebulous. The Brewers Association defines the term as a brewery that produces fewer than six million barrels of beer, with no more than 25 percent of the company owned or controlled by someone in the alcohol industry who is not a craft brewer (like a big beer company), and produces mostly all-malt beer.

CRAFT DISTILLERY

(n.) Generally used to describe a small, independently owned distillery, the term has no legal definition; is often used interchangeably with "microdistillery." Although small distilleries once thrived in the United States, Prohibition hobbled the industry and laws enacted after Prohibition discouraged the practice. As a result, large distilleries, often owned by multinational corporations, dominated the alcohol production scene and encouraged consolidation. Since the 1980s, however, there has been a rise of small, independently owned distilleries as some of the more restrictive laws have been lifted. The term "craft distillery" is usually used to describe these small distilleries, but there is no exact definition as to what distinguishes a craft distiller from a larger, more established distillery. The American Craft Distillers Association defines the term as a distillery that produces less than one hundred thousand proof gallons that can be taxed per year (a proof gallon is 50 percent alcohol at 60°F).

C

CREAM ALE

(n.) An American style of light ale designed to compare with American pale lagers. The modern profile skews crisp and light with a smooth mouthfeel and low to zero hop flavor, though prior to Prohibition the style had more character, with greater body and a higher quantity of hop influence. A proportion of corn or sugar is sometimes used in the grain bill to create cheaper versions of this style.

CREAM LIQUEUR

(n.) A liqueur with dairy products added. This is different than a crème liqueur, which is so named because of its viscous mouthfeel, which is often the result of added sugar. Because of the inclusion of dairy, cream liqueurs require refrigeration after opening and have a shorter shelf life than most other alcoholic beverages.

CREAM OF COCONUT

(n.) Sweetened coconut cream, an ingredient sometimes called for in cocktails such as the Piña Colada. Many commercial versions contain high-fructose corn syrup and artificial stabilizers. To better control the level of sweetness in a drink, use coconut cream and add sugar or simple syrup to taste instead.

CREAM SHERRY

(n.) A sweet style of sherry traditionally made by sweetening oloroso or amontillado sherry with Pedro Ximénez sherry. The result is dark, nutty, and rich. Note that cream sherry does not contain any dairy. The misleading "cream" in the name is a reference to the product's viscosity. It is best served as an after-dinner drink over ice or with a slice of lemon or lime.

CREMANT

(n.) A French designation for a sparkling wine not made in the Champagne region. These wines, which are often made in the Loire or Burgundy, typically offer good value compared to the pricey offerings of Champagne.

CRÈME DE CACAO

(n.) A sweetened liqueur flavored with cacao (cocoa bean) and vanilla. The word "crème" refers to the rich texture of the liqueur, which is often achieved by adding sweeteners. Usually mixed in cocktails such as the Grasshopper or the Brandy Alexander, this sweet, chocolate-flavored alcohol may also be consumed with a splash of soda water as a digestif. Both dark (brown) and white (clear) versions exist; if neither is specified in the recipe, use white. Brands to try include Tempus Fugit and Bols.

CRÈME DE CASSIS

(n.) A black currant–flavored liqueur. Though the deep red spirit is produced around the world, crème de cassis's spiritual homeland is Burgundy, France, where top versions are made by macerating black cur-

rants in a neutral spirit, then sweetening the tart liquid with sugar. Along with Champagne, the liqueur forms half of the ingredient list for the Kir Royale, an apéritif that was once fashionable in France. Brands to look for include Briottet.

CRÈME DE MENTHE

(n.) A mint-flavored liqueur that comes in white (clear) and green versions, the latter gaining its color from mint leaves or extracts. Typically made from a neutral spirit that is infused with mint leaves and then sweetened, crème de menthe does not actually have any cream in it; the word "crème" is a reference to the liquid's smooth texture. The spirit may be used in cocktails such as the Grasshopper or drunk as a digestif.

CRÈME DE NOYAUX

(n.) A sweet almond-flavored liqueur traditionally made from distilling apricot or peach pits, though cheaper versions may use almond flavoring. Some producers dye the product red,

C

while others produce clear or barrel-aged versions. Amaretto is an acceptable substitute.

CRÈME DE VIOLETTE

(*n.*) A liqueur flavored with the violet flower. European in origin and first produced in the nineteenth century, the sweet, floral, and deep-purple spirit was a staple ingredient in classic cocktails like the Aviation and Blue Moon. It was unavailable in the United States for many years until 2007, when Rothman & Winter's version made it to American shores. In recent years a handful of other brands have become available as well.

CRU

(*n.*) This French term means "vineyard" when translated directly, but is also used as a legal classification for wine made from a special vineyard or village in France. Depending on the wine region, however, it varies in meaning. For example, "grand cru" is the highest designation for a vineyard in Burgundy, with the next

step down being "premier cru." In Bordeaux, however, the top producers have a rating of premier cru. Though the ranking system was originally conceived to identify and classify quality wines, some dispute the usefulness or accuracy of the tiers.

CRUSH

(*n.*) A wine-industry term for the period of the year when grapes are harvested and made into wine.

CRUSHED ICE

(*n.*) Pulverized in a blender or by hand, crushed ice is an essential ingredient in juleps, cobblers, swizzles, and other drinks. The increased surface area of the ice allows it to more rapidly cool and dilute the cocktail. One easy way of making crushed ice at home is to place lump ice in a Lewis bag and pound the covered bag with a mallet or hammer.

CUBA LIBRE

FOR being a sweet, simple highball, the Cuba Libre comes with some heavy historical baggage. In the wake of the Spanish-American War, which transferred the Spanish colonies of Puerto Rico, parts of the Philippines, Guam, and the West Indies to the United States and released Cuba from Spanish rule in 1898, the fairly recent American invention of Coca-Cola found its way into Havana bars. Accounts of who first mixed it with Cuban rum and a squeeze of lime juice are sketchy, but the combination, which cheekily took its name from the rallying cry for Cuban independence ("Viva Cuba libre!"), soon spread northward to the United States. Essentially a sweet, simple highball that's dead easy to make, the Cuba Libre, otherwise known as the more pedestrian-sounding rum and Coke, would become one of the most popular mixed drinks of the century as rum would rise in popularity after Prohibition and during World War II, when European imports to the United States slowed and distilleries were repurposed for wartime activities.

Serves 1

2 ounces rum, white or golden
1 lime, halved
Coca-Cola Classic

Garnish: lime wheel or slice

Glassware: Collins

In a Collins glass, add rum and squeeze in lime halves. Add ice and top with Coca-Cola. Stir gently to combine. Garnish with a lime wheel or slice.

C

CRUSTA

(n.) New Orleans bartender Joseph Santini generally gets the credit for the mid-nineteenth-century creation of the crusta, now thought of as the intellectual bridge between the original stripped-down cocktail (the Old Fashioned) and everything that came after. The version laid out in Jerry Thomas's 1862 edition of the *How to Mix Drinks* reports that to the basic formula of a base spirit, sugar, and bitters, Santini added a lighter spirit (usually orange liqueur) and citrus. Brandy (usually French Cognac) was the popular base spirit for the drink at the time, but many others—gin, whiskey, and the like—are all acceptable substitutions. (For recipe, *see:* Brandy Crusta.)

CULT WINE

(n.) A term that emerged in the 1990s to describe highly sought after collectible wines, usually Napa Cabernets (such as those made by Screaming Eagle and Harlan Estate) or red Bordeaux (such as Château Angélus and Château Le Pin). These wines tended to receive high scores from wine critics and have limited allocations, which put upward pressure on the resale value. Many of the California wines were initially sold only through mailing lists, though they could later be found on the auction market.

CURAÇAO

(n.) One of the two main styles of orange-flavored liqueurs, along with triple sec. Invented by the Dutch in the nineteenth century, using dried peels from a strain of oranges grown in the West Indies and pot-distilled brandy, this sweetened spirit was traditionally made in a heavier style than triple sec. Modern versions may be clear or dyed blue or orange, and occasionally other flavors are added, such as coffee and chocolate. Though the brand is French, Grand Marnier is one of the most recognizable curaçao-style orange liqueurs on the market, though the inclusion of Cognac in the blend sets it apart, and as such, it is generally not interchangeable with others. High-end

C

bartenders tend to shun most curaçaos, though the cocktail renaissance has resulted in some higher-quality version coming out on the market, such as Pierre Ferrand dry curaçao.

CUVÉE

(n.) A wine term usually used to describe a blend or special bottling.

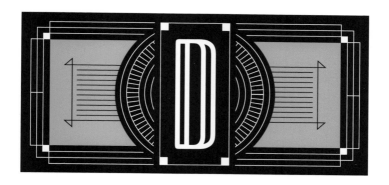

DAIGINJO

(n.) A subset of ginjo sake in which the rice grains have been polished to remove at least 50 percent of the outer husk. If the daiginjo sake bears the "junmai" label, it has not been fortified with added ethyl alcohol. Like ginjo sake, this style is best served slightly chilled to preserve the delicate aromatics.

DARK RUM

(n.) Deeper in color than golden rum, dark rum tends to be assertive in flavor and heavy in body. The color and flavor usually come from long aging times in charred oak barrels, which impart notes of chocolate, nuts, and coffee, though some lesser-quality versions achieve this effect through the addition of caramel or molasses flavorings.

DASH

(n.) An imprecise measurement used to indicate a very small amount of liquid, most often used in reference to liquids that are used sparingly, such as bitters or hot sauce. In a cocktail recipe, the term usually indicates what comes out of the bottle with one shake, though this amount can vary wildly from bottle to bottle,

DAIQUIRI

THOUGH the name "Daiquiri" may be inexorably linked to frozen drinks served at strip mall chain restaurants these days, the true recipe is a quality cocktail that can stand toe-to-toe with the best of them. The credit for the recipe, which is essentially a Rum Sour, usually goes to a U.S. engineer living in Cuba during the Spanish-American War, though it is likely that Cuban residents had been drinking something similar for some time. Famously associated with author Ernest Hemingway and the jet-set glamour of pre-embargo Cuba in the 1930s, the Daiquiri would rise in popularity in the United States during World War II, as Caribbean rum became much easier to procure than foreign whisky.

Serves 1

2 ounces light rum
1 ounce lime juice
¾ ounce simple syrup
 (1:1, sugar:water)

Garnish: lime wheel

Glassware: cocktail or coupe

Add all ingredients to a cocktail shaker. Add ice and shake until chilled. Strain into a chilled cocktail or coupe glass. Garnish with a lime wheel.

DARK 'N' STORMY

THIS simple mix of dark rum and ginger beer over ice has roots in colonial Bermuda, where England's royal navy opened a ginger beer plant in the late nineteenth century. The drink was traditionally made with a dark, heavy Demerara-style rum, part of the sailors' daily rations. A note: Gosling Brothers bought the trademark to the Dark 'n' Stormy name and recipe, so Gosling's Black Seal rum is the official liquor of record to use in this drink.

Serves 1

2 ounces dark or blackstrap rum
½–¾ ounce lime juice
4 ounces dry ginger beer
   (preferably Fever Tree or
   Fentiman's)

Garnish: lime wheel

Glassware: Collins glass

Add rum and lime juice to a Collins glass. Add ice and stir. Top with ginger beer and garnish with a lime wheel.

Note: *Adjust the lime/ginger according to the sweetness of the rum/ginger beer.*

and even from shake to shake. Some bartenders advocate measuring a dash more accurately, often by using an eyedropper or a standardized shaker bottle.

DEAD SOLDIER

(n.) A slang term for an empty bottle, usually used to refer to beer bottles, but it may also refer to wine or liquor bottles.

DECANT

(v.) The process of pouring a wine into another vessel, usually a decanter. This process can serve one of two purposes. For younger and more tannic wines, decanting can help aerate the wine and make it more palatable. For older wines, decanting helps ensure no sediment (material like dead yeast cells that may precipitate out of wine over time) will be poured into glasses. To properly decant an older bottle of wine, the pourer should arrange the bottle in front of a light source, such as a candle, so that he or she can see

when the sediment from the bottom of the bottle reaches the neck while pouring.

DEMERARA SYRUP

(n.) A variation on simple syrup made with Demerara (turbinado) sugar. The syrup should carry notes of caramel, have a golden color, and taste richer than syrup made with white sugar.

DESSERT WINES

(n.) An unregulated term that groups together sweet wines, which are usually intended for consumption after dinner, either with dessert or as dessert. Common examples include ice wine; sweet styles of port, Madeira, and sherry; Sauternes; Tokaji; and Muscat wines.

DIGESTIF (DIGESTIVO)

(n.) Conceptually paired with the apéritif as bookends to a meal, the digestif is an after-dinner drink, usually a fortified wine or distilled

DEATH IN THE AFTERNOON

THE title of Ernest Hemingway's 1932 novel *Death in the Afternoon* is both a direct reference to the gruesome finale of Spanish bull-fights and a more oblique one to his meditations on mortality. The fact that he ascribed the same title to a cocktail made of a shot of absinthe topped with Champagne, which he submitted to a celebrity recipe book in 1935, is something to ponder. The original formula for absinthe was certainly a more powerful concoction than it is now, but the more likely explanation for the macabre name: in his recipe he prescribed drinking three to five of these at a time.

Serves 1

¼–½ ounce absinthe
1 dash simple syrup, optional
　(1:1, sugar:water)
Sparkling wine (dry), chilled

Glassware: flute

Add absinthe and simple syrup to a flute. Slowly top with chilled sparkling wine.

Note: *A good, dry sparkling wine or Champagne works well here. Because absinthe has a very particular flavor profile, some may prefer more or less. Though the original recipe calls for a prodigious one-and-a-half ounces of absinthe, it's easier to remain standing after drinking one of these, so contemporary versions call for a lighter pour.*

liquor, served neat in small amounts. The ritual originated in Europe (digestif from France, digestivo from Italy), where a small amount of liquor after dinner was thought to help digestion. This category can encompass a wide range of alcohols, including port, sherry, Madeira, amari, whiskey, liqueurs, and brandy.

DISTILLATION

(n.) A chemical process used to make high-alcohol spirits, distillation separates ethanol (drinking alcohol) from water. The basic steps: A mix of ethanol and water, usually derived from fermentation, is heated. Water and ethanol have different boiling points, so the alcohol evaporates into steam first, which can then be condensed and collected.

Archaeological evidence of distillation dates to the ancient Greeks, who used the process in attempts at alchemy. During the Middle Ages, further refinements were made in the Middle East by those preparing perfumes and medicinal products. The first recorded examples of the distillation of alcohol for drinking are from the twelfth century. Europeans began to make high-alcohol products flavored with herbs for medicinal purposes, which gradually became used recreationally.

In the production of high-alcohol spirits, there are two main types of stills, the instruments used in distilling. Pot stills, which are similar to what the ancient Greeks and Arabs used, can distill one batch of alcohol at a time. The column still, which was patented in Ireland in 1822, allows distillers to condense multiple distillations into one process, thereby achieving a higher-alcohol product.

DOSAGE

(n.) A sweet liquid made from sugar and wine or a sweet wine that is added to Champagne or sparkling wines before capping. The practice originated in Champagne, where some thought extra sweetness helped make highly acidic wines more palatable. Certain sweet styles of sparkling wine (doux or demi-sec, for example) require a larger dosage,

D

while on the dry end of the spectrum, wines labeled "extra brut" or "brut" will have little to no added sugar.

DOUBLE

(*n.*) A drink order requesting twice the amount of said drink, usually referring to a shot of a spirit (e.g., "A double whiskey, please," or "Whiskey, make it a double"). This can get tricky when ordering a mixed drink with twice the amount of alcohol when you don't want twice the mixer (such as a double vodka and soda), so be prepared to clarify your order.

DOUBLE STRAIN

(*v.*) This cocktail-making technique for shaken drinks requires two strainers (usually a Hawthorne strainer and a fine-mesh strainer) for pouring the liquid from the shaker into the service glass. The second strainer ensures that no chips of ice, seeds, fruit pulp, or other nonliquid ingredients end up in the finished drink.

DRAFT (DRAUGHT)

(*n.*) A beer that has been poured from a tapped keg or cask; usually used to distinguish these beers from those that have been canned or bottled.

DRAM

(*n.*) Derived from the Scottish Gaelic term meaning "drink," a dram originally indicated a liquid measurement equaling ⅛ ounce, or ¾ teaspoon. Colloquially, the term was co-opted to mean a small sip or drink of alcohol, usually referring to whiskey. In the eighteenth century, dram houses—essentially taverns where patrons could buy liquor—sprang up in England as the production of gin increased. The term "dram shop" remains a legal definition meaning a bar or tavern in the United States today.

DRY

1. (*adj.*) A drink order, usually in reference to the contemporary recipe for dry Martinis, that specifies dry

DUBONNET

ELEGANT in its simplicity, this crowd-pleasing drink features just two ingredients: dry gin and the titular Dubonnet, a sweetened wine apéritif. Dating to the early twentieth century, the combo was supposedly a favorite of Queen Elizabeth, who reportedly could down a few of these at a time. The spare skeleton of a recipe allows for a host of variations; try swapping other spirits for the gin or adding different bitters (orange works particularly well).

Serves 1

1½ ounce Dubbonet
½ ounce gin

Glassware: cocktail or coupe

Add all ingredients to a mixing glass, add ice, and stir. Strain into a chilled cocktail or coupe glass.

D

vermouth to be mixed with gin in a ratio of 1:5 or 1:6.

2. *(adj.)* A wine that has little to no sugar.

3. *(adj.)* A colloquial description for a county or region that does not permit the sale of alcohol.

DRY HOPPING

(v.) A beer-making technique in which hops are added to a beer after it has been cooked and fermentation has begun. In most beer recipes, hops are added during the boil (when beer is cooked) so that hop resins—which provide the bitter flavor—will have a chance to become soluble and flavor the beer. The boiling process, however, minimizes the amount of complex hop flavor and aroma esters—all the citrusy, grassy, spicy character—that can be transferred to the beer. Hops added late in the boiling process provide some of these esters, but adding hops after the cooking process is done allows for the most delicate flavor and aroma molecules to survive. This practice is most common in beers with a hoppy profile, such as IPAs or pale ales.

DRY SHAKE

(n.) A cocktail-making technique in which drinks containing egg whites are shaken before ice is added so a more complete emulsification may be achieved.

DUNKEL

(n.) A generic term for dark lagers, from the German word for "dark." These beers are generally smooth, malty, and dry, with a low hop profile. The dunkel style comes from Bavaria, where it was the first style of beer to be regulated by the Reinheitsgebot (German Purity Law of 1516), which stated that beers could be made only from water, barley, and hops, but it is now made around Germany. The term "dunkel" may also be attached to other styles of beer, such as *dunkelweizen*, to refer to unusually dark versions of the style.

EARLY WINE

(n.) A class of wines bottled and sold soon after harvest, as opposed to wines that have been aged for at least one winter. The most famous example of this category, which is known as *vin de primeur* in France, is Beaujolais nouveau, which is a red wine made in Beaujolais that is fermented quickly after the harvest and released for sale on the third Thursday in November in the same vintage calendar year. Because the wine is made rapidly, it tends to be fruity and light in body. American producers are also experimenting with this style of wine.

EAU DE VIE

(n.) This type of brandy is made from distilling fermented fruit, most often tree fruits and berries, such as plums (mirabelle), pears (poire), raspberries (framboise), and cherries (Kirsch). The final product is usually bottled unaged to preserve the fresh and vibrant fruit flavors. Alpine locales may produce the most famous versions, but the spirit is made around the world. Historians believe that eaux de vie, which have roots as old as alcohol distillation itself, were first used for medicinal purposes, hence the name, which means "water of life." Although they are consumed primarily as a digestif, a growing number of bartenders are using these in cocktails.

ENOLOGY (OENOLOGY)

(n.) The study of wine making; often paired in academic programs with viticulture, the study of grape growing and harvesting.

ESTUFAGEM

(n.) An aging process for Madeira in which wines are heated in stainless steel tanks. This is done to mimic the more natural but time- and effort-intensive canteiros system, in which wines are aged in hot lofts or attics for years at a time. The estufagem system is generally considered inferior.

EXPRESS

(v.) A method to extract the oils in a twist of citrus peel by squeezing or twisting the peel over a cocktail.

EXTRA AÑEJO

(n.) A category of tequila that has been aged in wood barrels for a minimum of three years. These tend to have a smooth, almost Cognac-like character.

EL PRESIDENTE

THIS Cuban cocktail is believed to have become popular with alcohol-seeking Americans traveling to the island nation during Prohibition. After the ban was lifted, the rum-based drink found its footing stateside as well. It makes for an interesting historical recipe with a markedly different turn than most tropical drinks with the addition of vermouth, which lends a note of levity to an otherwise lighthearted rum concoction spiked with grenadine and curaçao.

Serves 1

1½ ounces light rum
¾ or 1½ ounce dry vermouth
½ oz or 1 barspoon orange
  curaçao
1 dash grenadine

Garnish: orange peel

Glassware: coupe glass

Add all ingredients to a mixing glass, add ice, and stir well. Strain into a chilled coupe glass and garnish with an orange peel.

FALERNUM

(n.) A sweetened syrup or liqueur made from lime zest, cloves, sugar, ginger, and almonds that most likely originated in Barbados in the nineteenth century. It can be either non-alcoholic or alcoholic and is often yellow in color. Though several lay claim to its invention, the mix was likely made in many households before commercial production began. The syrup plays an essential role in many tiki drinks such as Zombie Punch and the Bermuda Rum Swizzle. It can be hard to find quality versions of the syrup in stores, so many bars and restaurants make their own version in-house. Brands to try include John D. Taylor's and Fee Brother's.

FAT WASH

(n.) The process by which spirits are infused with flavor from a particular fat. A fatty substance, commonly bacon, duck fat, or sesame oil, is heated and added to a spirit, then the mixture is chilled. After the fat has solidified, it is skimmed off and the spirit is strained.

F

FERMENT

(v.) To induce a chemical reaction that results in the creation of alcohol (to make wine, beer, or sake, for example) or lactic acid (to make sour foods such as kimchi, sauerkraut, yogurt, or pickles). During the fermentation process for alcohol, yeast consumes sugar from either fruit or starches, which produces alcohol and carbon dioxide.

FERNET-BRANCA

(n.) A dry, bitter amaro made in Milan, Italy, by the Fratelli Branca distillery (Fernet is a type of amaro; Branca is the brand name). First produced in 1845 as a medicinal elixir thought to aid digestion and soothe stomach troubles, it became a popular digestivo recommended for consumption after overly large dinners. The dominant characteristics— bracing bitterness and notes of eucalyptus and menthol—come from a proprietary blend of more than forty ingredients, including cinchona bark, saffron, and chamomile. In the early 2010s the brand experienced a surge of popularity in American metropolises such as San Francisco and New York, and to order a shot is generally considered an insider move. The drink is most often served neat, occasionally with a ginger ale back, though many bartenders are experimenting with mixing it in cocktails.

FIELD BLEND

(n.) A wine made from different types of grapes that were grown in the same vineyard or field.

FIFTH

(n.) This unit of measurement equals one-fifth of a gallon. In the United States, where imperial measurements are used in lieu of metric, liquor was sold in either quarts (one-quarter of a gallon) or fifths (one-fifth of a gallon) until 1980. Today it is much more common to see bottles sold in liter or 750-milliliter sizes.

F

FINGER

(n.) This unit of measurement is determined by a finger width against a glass (e.g., "I'd like two fingers of whiskey.") The usage is growing infrequent, as finger width is not a reliable unit of measure.

FINISH

(n.) A term used to refer to the last flavors detected before swallowing or spitting a cocktail, liquor, beer, or wine. For example, rye may have a spicy finish, while an amaro-based cocktail might have a bitter finish. This differs from length, another tasting term, which refers to how long the flavors linger in your mouth.

FINO

(n.) A light, crisp style of sherry made by allowing a layer of flor (yeast) to develop over the wine as it ages, which protects it from oxidation. This dry, pale fortified wine is best served chilled and should be consumed soon after opening the bottle.

FIOR D'ALPI

(n.) A style of Italian liqueur made with a neutral spirit and herbs.

FIZZ

(n.) Essentially a sour made tall with the addition of soda water, the fizz emerged in the United States in the late nineteenth century. Any base spirit can be used (gin may be the most famous), but the drink must also include citrus, a sweetener, and soda water, which is then shaken with ice and strained into a tall narrow glass, such as a highball glass. The agitated ingredients might form a frothy head on the drink, which is more apparent when thickeners such as egg whites are included. Variations abound (the most recognizable perhaps being the Gin Fizz), with addition of egg or egg whites, fruit, cream, or additional spirits all accepted within the canon. There's a debate among cocktail authorities as to how fizzes differ from Collins drinks, which basically contain the same ingredients. Though the lines

FLAME OF LOVE

REPORTEDLY created by Hollywood bartender Pepe Ruiz for Rat Pack crooner Dean Martin, who suffered from Martini ennui, this unusual mix of vodka and sherry requires some showy flair on the part of the bartender, who should flame the orange peel and then express it into the serving glass both before the drink is poured.

Serves 1

2 ounces vodka
½ ounce fino sherry
8 orange peels

Garnish: orange peel

Glassware: coupe glass

Add vodka and sherry to a mixing glass. Add ice and stir well. Strain into a chilled coupe glass. Flame orange peels over top of the glass. Garnish with an unflamed orange peel.

are blurry, there is some consensus that fizzes are shaken and strained while Collinses get prepared in the serving glass with ice and stirred.

FLAG

(n.) A garnish made of two or more fruits (think maraschino cherry and an orange wedge) skewered together on a cocktail pick.

FLAMING DRINKS

(n.) A category of cocktails and shots that are set on fire before service. Though the flavor may be altered by some of the alcohol burning off, the primary reason for doing this—in every drink from classic cocktails such as the Blue Blazer to spring break–worthy shots such as the B-52—is dramatic presentation. Experts recommend taking appropriate safety measures (removing dangling sleeves or clothes and finding a fire extinguisher, for example) before executing these at home.

FLIP

(n.) Although egg whites might show up in sours or fizzes, any drink with a whole egg could be considered a flip, a category that has been floating around since the seventeenth century. The early versions involved heating sugar or molasses-sweetened beer until the sugar caramelized. Sometime in the nineteenth century, eggs got added to the mix. The modern version usually works like this: a base spirit, a whole egg, and a sweetener, shaken and served with grated nutmeg. Eggnog may be the most famous drink to come out of this category, but the formula allows for a host of variations. (For recipe, *see:* Sherry Flip.)

FLOAT

1. *(v.)* A bartending skill used to layer cocktail ingredients in the glass, as seen in drinks such as the Mai Tai, black and tan, or pousse-café. Typically a bartender will pour the heavier liquid in the glass first, then slowly pour the second liquid into the glass

FOG CUTTER

A **STAPLE** on the Trader Vic's drink menus, this umbrella drink is a little unusual for a drink in the tiki canon, as it calls not for a mix of dark and light rums, but rather a blend of brandy, gin, and light rum. In addition, some versions call for it to be topped off with a float of sherry (a sweetened style works best with the drink's fruity flavors, so choose cream or East India). The whole mix is potent stuff; it's best to take the title of the drink as tongue in cheek.

Serves 1

1½ ounces light rum
½ ounce gin
½ ounce brandy
2 ounces orange juice
1 ounce lemon juice
½ ounce orgeat
½ ounce sherry

Garnish: sprig of mint

Glassware: highball or Collins

Add all ingredients except the sherry to a cocktail shaker and add ice. Shake, then strain into a highball or Collins glass filled with crushed ice. Float the sherry on top, garnish with the mint, and serve with a straw.

over the back of a barspoon so that the second component floats on top of the first.

2. *(n.)* A tall, fizzy beverage poured over scoop of ice cream, such as in a root beer float.

FLUTE

(n.) A wineglass with a narrow tulip-shaped or cylindrical bowl that is used for serving sparkling wine or cocktails made with sparkling wine. The glass most often comes with a stem to keep body heat from transferring from the person holding the glass to the chilled sparkling wine, but stemless glasses, considered less fussy, can also be found.

FLYING WINE MAKER

(n.) Slang for a consulting wine maker who makes wine in many countries, often traveling between the hemispheres to maximize the number of harvests in which she or he can participate. In some circles this term is considered derogatory.

FORTIFIED WINE

(n.) A wine-based product that has been made with added distilled liquor and bottled at an ABV between 16 and 24 percent. The added alcohol, usually in the form of grape brandy, helps preserve the wine. Producers can change the style of the product by timing the addition of the extra alcohol: it can either arrest the fermentation of the wine as high alcohol levels kill yeast cells, leaving a sweeter product with more residual sugar; or it can be added once fermentation is complete or nearly complete, leaving a dry product. Some examples of fortified wine are port, sherry, vermouth, and Madeira.

FRAPPÉ

(n.) Conceived as a stripped-down version of the absinthe cocktail in the late nineteenth-century United States, the frappé is made by pouring absinthe over crushed ice in a small bar glass, with an optional dash of water. Some historians argue for

F

the addition of soda water, what cocktail writer David Wondrich terms "the California style."

FRAPPÉ GLASS

(*n.*) A squat stemmed glass used to hold frappés. Usually around 8 ounces, the glass may have an hourglass or tulip shape.

FREE POUR

(*v.*) A bartending skill in which the act of portioning a cocktail's ingredients is done by pouring spirits straight from the bottle rather than measuring with a jigger. A bartender with a steady and consistent rate of pour can theoretically measure the amount dispensed by timing, and certain pour spouts are designed to assist in this endeavor. Though the effect is theatrical, many bar owners discourage this practice because of the increased chance of waste from inaccurate measurements.

FRENCH OAK

(*n.*) A type of wood commonly used to make casks and barrels. Products aged or fermented in French oak gain a spicy flavor and soft, silky tannins.

FRESH/WET HOPPING

(*v.*) A beer-making technique in which fresh, undried hops are used to flavor the beer. Most hops destined for beer are dried for easy storage and year-round use. Fresh, or "wet," hops have a limited shelf life and must be used soon after being harvested. Some brewers have seized on the seasonal nature of fresh hops and offer harvest-time beers made with freshly picked hops. The fresh hop flavor tends to skew more vegetal and grassy than dried hops, and some say that the delicate aroma esters from fresh hops will last in the beer for a few months.

FRENCH 75

NAMED after a French gun used in World War I—a not-so-subtle reference to its metaphoric lethalness—this Champagne cocktail was made famous at Harry's New York Bar in Paris in the early 1900s. Some historical records cite Cognac as the original base spirit, which would make sense on account of the drink's Gallic origins. Somewhere in translation, however, gin became the official liquor, a move that makes the drink kissing cousins with the Tom Collins.

Serves 1

2 ounces Cognac or gin
½ ounce lemon juice
¼ ounce simple syrup
    (1:1, sugar:water)
3 ounces sparkling wine
    (preferably dry Champagne)

Garnish: long, curly peel of lemon

Glassware: coupe or flute

Add first three ingredients to a cocktail shaker. Add ice and shake until chilled. Strain into a coupe or a flute and top with sparkling wine. Garnish with a long curling peel of lemon.

Note: *Whether making a Cognac or gin French 75, a dry sparkling wine is preferred. Should you be using bubbly with a bit more residual sugar, adjust the simple syrup measurement down accordingly. Use a channel knife to create the perfect long, loopy peel of lemon.*

FRENCH MARTINI

NEITHER truly a Martini nor really all that French, this inaptly named cocktail, with its pink hue and service in a Martini glass, could be seen as the understudy to the more famous Cosmopolitan. The vodka-based drink gets its pink color from a dollop of Chambord, a black raspberry liqueur, and its fruity disposition from a heavy hand with pineapple juice, which creates a nice froth on the finished drink. Created by the owners of Chambord to promote the brand, the drink gained traction in the 1990s, when the not-a-Martini-but-served-in-a-martini-glass trend took flight.

Serves 1

2 ounces vodka
1¾ ounce pineapple juice
¼ ounce crème de cassis

Glassware: coupe

Add all ingredients to a cocktail shaker. Shake with ice and strain into a chilled coupe glass.

F

FROSTED GLASS

1. *(n.)* A serving glass put in the freezer or on ice until a frost forms on the surface. This technique helps to keep drinks chilled. Depending on the temperature of the freezer, it can take more than an hour to achieve this effect.

2. *(n.)* A serving glass with salt or sugar on the rim, as seen on drinks such as the Margarita and Sidecar, respectively. *See*: Rim.

FRUIT BEER

(n.) A beer flavored with fruit or fruit extracts; the fruit may be added either before fermentation, which adds to the fermentable sugars, or after the beer is finished fermenting (usually in extract form), which results in a more pronounced flavor. Before the beer formula of grains, yeast, hops, and water became the norm, spices, vegetables, and fruits were all common additions. Certain styles became linked to particular fruits, such as Belgian kriek, a lambic made with sour cherries. Modern-style fruit beers, often built around an ale base, can verge on cloying if the brewer is too heavy-handed when adding the extract, but the best will strike a good balance between fruit flavor and beer character. Common fruits used in beers include a slate of berries, from raspberries to blueberries, but one can also find versions made with peaches, apricots, apples, cherries, and mangoes.

GAMAY

(n.) A grape used to make red wines. Gamay's homeland is Beaujolais, France, where it dominates production of a range of wines from Cru Beaujolais to Beaujolais nouveau. Thought to have been cultivated in the region since the fourteenth century, the grape is prized for its tendency to ripen early and produce fruity, acidic wines. Though it has long lived in Pinot Noir's shadow on account of Beaujolais's proximity to Pinot Noir–dominated Burgundy, Gamay is coming into its own, with vintners around the world experimenting with the grape.

GAMMEL DANSK

(n.) A Danish potable bitter invented in the early 1960s. The proprietary recipe for the copper-colored liquor calls for twenty-eight different herbs and spices, including ginger, aniseed, and nutmeg.

GARNISH

1. *(n.)* An object placed on or in a finished cocktail that performs a decorative function, though some may also add flavor. Many garnishes are built into traditional cocktail recipes; some have even come to distinguish one cocktail from another, such

GIBSON

A **GOOD** example of how powerful a garnish can be, in this drink the lowly cocktail onion transforms a bitters-less Martini into an entirely new drink: the Gibson. The usual historical squabbles exist about the drink's origins (stories suggest it was created at San Francisco's Bohemian Club in the 1890s for Walter D. K. Gibson, or for the illustrator Charles Dana Gibson, to name just a few), but no one can seem to pinpoint when or why the pickled onion made it into the recipe: the earliest versions did not call for it. By the mid-twentieth century, though, the Gibson—with the onion in place—challenged the Martini in terms of cultural cachet, although its popularity seems to have dwindled in recent years.

Serves 1

2 ounces gin
1 ounce dry vermouth

Garnish: cocktail onion
(see note)

Glassware: cocktail or coupe

Add all ingredients to a mixing glass. Add ice and stir until chilled. Strain into a chilled cocktail or coupe glass. Garnish with a cocktail onion.

Note: *To pickle cocktail onions, peel a handful of pearl onions and place in a jar filled with white vinegar and a pinch of sugar. Let infuse for several hours or up to one week in the refrigerator.*

GIMLET

L EGEND has it this warm-weather cocktail—essentially a Gin Sour made with lime juice—was created in the mid-nineteenth century to encourage Royal Navy sailors to consume their rations of scurvy-stopping lime juice. The name? Possibly attributable to a Thomas Desmond Gimlette, a naval medical officer who served during that era, although his obituary mentions nothing of the drink. Rose's Lime Juice Cordial, a syrup of sugar and lime juice, was invented around the same time to preserve lime juice during long journeys at sea, and fundamentalist versions of the drink still call for it. The Rose's of today, however, is a different animal, with high-fructose corn syrup and additives—stuff that wouldn't make it past the front door of any self-respecting craft cocktail establishment. The recipe below skews secular, interpreting lime cordial as a mix of fresh lime juice and sugar.

Serves 1

2 ounces gin
¾ ounce lime juice
¾ ounce simple syrup
   (1:1, sugar:water)

Garnish: lime wheel

Glassware: cocktail or coupe

Add all ingredients to a cocktail shaker. Add ice and shake until chilled. Strain into a chilled cocktail or coupe glass. Garnish with a lime wheel.

Note: *Before fresh juice was standard in cocktails, Rose's Lime Cordial was the traditional substitute for simple syrup and lime juice. Some still insist that a Gimlet is not a Gimlet without Rose's, but fresh citrus is now generally preferred whenever possible.*

G

as the cocktail onions that turn a Martini into a Gibson. Candidates for adornment include edible items, such as slices of citrus, shaved citrus peel, olives, or cherries, as well as ornamental flourishes, such as miniature paper cocktail umbrellas.

2. *(v.)* The act of placing a garnish on a drink.

GELATIN

(n.) An ingredient used by molecular mixologists to make foam for cocktails or to turn a liquid semisolid (think Jell-O shots).

GENTIAN

(n.) A bittersweet liqueur made from the root of gentian plants and other botanicals. Usually light in color, it is bottled at around 20 percent ABV. Popular in the French Alps, the drink is most often consumed as an apéritif on the rocks with a squeeze of lemon. Brands to try include Avèze and Bittermens.

GEOGRAPHIC INDICATION

(n.) A term for a product, usually a wine, produced in a bounded geographic area and made according to local laws regarding grape variety or materials, production rules, and aging requirements. Only products that comply with the regulations may bear the geographic indication. While having a geographic indication is generally an indication of quality, some good producers choose not to follow a region's rules in order to make their product according to their own specifications and therefore must give up having the indication on the label, even though the product is made within the geographic boundary.

GIN

(n.) Gin's legal definition requires it to be a neutral spirit flavored with juniper berries and proprietary blends of botanicals and bottled at over 80 proof. Common botanical additions include citrus peel, coriander,

GIN DAISY

THIS drink is a variation on the basic daisy formula: a sour kicked up a notch with the addition of seltzer or soda water. Like any of the classics, the Gin Daisy is divided into two distinct genres: the old school and the new school. The former relies on orange liqueur for its citrusy backbone, while the latter knocks down the quantity of gin and substitutes grenadine for a fruitier flavor.

OLD SCHOOL:

Serves 1

1½ ounces gin
¾ ounce lemon juice
¾ ounce orange liqueur
Soda water

Garnish: lemon peel

Glassware: Collins

Add gin, lemon juice, and orange liqueur to a cocktail shaker. Add ice and shake until chilled. Strain over ice into a Collins glass and top with soda. Garnish with a lemon peel.

NEW SCHOOL:

Serves 1

1½ ounces gin
½ ounce lemon juice
¼ ounce grenadine
¼ ounce simple syrup
   (1:1, sugar:water)
Soda water

Garnish: orange slice

Glassware: Collins

Add gin, lemon juice, grenadine, and simple syrup to a cocktail shaker. Add ice and shake until chilled. Strain over ice into a Collins glass. Garnish with a slice of orange.

GIN FIZZ

THE gin iteration of the classic nineteenth-century fizz template may be the most famous, but rightly so, especially when it comes to warm-weather drinking. The herbal, citrusy character of the liquor shows well alongside the sweet-sour combo of citrus and simple syrup, all lightened by the spritzy tang of soda water. Kissing cousin to the Tom Collins, this fizz recipe leans slightly heavier on the gin for a more assertive kick.

Serves 1

1 ounce soda water
2 ounces gin
1 ounce lemon juice
¾ ounce simple syrup
1 egg white

Glassware: fizz

Add soda water to a fizz glass and set aside. Add the remaining ingredients to a shaker and dry shake. Add ice to shaker and shake well. Strain into a fizz glass.

cinnamon bark, angelica root, cardamom, and a slate of others.

First created in the seventeenth century as a Dutch medicinal tonic, gin saw its popularity spike in England in the early eighteenth century, when political maneuvering made it the country's cheapest alcoholic beverage. Public drunkenness among the lower classes became such an issue that in 1850 the English passed a law to allow only large distillers to produce gin, which largely worked in raising prices and stemming the tide of drunkenness. More advanced distilling techniques and gains in stature with the upper classes would allow gin to go on to become one of the most important spirits in cocktail making, forming the backbone of the gin and tonic, the Martini, and the Negroni, among many other drinks.

Several styles exist under the gin umbrella:

London dry may be the most recognizable to modern drinkers, with its dry, light-bodied, and fragrant character, which is well suited for a classic Martini.

Plymouth gin (both a style and a brand name) is similar in style to London dry, but it has a slightly fuller body and must be made in Plymouth, England.

Old Tom gin, a sweeter style, was most popular in England in the nineteenth century, though it is making a comeback on the artisanal scene today. Certain cocktails call for this style, such as the Dutch Kills, as well as historically correct versions of the Martinez and Tom Collins.

Genever gin, based on the original Dutch formula, is the forerunner to modern gins. Distilled from a malted grain base, then blended with a spiced high-proof spirit, genevers tend to have a more subtle botanical influence and may be aged in oak. Within this category are further style subsets, including *jonge,* a slightly sweetened variation that must contain less than 15 percent malted grain base; *oude,* a sweeter type, with more than 15 percent malted grain base; and *korenwijn,* which must contain more than 51 percent malted grain base.

GIN RICKEY

THIS variation on the fizz traces its origins to a whiskey-based drink created by Joe Rickey, a lobbyist from Missouri who moved to the nation's capital in the late nineteenth century. He began requesting whiskey cocktails sans sugar from local bars. The drink was a hit and soon found nationwide popularity, so much so that Rickey eventually got into the drinks business himself selling soda water. This version replaces whiskey with gin, which has arguably become the drink's most famous riff.

Serves 1

2 ounces gin (preferably London dry)
½–¾ ounce lime juice
Soda water

Garnish: lime wheel

Glassware: Collins

Add gin and lime juice to a Collins glass. Add ice and top with soda water. Garnish with a lime wheel.

G

While most gins are somewhere in the 42 to 45 percent alcohol range, navy-strength gins skew much higher, around 57 percent. And it should be noted that sloe gin is not really a gin at all, but a sweet liqueur made from sloe berries.

Gin's popularity may have faded in the mass market—it has slipped in sales slightly during the 2000s—but it remains a favorite with the craft cocktail crowd for its bold flavor, historical importance, and multiplicity of expressions. A recent explosion of craft distillery gins highlights locally available botanicals and base distillates. Brands to try include the Botanist, London Distillery, Spring 44, Death's Door, New York Distilling, St. George, Aviation, Greylock, Junipero, and Leopold's.

GINGER ALE

(*n.*) A sweetened carbonated soft drink containing ginger or ginger extract that is much milder than ginger beer. The original formulation, said to be first made in Ireland in the nineteenth century, was stronger than the ubiquitous version popular today, which comes from a recipe conceived in Canada in 1904.

GINGER BEER

(*n.*) What began as an alcoholic beverage fermented from ginger and sugar in England in the 1800s has evolved into a nonalcoholic carbonated ginger-flavored soft drink. The pungent ginger flavor is usually more assertive in ginger beer than in ginger ale. Traditionally brewed ginger beers are worth searching out for inclusion in cocktail recipes such as the Moscow Mule and Dark 'n' Stormy.

GINJO

(*n.*) A grade of sake that has been made with a special yeast and rice grains that have been polished to remove 40 percent of the outer grain, which results in a light, delicate profile. This type of sake is also brewed at colder temperatures and undergoes a longer fermentation than lower-quality sakes. If the ginjo sake also bears the "junmai" label, it has not been fortified with added ethyl alcohol. It is best drunk slightly chilled.

GLÖGG

(n.) A Nordic style of mulled wine that can either be purchased commercially or made at home. Recipes vary widely, but a typical version involves heating red wine with baking spices such as cinnamon and cloves, sugar, and citrus. Some versions call for fortified wines or spirits.

GLÜHWEIN

(n.) A style of mulled wine popular in Germany, Austria, and Switzerland and traditionally drunk during the Christmas holidays. It usually consists of red wine heated with a mix of baking spices (allspice, cinnamon, and anise are common), citrus, and sugar. If a shot of rum or liquor is added, it is called "Glühwein *mit schuss*" (Glüwein with a shot). *See:* Mulled Wine.

GOLD FIZZ

(n.) Swap egg yolk for whites to get this rich variation on the Silver Fizz. Whiskey is an acceptable substitute for gin here.

GOLDEN RUM

(n.) This medium-bodied style of rum is pale gold to amber, the color a result of either aging in charred oak barrels or added caramel flavoring or color. The best versions have complex notes of vanilla, coconut, and caramel from a long period in oak barrels.

GOLDWASSER

(n.) A type of herbal or spiced liqueur that is most notable for containing small gold flakes. The concept is thought to have arisen from the notion that gold, like the herbs and botanicals used in liqueurs, had certain medicinal properties. Though this has been disproven, the style, which is also known as *liqueur d'or*, persists under several brands, such as Danziger Goldwasser and Goldschläger.

GOLDEN CADILLAC

PART of the cream cocktail family, this sweet drink is a mix of Galliano, white crème de cacao, and heavy cream, all shaken to a frothy head. Poor Red's BBQ, a roadside bar in El Dorado, California, lays claim to the recipe. Local lore says that in 1952, a pair of newly engaged patrons at the bar requested a special drink to match their gold Cadillac. This version of the heavy-handed drink was created at the East Village 1970s mecca of the same name. Instead of heavy cream, it substitutes coconut cream for a semi-tropical twist.

Serves 1

1 ounce Galliano
1 ounce crème de cacao
1 ounce coconut cream

Glassware: cocktail or coupe

Add all ingredients to a cocktail shaker. Add ice and shake until chilled. Strain into a chilled cocktail or coupe glass.

Note: *Coconut cream can be replaced with heavy cream in the same proportion.*

GOSE

(n.) A salty, sour German style of beer. Native to the town of Goslar, Germany, and named for the river Gose that runs through it, the distinctive top-fermented wheat beer made with salt and coriander would eventually come to be associated with the town of Leipzig, where it became popular in the eighteenth century. During World War II, when brewing ceased in Germany, the style was briefly lost, but it was resurrected in the 1980s with a revival of one of the Leipzig's most famous *gosenschenke*, or gose taverns. Contemporary brewers, both in Germany and the United States, are now experimenting with the style to great effect. The beer can get its sour flavor from either the traditional method of spontaneous fermentation, the addition of lactic acid, or by making a sour mash to encourage the natural development of acidity.

GRAFT

(v.) The process of attaching one cultivar of plant to another. This horticultural technique is commonly used in vineyards, where vines of different grape varieties may be attached to established rootstock. The reasons for doing this are varied: the rootstock may have natural pest resistance (which was especially important during the phylloxera outbreak in the nineteenth century), or the vintner may want to take advantage of the rootstock's maturity while converting their vineyard to trendier or more commercially successful grapes.

GRAIN ALCOHOL

(n.) A neutral spirit distilled from grains at 95 ABV percent or higher. On account of its high proof and expressionless character, this product is often used to make liqueurs and infused alcohols and is mixed into certain cocktails and punches.

GRASSHOPPER

THIS mint-green cream-based drink was reportedly invented pre-Prohibition in a 1919 New York City cocktail contest in which Philbert Guichet, owner of Tujague's in New Orleans, took home second place for this recipe. A combination of equal parts crème de menthe, crème de cacao, and heavy cream, shaken with ice and strained into a cocktail glass, it falls into the category of sweet after-dinner drinks. This frothy concoction gained traction midcentury, especially in the American South. The core ingredients can be varied in a many ways: swap vodka for cream to get a Flying Grasshopper, or add coffee for a Brown Grasshopper.

Serves 1

1 ounce crème de menthe
1 ounce crème de cacao
1 ounce cream

Glassware: cocktail or coupe

Add ingredients to a cocktail shaker. Add ice and shake until chilled. Strain into a chilled cocktail or coupe glass.

G

GRAND MARNIER

(n.) A French brand of orange-flavored liqueur used in mixed drinks, served neat as a digestif, or used in desserts (most famously, flambéed in crepes suzette). Created in 1880 by Cognac producer Alexandre Marnier-Lapostolle, the liqueur includes Cognac, distilled orange essence (citrus was still an exotic scent at the time), and sugar. It's then aged in new French oak vats for six to eight months and bottled at 80 proof. Considered one of the higher-quality orange liqueurs, this product can be used in making the Margarita, Cosmopolitan, and Sidecar.

GRAPPA

(n.) An Italian brandy distilled from grape pomace, the skins and seeds leftover from the wine making process. Grappa is most commonly served as a digestivo, though it also makes an appearance in caffè corretto, which is a shot of espresso and a shot of liquor that can be served at any time of day.

There are a few competing theories about grappa's birthplace, but the general consensus seems to be it was created in the Alpine region of northern Italy as a way to stretch castaway materials. For centuries, production was crude and rustic: wineries would ship pomace to distilleries in return for a few bottles of the final product, which usually were not distilled with care. As such, grappa developed a poor reputation in the international marketplace. Beginning in the 1970s, however, some producers began to experiment to great effect with versions made from single grape varieties, pomace from top vineyards, quality distillation, and aging in oak barrels. Notable producers include Nardini, Nonino, and Poli.

GRENACHE

(n.) A red wine grape grown primarily in Spain, France, and Italy, though examples can be found throughout the world. The grape typically exhibits notes of strawberries, candied fruit, and cinnamon. It tends to be medium bodied, with a translucent

red color, though it can reach high levels of alcohol when grown in hot regions, like the Calatayud in Spain. In Spain, where the grape is known as Garnacha, it can be found in a wide range of bottlings, from value reds to high-end single-vineyard offerings from Priorat. In Italy, where the grape goes by the name Cannonau, it is grown mostly in Sicily and Sardinia. In France, it is grown primarily in the Rhône, where it is often included in blends with Syrah and Mourvèdre (slangily known as GSM blends.) Wine makers in the Central Coast region of California, known for their Rhône-style wines, have found some success with the grape as well.

GRENADINE

(*n.*) Historically made from tart-sweet pomegranate juice and sugar, grenadine is perhaps the most enduring in the category of concentrated fruit syrups, such as pineapple or raspberry, which were popular cocktail ingredients in the late nineteenth century. The name likely comes from *grenade*, which is French for "pomegranate," and France is also thought to be the country that gave rise to the syrup's popularity. Today grenadine makes an appearance in cocktails such as the Pink Lady and nonalcoholic drinks such as the Shirley Temple. A note of caution: Widely available grenadines are made from high-fructose corn syrup and dye—i.e., not from actual pomegranates—so seek out quality artisanal examples such as that made by Small Hand Foods, or consider making your own.

GRIST

(*n.*) A brewing term that refers to grains that have been coarsely milled or cracked so that they can be used in fermentation.

GROG

(*n.*) A hot beverage made of rum, hot water, citrus juice, sugar, and spices. The drink purportedly dates to the mid-1700s, when a British navy captain became known for

GREYHOUND

THIS highball standard is as simple as they come, with just two ingredients—grapefruit juice and vodka—served over ice and stirred. The easy template makes a solid base for a host of variations: add a salted rim for the Salty Dog, swap gin for vodka for a more herbaceous spin, or add a splash of vermouth or amaro, such as Punt e Mes or Campari for the Italian Greyhound.

Serves 1

2 ounces vodka
4 ounces grapefruit juice

Garnish: grapefruit wheel
or twist

Glassware: rocks

Add ingredients to a cocktail shaker. Add ice and shake until chilled. Strain into a rocks glass and garnish with a grapefruit wheel or twist.

stretching rum with water to ration it. Lime and lemon juice were added to the drink to ward off scurvy. The name is said to be a nod to the captain's nickname, "Old Grog," for his signature grogram cape.

GROSSES GEWÄCHS

(n.) A dry German wine made from a top vineyard site, somewhat analogous to Burgundy's Grand Cru designation.

GROWLER

(n.) A reusable container used to transport and temporarily store beer dispensed from a keg or cask. Growlers are most often made from glass and have either a screw-top or swing-top closure. The most common size is a half gallon (64 ounces), which holds four pints of beer, though other sizes, including a gallon (128 ounces) and a quarter gallon (32 ounces), are sometimes available. If sealed properly, a growler can hold the carbonation of a beer indefinitely (like a sealed bottle of beer), though if it is repeatedly opened, the carbonation will dissipate.

GUM (GOMME) SYRUP

(n.) A cocktail ingredient made with sugar, water, and gum arabic. Often used by bartenders in the 1800s, this syrup gives cocktails a smooth mouthfeel and a heavier texture than plain simple syrup. To achieve the thickening texture without the gum arabic, some bartenders mix a syrup with a 2:1 ratio of sugar to water.

GYPSY BREWER

(n.) A brewer who rents brewing time and equipment in an established brewery's brick-and-mortar place of production; also known as a tenant brewer. The gypsy brewer is able to produce beer without investing in owning equipment or maintaining a lease, while the host brewery is able to make money from their extra capacity during times they would not be making beer.

HAND-CARVED ICE

(n.) Ice that has been cut from a larger block by hand (or chain saw). Though this was once the only way to obtain ice for making cocktails, hand-carved ice fell out of favor with the advent of mechanical ice-making machines. Recently, however, hand carving has become popular again as a way to ensure quality of the ice (ice-making machines often produce low-quality ice, save for the Kold-Draft models) and enhance the presentation of a cocktail through the use of distinctive shapes.

HAND PUMP

(n.) A piece of equipment used to dispense cask-conditioned beer without the use of carbon dioxide, also known as a "beer engine." Cask ale aficionados (also known as "real ale" in England) often contest that this method, or the use of gravity to dispense beer, allows for a beer profile unadulterated by forced carbonation. For a commercial operation, the hand pump can usually attach to a bar, with a long pull handle visible to customers above the bar and the siphon system below. To work the hand pump, the user pulls the handle, which siphons beer into a piston that will

HARVEY WALLBANGER

T HE oft-told story that this mix of vodka, orange juice, and Galliano was created by a top Los Angeles bartender in the 1950s for a local surfer has been largely debunked by cocktail writer Robert Simonson. The drink more likely originated, he says, with Galliano's marketing team in the early 1970s, complete with a cartoon surfer mascot for the advertising campaign. What is undeniable, however, is that the Wallbanger became one of the iconic drinks of the 1970s, inspiring lines of premade mixes and branded paraphernalia, which helped propel Galliano to the position of the number one liqueur imported to the United States that decade.

Serves 1

1½ ounces vodka
½ ounce Galliano
2 ounces orange juice
1 dash Angostura bitters

Garnish: orange wheel, salted

Glassware: cocktail or coupe

Add all ingredients to a cocktail shaker. Add ice and shake until chilled. Strain into a chilled cocktail or coupe glass. Garnish with a salted orange wheel.

empty into a pour spout. Depending on the size of the piston, the user may need to pump the handle several times to draw a full pint.

HAND SELLING

(v.) The sommelier practice of high-lighting or pointing out a wine that might be overlooked in order to entice a customer to try it; usually necessary for an obscure or unique bottling.

HARD SHAKE

(v.) A highly choreographed and controversial version of the hand shake said to increase the integration of ingredients and improve a drink's texture and the quality of the ice chips that float on a shaken and poured cocktail. Developed in Japan by bartender Kazuo Uyeda, the process involves rapidly moving a filled cocktail shaker held at a precise angle through three separate points relative to the cocktail maker's body (around head height, slightly lower than head height, and then slightly lower), which supposedly maximizes the amount of contact between the ice and the liquid, making a better cocktail. Whether this process works better than a standard hand shake is a point of contention in the bartending world; a 2009 panel at the annual Tales of the Cocktail event in New Orleans reported that experiments have not yet been able to discern a difference in a finished cocktail, though some experts insist that researchers have not come up with the appropriate test yet.

HAWTHORNE STRAINER

(n.) Comprised of a flat perforated disk with a coiled metal spring attached to the rim, this strainer is best suited for use with a mixing tin. The coiled spring helps catch solids such as muddled herbs or fruits as well as smaller chunks of ice. The name comes from a company that used to produce them. To use this strainer, place the disc over the mouth of the mixing tin, coil side down. Slide the front end of the strainer (the one with more perforations) against the rim of

H

the tin. Securing the strainer with one or two fingers, lift and tilt the mixing tin over the serving glass and pour.

HEAD

(n.) The foamy top of a beer formed during or after pouring it into a glass. This foam is caused by carbonation, the type of grains used, the method of brewing, and, in some cases, the additives of enzymes and gums. The resulting head will also differ in density, texture, and size depending on the style of the beer. For example, pilsners are supposed to have a thick, creamy white head, whereas Irish red ales characteristically have a short off-white or tan head. Certain beers, such as Guinness, are carbonated with a mixture of nitrogen and carbon dioxide, which makes a stable, creamy head, since nitrogen dissolves less easily in beer than carbon dioxide does. Glassware can also influence the shape and size of the head: tall, narrow glasses preserve the foam, whereas the carbon dioxide in short, wide-mouthed glasses will dissipate more quickly.

HEADS

(n.) When alcohol is distilled, it come out of the still in three sections. The first, called the heads, contains ethanol as well as toxic compounds such as methanol. For this reason, the heads are discarded.

HEARTS

(n.) The desirable ethanol produced during distilling between the "heads," which comes out of the still first, and the "tails," which comes last, both of which contain toxic compounds.

HEFEWEIZEN

(n.) A Bavarian style of lightly hopped wheat beer. Commonly brewed with at least 50 percent wheat in the grain mix, the beer is usually pale gold and hazy from being bottled unfiltered. A special strain of yeast used for this style produces distinctive flavors of bananas, bubblegum, and cloves. The practice of serving it with a lemon wedge is an American invention that

HEMINGWAY DAIQUIRI

WITH his prodigious enthusiasm for drinking (and then writing about it), Ernest Hemingway shows up frequently in cocktail mythology, perhaps never more famously than in the origin story of this drink. The Floridita, a Havana bar the author frequented in the 1930s, served Hemingway these doctored-up Daiquiris, made unique by the addition of maraschino liqueur and the lack of simple syrup (by Hemingway's request). He reportedly could pack away tens of these at a time, ordering doubles, or what would come to be known as the Papa Doble in his honor. Another interesting fact: The bartenders would blend the drink with ice, then strain it out in what sounds like a foreshadowing of the frozen Daiquiri.

Serves 1

2 ounces light rum
½ ounce maraschino liqueur
¾ ounce lime juice
½ ounce grapefruit juice

Garnish: lime wheel

Glassware: cocktail or coupe

Add all ingredients to a cocktail shaker. Add ice and shake until chilled. Strain into a chilled cocktail or coupe glass. Garnish with a lime wheel.

H

purists believe masks the true flavor of the beer.

HERBSAINT

(n.) An anise-flavored liqueur first introduced in 1934 as a replacement for absinthe, which was banned in 1912 in the United States for its purported psychedelic properties. Made by New Orleans's Legendre & Co., the bright-green spirit approximated the taste of absinthe but without the problematic wormwood. The Sazerac Company bought the brand in 1949 and the recipe has been retooled a few times (fans of the original say the color has diminished some and the flavor become less complex). In 2009 the company released a bottling of the original Legendre recipe.

HIGH CORN

(n.) An unofficial term for bourbons made almost entirely with corn. By law, bourbon must be made with at least 51 percent corn, with the rest of the grain bill traditionally rounded out with barley and rye. Most bourbons on the market use 60 to 70 percent corn, but a rare few go higher. The more corn in the mix, the sweeter the bourbon tends to be. Examples in this category include Tuthilltown's Baby Bourbon, which is made entirely with New York State corn, and Old Charter.

HIGH RYE

(n.) An unofficial term for bourbons made with a high percentage of rye in the grain bill. These examples tend to be spicier and richer than those made with the traditional amount of rye, as the grain itself is spicier, carrying notes of pepper, cinnamon, and clove. Examples of this style are Four Roses Single Barrel, Bulleit, and Basil Hayden.

HIGHBALL

1. *(n.)* A spirit (most often whiskey) mixed with a carbonated beverage in a roughly 1:2 ratio and served in a tall glass over ice. The name supposedly originated with New York bartender Patrick Duffy in the late

nineteenth century, but the simple mixture has ancestral roots in many a mixed drink, including fizzes, Collinses, and bucks.

2. *(n.)* A tall glass in which highball cocktails are served.

HIGHBALL GLASS

(n.) Usually slightly shorter and wider than a Collins glass, this all-purpose tumbler holds anywhere from 8 to 12 ounces, though examples can be found that push 20 ounces. The base tends to be reinforced to withstand muddling. The shape makes this glass ideal for tall drinks with ice.

HIGHLANDS

(n.) A large whisky-producing region in Scotland that produces single malts such as Macallan, Glenmorangie, and Glen Garioch.

HONJOZO

(n.) Similar to junmai, honjozo is a sake style made from water, koji mold, yeast, and rice that has been polished to remove at least 30 percent of the outer husk. It also includes a small amount of added ethyl alcohol, which helps enhance the aromatics and gives the impression of a drier sake.

HOOCH

(n.) An American slang term for alcohol of poor quality; often used in reference to bootlegged or homemade alcohols.

HOPS

(n.) These cone-shaped flowers from the hop plant, *Humulus lupulus*, contribute flavor and aroma to beer. The flowers are harvested from the vine and usually dried before use, though some brewers are experimenting with adding fresh hops to their beers.

Thought to have been adopted as an ingredient by French and German breweries during the Middle Ages, in part because of the hop resin's preservative qualities, these pungent, bitter flowers would become an

HORSE'S NECK

THIS refreshing mix of bourbon, bitters, and ginger ale takes its name from the oversized loop-di-loo of citrus peel garnish that gets coiled around the inside of the glass (a channel knife will help you make the perfect spiral). Nominally part of the cooler family of cocktails, this sweet and spicy drink can easily be made without alcohol for teetotaler, as it was during Prohibition.

Serves 1

2 ounces bourbon
3 dashes Angostura bitters
Ginger ale or soda

Garnish: long, loopy lemon peel

Glassware: highball or Collins

Using a channel knife, peel a lemon in one long spiral. Twist around your finger or a barspoon to create a coil. Drop the lemon coil into a highball or Collins glass, leaving the end hanging over the lip, and fill the glass with ice. Add bourbon and bitters. Top up with ginger ale or soda.

HOT BUTTERED RUM

Is there anything sexier than a glass of melted butter mixed with warm golden spirits? Gout be damned, this hot lipid–laden drink is a cold-weather panacea that resulted from colonial New Englanders' penchant for putting rum in everything. Americans have been whipping up a spiced butter batter and dousing it with rum and hot water since before they were Americans. This fancified version, created at the Boston cocktail bar the Hawthorne, brings the winter warmer to its full velvety potential with the crucial addition of ice cream and black tea.

Serves 18–20

2 sticks butter, softened
1 cup brown sugar
¼ cup honey
¼ cup vanilla ice cream
1½ tablespoons cinnamon, ground
1½ tablespoons nutmeg, ground
1½ tablespoons clove, ground
1½ tablespoons allspice, ground
1 teaspoon cayenne pepper
1 teaspoon salt
Dark rum
Black tea, hot

Garnish: star anise, optional

Glassware: mug or rocks

Add first ten ingredients to a mixing bowl and blend with an electric mixer. Refrigerate until ready to use. When ready to serve, warm the mugs by filling with hot water. Let stand for a minute or two and discard. Add 1 tablespoon of batter to each mug. Top with 2 ounces hot tea and stir to mix. Add 1 ounce of each rum and then top with 2 ounces more hot tea. Rum will form a ¼-inch cream over the top of the drink. Garnish with a whole star anise.

H

essential beer ingredient, and the flavor and aroma differences of local varieties helped define certain beer styles. For example, German beers traditionally use combinations of milder aromatic hops, such as Saaz or Hallertau, while British beers tend to employ Fuggle or Goldings varieties. Pacific Northwest beers often gain their highly bitter character from local Cascade hops.

The most recognizable characteristic of hops is their bitter flavor; a beer that tastes "hoppy" has a pronounced bitterness. This bitter quality is measured in finished beers on the International Bittering Unit (IBU) scale. Hops can add different aromatic or flavor properties, ranging from citrusy to grassy to spicy. Hops added early in the cooking release more bitter components as their resins become soluble, whereas hops added near the end or after the beer has been cooked tend to leave more aromatic notes.

HORIZONTAL TASTING

(n.) A wine-tasting event in which a group of wines made in the same year are compared against each other. The wines usually have something else in common, such as being made from the same grape, in the same region, or by the same producer.

HOUSE

(adj.) Usually inexpensive spirits or wine that a bar or restaurant serves unlabeled, often referred to as "well." The quality of the establishment is usually directly correlated with the level of quality one can expect from their house products.

HURRICANE GLASS

(n.) A bulbous short-stemmed glass modeled after hurricane lamps and designed specifically for the Hurricane cocktail, though it is frequently used for serving tropical-style drinks as well; usually holds 16 to 20 ounces.

HURRICANE

REGARDLESS of its exact origins (either New York's Hurricane Club or New Orleans's Pat O'Brien's), most agree that this powerful fruity drink—a mix of rum, passion fruit syrup, and lime juice—was popularized by Pat O'Brien at his eponymous bar in New Orleans in the 1940s, when a raging war in Europe meant Caribbean rum was much easier to come by than the preferred whiskey or Cognac. The iconic billowy glass, and thus the drink's name, was a nod to old-fashioned hurricane lamps.

Serves 1

1 ounce light rum
1 ounce dark rum
1 ounce lemon juice
1 ounce passionfruit syrup

Garnish: orange wheel and brandied cherry

Glassware: hurricane

Add ingredients to a cocktail shaker. Add ice and shake until chilled. Strain into a hurricane glass over crushed ice. Garnish with an orange wheel and a brandied cherry.

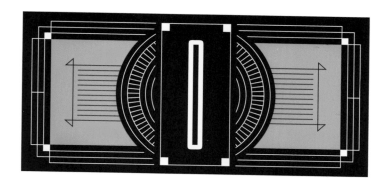

IBU (INTERNATIONAL BITTERING UNITS)

(n.) A unit of measurement that rates the bitterness of beer on a scale from 0 (no bitterness) to 100. Beer gains bitterness from the amount and type of hops used during brewing; certain styles of beers are expected to place higher on the scale. For example, a blonde ale might score around 15 IBU, while an India pale ale reaches above 40. The presence of bitterness doesn't necessarily result in the perception of bitterness: a higher malt character can often balance or mask bitter flavors, so judging a beer solely by its IBU score is largely ineffective.

ICE BEER

(n.) An American style of lager that has been partially frozen to remove some of its water, thereby slightly raising the alcohol content. German Eisbocks, the antecedent for this type of beer, are generally considered to be superior.

ICE PICK

(n.) With a long, narrow, sharp shaft attached to a sturdy handle, this cocktail-making tool is used to break apart ice cubes or blocks of ice.

ICE SHAVER

(n.) Used to make juleps, swizzles, or other drinks that call for crushed ice, this handheld tool shaves ice chips from a block of ice. Electric shavers, popular for making cocktails on a larger scale, are also available.

ICE SPEAR

(n.) A long, rectangular piece of ice designed to fit a Collins or highball glass, used according to the theory that the ice will melt more slowly and cool the drink uniformly from top to bottom, resulting in a better drink than one made with quick-melting cubes that float on the top of the drink.

ICE SPHERE

(n.) Also known as an ice ball, this large piece of ice, usually 2 to 3 inches across, is frozen in a spherical mold. They are most often used in whiskey-based cocktails or whiskey served on the rocks, since it is thought that a large piece of ice will melt more slowly than cubes, creating less dilution (though this is debatable). The shape also adds an element of theatricality to the presentation. Several models of makers exist, from low-tech plastic molds to high-end stainless steel presses, though some prefer to hand-carve the shape.

ICE WINE

(n.) A sweet dessert-style wine made from grapes left on the vine through a hard freeze. The grapes are harvested and pressed while still frozen so the low temperatures can concentrate the sugar in the grapes. Also known as Eiswein, this style can be produced only in grape-growing regions that are cold enough to experience a frost, such as Germany and the Niagara region of the United States and Canada.

IMPERIAL

(adj.) An unregulated beer term that usually indicates a beer will be bolder in flavor and more alcoholic than the

IMPROVED WHISKEY COCKTAIL

FIRST included in an appendix of an 1876 reprinting of Jerry Thomas's essential tome, *How to Mix Drinks*, this variation on the basic whiskey cocktail is indeed improved, if by "improved" you mean "has more ingredients." In his book *Imbibe!*, cocktail historian David Wondrich notes that including absinthe in drinks was quite fashionable at the time.

Serves 1

1 sugar cube (see note)
1 barspoon maraschino liqueur
1 dash Angostura bitters
1 dash Peychaud's bitters
1 dash absinthe
2 ounces bourbon or rye

Garnish: lemon or orange peel

Glassware: rocks

In a rocks glass, muddle the sugar cube (or sugar or simple syrup) with maraschino, bitters, and absinthe. Add whiskey and stir. Add ice (preferably a large cube) and stir until well chilled. Garnish with a lemon or orange peel.

Note: *If you don't have sugar cubes on hand, a teaspoon of sugar or a generous ¼ ounce of simple syrup will do the trick.*

nonimperial version. This adjective can be applied to a number of amped-up styles, from India pale ales to stouts to pilsners, and is usually achieved by increasing the quantity of hops and grains used in brewing, which yields a more flavorful product with an alcohol content of 8 to 12 percent ABV.

INDIA PALE ALE

(n.) A stronger version of pale ale, often with a higher alcohol content and more hop flavor. Colloquially abbreviated to IPA, this bitter ale is likely a descendant of a British well-hopped pale ale style called "October," which was traditionally brewed in the autumn and allowed to mature for a year or two. The October beer from English brewer George Hodgson became popular in the country's Indian outposts in the early nineteenth century, as it apparently matured well on the long sea journey, and the style—then called India pale ale or "pale ale as prepared for India"—caught on at home.

Modern versions typically have strong regional differences. American IPAs, especially those made on the West Coast, tend to have more assertive hop flavoring and are often quite bitter, herbal, and citrusy. English IPAs are lower in alcohol, due in part to taxation policies. Belgian IPAs tend to follow the American style.

INFUSE

(v.) The practice of steeping herbs, spices, or fruits in alcohol to transfer flavor to the liquid. There are two basic ways of flavoring alcohol: during the distillation process, in which spices and herbs are added to the mash or sugar solution before undergoing distillation, and infusion, in which flavorings are soaked in distilled liquor. With infusion, through the process of osmosis, color, flavor, and sugar can be imparted to the spirit. Flavor absorption rates differ from agent to agent, but generally, the longer the flavoring agents are kept in the alcohol, the more flavor will be transferred. If left too long, bitter or medicinal flavors may

dominate. Although some commercial spirits are made by infusion (Chambord, some flavored vodkas), the technique has long been employed for doctoring spirits at home. Recently, bartenders have been experimenting with using nitrous oxide to infuse spirits, a process that is thought to result in clearer, less muddied flavors.

INTENSITY

(n.) A subjective term used in the wine-tasting world that can refer to flavor, aroma, or color. More pronounced traits (an opaque color, for instance) are said to have greater intensity.

INTERNATIONAL VARIETY

(n.) A wine grape variety planted throughout the wine regions of the world and thus recognizable to many consumers. This group traditionally includes Riesling, Sauvignon Blanc, Chardonnay, Pinot Noir, Merlot, and Cabernet Sauvignon, among a handful of other varieties. A common critique of vineyards planted to these grape varieties is that they edge out planting of indigenous varieties, but they continue to be popular with consumers who have grown familiar with particular grapes.

IRISH COFFEE GLASS

(n.) Made of tempered glass, this mug with a handle and a short stem may be used for serving hot cocktails, such as Irish coffee, toddies, or Hot Buttered Rum; usually 8 to 10 ounces.

IRISH CREAM LIQUEUR

(n.) A cream liqueur made with Irish whiskey and cream, usually served straight or over ice as an after-dinner drink or mixed into shooters or cocktails. Baileys is the most famous example in this category.

IRISH RED ALE

(n.) A medium-bodied red or amber-colored ale with a low hop profile. Many versions are smooth and easy drinking and have a caramel tinge to the malty flavor; some,

I

such as Murphy's, are brewed as lagers. The style comes from Ireland but is popular among American craft breweries.

IRISH STOUT

(*n.*) A relatively dry, bitter style of stout made throughout the world. Porter and stout were traditionally made in England from brown malt, which gave the drink a deep, rich color and flavor but less alcohol per volume than pale malt. In the mid-nineteenth century, Irish brewers were quicker than the English to adopt the use of a new style of malted barley, which gave off a similar deep color when used in smaller quantities than the common style of brown malt and could be mixed with pale malt for a more economical dark beer. The Irish style—popularized by Guinness and Murphy's—skewed drier and bitterer than its English counterpart.

IRISH WHISKEY

(*n.*) Similar in many ways to its Scottish brethren, Irish whiskey generally skews lighter in flavor. Legally, Irish whiskey must be made in Ireland, distilled from a yeast-fermented mash predominantly of barley, and aged for three years in wooden casks. The malted barley is usually dried in kilns and ovens, not over smoky peat fires, as is done in parts of Scotland. Many are triple distilled, and some are made using the "single pot still" method, in which a mix of malted and unmalted barley is used in the mash. If made from two or more distillates, it can be labeled "blended."

Depending on which version of the creation myth you believe, the Irish may have invented whiskey, with Celtic monks bringing distilling back to their homeland from their travels throughout Europe before the Middle Ages (though don't tell that to the Scots, who also lay claim to creating the product). By the nineteenth century, Irish whiskey's reputation was so good that Scottish producers would send over their whiskey to have it be labeled as Irish so that it would command higher prices on the British market.

In the early twentieth century, production was hit hard by a British embargo after the Irish War of Independence of 1919–21, and soon after Prohibition in the United States shut off another big market. Consolidation ensued, and today Ireland has only four working distilleries, all owned by major conglomerates, though each produces a number of brands. Fortunes have changed recently for Irish whiskey: in 2012 it was the fastest-growing spirit category in the United States according to the Distilled Spirits Council. Jameson and Bushmills are the most recognizable brands, but also look out for Green Spot, Redbreast, and Midleton.

ISINGLASS

(n.) A fining agent made from fish bladders used to clarify wine and beer. The proteins from the isinglass bind with particulates in the alcohol and precipitate out of the product, speeding the clarification process. Though no measureable amount of fish remains in the beer or wine, some vegetarians find the use of this product unacceptable.

ISLAY

(n.) An island off the coast of Scotland known for its particularly peaty and bold style of Scotch. Some attribute a saline or seaweed character to the Scotch produced on the island to the distilleries' proximity to the ocean and the seaweed that inflects the soil. Other islands that produce Scotch include Orkney, Shetland, Skye, Mull, Jura, and Arran, but Islay Scotches have the highest profile.

IZARRA

(n.) A family of herbal liqueurs made in the Basque region of France since 1904. The green version tastes slightly minty, while the yellow bottling has a nutty profile. Both are usually served neat, over ice, or mixed in cocktails.

JÄGERMEISTER

(*n.*) A bitter liqueur produced by Mast-Jägermeister in Hanover, Germany. Curt Mast, son of vinegar- and wine-store owner Wilhelm Mast, created the proprietary blend of more than fifty-six ingredients, with dominant flavors of star anise and cardamom, during Nazi-era Germany. A neutral spirit is infused with the spices and herbs, then aged for a year in oak barrels, and caramel and sugar are added before bottling in the brand's signature green bottle with Gothic lettering. The deer logo is a tie-in to the name, which means "master of the hunt."

Seen largely as a digestif for older people in its native homeland, the liqueur got a boost in popularity in the 1970s when New Yorker Sidney Frank began promoting the drink as a party shot in bars and nightclubs, complete with female ambassadors called Jägerettes. In certain circles the spirit has gained notoriety for its role as one-half of the Jägerbomb, a drink order that combines a shot of Jägermeister and a carbonated energy drink (often Red Bull). Often served at nightclubs and establishments that serve university-age students, the "bomb" phenomenon has helped propel Jägermeister to a position as the third most popular spirit in England as of 2012.

J

JAMESON IRISH WHISKEY

(n.) A blended Irish whiskey made by Pernod Ricard's Irish Distillers branch. Scotsman John Jameson purchased Dublin's Bow Street Distillery in 1780 and rapidly increased the sales of their whiskey. The early twentieth century proved challenging for the distillery, as Prohibition in the United States, English tariffs on Irish products, and the temperance movement in Ireland dampened demand, but today the spirit is one of the most popular whiskeys in the world; sales figures from 2012 show the brand sold more than four million cases globally.

Now produced in Cork, Ireland, the basic whiskey is made from a mix of maize and malted and unmalted barley, which are fermented and then triple distilled in pot stills (the barley) and column stills (the maize). The alcohols are aged separately in a mix of casks that have come from sherry, port, and bourbon production before being blended and bottled at an ABV of 40 percent.

JIGGER

(n.) A bartending tool used to measure small quantities of liquid. In nineteenth-century recipes, this measurement was imprecise, but some speculate it correlated with either the pony glass or something around 2 ounces. Today the most common versions are made from stainless steel in a conical hourglass shape and come in a range of measurements, from ½ to 2 ounces. When a recipe specifies one jigger, it most likely is calling for 1½ ounces.

JONGE

(n.) A style of genever gin invented in the twentieth century to appeal to younger drinkers accustomed to the neutrality of vodka. The flavor is subtle and clean tasting, and it is therefore often used in mixed drinks.

JACK ROSE

ONE of writer David A. Embury's six essential cocktails listed in his *The Fine Art of Mixing Drinks* 1948, this classic drink is distinguished by being the only one that calls for applejack, a high-proof spirit dating to the colonial era. Grenadine and lime juice help blunt the applejack's edges while adding both a pretty pink color and a sweet-sour flavor. The name is thought to be a mash-up of the word *apple-jack* and a poetic nod to the drink's color.

Serves 1

2 ounces applejack
1 ounce grenadine
½ ounce lemon juice
½ lime juice

Glassware: cocktail or coupe

Add all ingredients to a cocktail shaker. Add ice and shake until chilled. Strain into a chilled cocktail or coupe glass.

JAPANESE COCKTAIL

QUICK scan of the ingredients list reveals nothing overtly Japanese about this cocktail. No sake or shochu. No Japanese whiskey or yuzu. But such is the way cocktail writer Jerry Thomas titled this classic mix of Cognac, orgeat, and Angostura bitters in his 1862 edition of *How to Mix Drinks*, and so the name remains. The orgeat helps take the edge off the brandy, while the bitters bring a hint of herbs and spice to this drink, which is elegant in its simplicity.

Serves 1

2 ounces Cognac
½ ounce orgeat syrup
2 dashes Angostura bitters

Garnish: lemon peel

Glassware: coupe

Add all ingredients to a mixing glass, add ice, and stir well. Strain into a chilled coupe glass and garnish with a lemon peel.

J

JOVEN

(n.) A designation for tequila made either by blending blanco tequila (young, clear tequila not aged in barrels) and a smaller amount of aged tequila, or by adding caramel coloring to blanco tequila for a golden color; sometimes called "gold" tequila. The flavor is usually mellower than that of a blanco tequila.

JUICE

1. *(n.)* The liquid extracted from fruit and vegetables. For tools to juice citrus, *see:* Citrus Reamer, Citrus Squeezer.

2. *(n.)* A slang term for wine, often used by sommeliers and wine professionals, as in, "I'm drinking good juice tonight."

JULEP

(n.) Though Persian literature dating to 900 AD shows that the term originally referred to a nonalcoholic medicinal tonic, by the late 1700s "julep" had a decidedly more recreational connotation in the United States, and the recipe consisted of a mix of spirits, sugar, and mint served over crushed ice with and often fruit garnishes. The most recognizable form of the julep is the bourbon-based Mint Julep, a Southern staple dating from the early 1800s.

JULEP CUP

(n.) A silver or tin cup in which Mint Juleps are traditionally served. Kentucky silversmiths have been making these since the eighteenth century. Though it's not necessary to make a julep, the metal cup has one major benefit: it holds frost better than its glass or plastic counterparts. Antique cups have become collectors' items and can fetch upwards of $1,000 each at auctions.

J–K

JULEP STRAINER

(n.) This one-piece strainer consists of a shallow bowl with even round perforations and an attached handle. Designed specifically for juleps in the era before drinking straws were invented, the strainer would fit into the cocktail glass and hold back the crushed ice while the drinker took a sip. Today the strainer can be used for making any cocktail, but it is particularly well suited to straining liquids from a mixing glass. To use, invert the strainer over the cocktail glass so the bowl holds back the ice. Holding the strainer with your index finger over the glass, lift and tilt the mixing glass over the serving glass and pour.

JUNMAI

1. *(n.)* A prefix that indicates no alcohol has been added to a sake.

2. *(n.)* A grade of sake made from only water, koji mold, yeast, and rice; no added ethyl alcohol is allowed.

KABINETT

(n.) A German classification for wines made from ripe grapes in a style that is lighter and leaner than Spätlese, the next step up on the hierarchy. The wines may be dry, medium-dry, or sweet and are usually low in alcohol. Dry wines will bear the label "trocken."

KAHLÚA

(n.) This syrupy sweet coffee liqueur made from a sugarcane spirit base is flavored with coffee beans, caramel, and vanilla. Created in Veracruz, Mexico, in 1936, the dark-brown spirit was first imported to the United States in 1962. Most commonly mixed into cocktails such as the White Russian, it may also be served on the rocks.

KOLD-DRAFT

(n.) A brand of commercial ice machines often found in top cocktail bars. Cubes come in two sizes, full (1¼ inch by 1 inch by 1¼ inch)

KIR ROYALE

A **VARIATION** on a kir, a French apéritif made with crème de cassis and white wine, the "royale" designation means sparkling wine should be subbed in for still. Legend says the drink's namesake was Canon Félix Kir, a Burgundian priest who became mayor of Dijon after World War II and would serve this popular drink made from the locally produced black currant liqueur and wine. The bubbly version is typically consumed as an apéritif or on special occasions in France.

Serves 1

4 ounces Champagne or
    sparkling wine
¼ ounce crème de cassis

Glassware: flute

Add crème de cassis to a flute and top with Champagne or sparkling wine.

K

and half (1¼ inch by 1¼ inch by ⅝ inch). The ice is prized for its density, purity, and uniform size, and many bartenders believe that shaking drinks with the ice results in a cocktail that is both colder and less diluted than those made with lower-quality ice.

KÖLSCH

(n.) A German style of ale, native to the town of Cologne. Pale yellow or straw in color, this crisp, subtly flavored beer has the distinction of being brewed using ale yeast and fermented at a warm temperature, at which the yeast performs best. It is then cellared in cold storage, as is typically done with lagers. Born in the early twentieth century, the Kölsch style became a protected designation in 1997 and now can be made only in Cologne, though several U.S. breweries produce a similar product.

KORENWIJN (CORENWIJN)

(n.) A style of genever gin that has been aged in oak barrels for one to three years and has a malty profile.

KOSHER WINE

(n.) A classification for wines produced according to the rules of kosher food production: a rabbi must supervise production, all yeasts and other ingredients must be kosher, no preservatives or artificial colors may be added, the facility and equipment that makes the wine must be certified by a rabbi, and all personnel that handles the product must be Sabbath-observant Jews. Kosher for Passover wines may not include corn syrup and other additives, which mainly affects Concord grape–based wines such as Manischewitz, which produces a special version of the wine for the holiday.

K

KRIEK

(n.) A Belgian style of lambic beer that has been fermented with cherries. Traditionally, whole cherries, either Morello cherries that are grown in the area around Brussels or sour cherries, are added to fermenting lambic beer. The cherries ferment alongside the beer, so there is little residual sugar left from the addition. The result is a cherry flavor that meshes with the sour profile of the lambic base.

KRISTALWEIZEN

(n.) A German wheat beer. Essentially a hefeweizen that has been filtered, this crisp, clear, pale golden beer will carry some of its hazy cousin's traits, such as the characteristic banana aroma, but none of the cloudiness.

KÜMMEL

(n.) An aniseed-flavored spirit created in northern Europe around the sixteenth century. The clear liquor, made with citrus peel, cumin, and anise, is now produced across Europe from France to Russia and is popular in the United Kingdom as a golf clubhouse beverage.

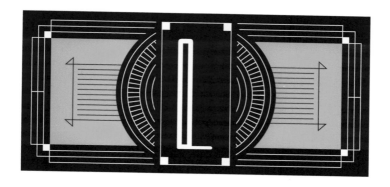

LAGER

(n.) A large umbrella category for beers that have been fermented and aged at low temperatures. The process requires using strains of yeast that can reproduce in cooler temperatures. Lagers come in a range of styles, from light to dark, including pilsner, bock, dunkel, and Vienna. In general, the category skews crisper and cleaner tasting than ales, which tend to have the fruitier profile of ales.

LAMBIC

(n.) A Belgian-style beer fermented using wild yeasts and bacteria, which give the beer a sour, earthy, oxidative character. This distinctive style of beer evolved in the farmlands south of Brussels, where brewers would ferment the beer in open-air vats, then age it in barrels for one to three years. Between eighty and one hundred types of bacteria and yeast are thought to influence the flavor, most famously Brettanomyces, a strain of wild yeast that produces barnyard, leather, and funky flavors. A number of substyles exist, the most common of which are gueuze and fruit. Gueuze, a blend of

L

old and new lambics that are refermented in the bottle, are generally golden in color, are sour and earthy in flavor, and have a high carbonation. Fruit lambics, which have had fruit added to the beer, take on the aroma from that particular fruit but also carry the distinctive sour, barnyardy lambic character.

LAMBRUSCO

(n.) A sparkling red wine made in Italy from the Lambrusco grape. Most production of this unique fizzy red wine is centered in Italy's Emilia-Romagna region. Though Lambrusco had a reputation for being overly sweet on account of low-quality imports to the United States in the 1970s, dry, earthy styles are gaining in popularity. The color can range from light red to maroon, and some white and rosé styles are also vinified from the grape. Most Lambruscos are made using the Charmat method, in which the wine undergoes secondary fermentation in a tank to become carbonated before being put into bottles. If the wine is intended to be sweet, producers will halt the fermentation before it is complete, leaving residual sugar and a frothy texture. The flavor skews to the red berry end of the spectrum, often with a slightly bitter edge.

LARGE FORMAT

(n.) A category of wine bottles larger than the standard 750-milliliter size, including the magnum (1.5 liters), Jeroboam (3 or 4.5 liters), imperial or Methuselah (6 liters), and Salmanazar (9.0 liters), among others. Wineries usually make only a limited number of large-format bottles, which can turn some bottles into collector's items.

LAYER/LAYERING

(v.) A cocktail-making technique in which different ingredients are added in such a way that they float on top of one another, creating a layered effect; also known as "floating." To layer ingredients, pour the densest ingredient in the cocktail into the glass first. Then hold a spoon with the back

LAST WORD

L **EGEND** has it that this gin-based cocktail was created at the Detroit Athletic Club during Prohibition but that it fell out of favor after World War II. It was rediscovered in 2004 by Seattle bartender Murray Stenson, who put the electric-green drink on the menu at the Zig Zag Café. As the popularity of all things Prohibition related soared during that decade, the profile of the prophetically titled drink rose again.

Serves 1

¾ ounce gin
¾ ounce green Chartreuse
¾ ounce lime juice
¾ ounce maraschino liqueur

Garnish: brandied cherry

Glassware: cocktail or coupe

Add all ingredients to a cocktail shaker. Add ice and shake until chilled. Strain into a chilled cocktail or coupe glass. Garnish with a brandied cherry.

L

facing up so that it nearly touches the first ingredient, then add the next densest liquid to the glass, pouring it slowly over the back of the spoon. Continue this process for the remaining liquid ingredients and serve the drink carefully. This technique is commonly used in pousse-café-type drinks, shooters such as the B-52, and beer cocktails such as the black and tan.

LEES

(n.) The dead yeast and particles that form a sediment after precipitating from the liquid during fermentation. In beer making this is sometimes called the "trub." For some products, aging the wine or beer on the lees leaves desired body or flavor characteristics; for others it can produce off flavors, and producers will transfer the almost-fermented or fermented liquid to a new container to avoid the lees. Battonage is a process that involves stirring the lees during fermentation, which can add a yeasty flavor and increase the body of certain wines. In French, wines that have been aged on the lees are described as "*sur lie.*"

LEGS

(n.) The drips of wine along the bowl of the wineglass that appear after swirling the liquid around. Though some wine tasters encourage visual examination of the legs as a barometer of a wine's quality ("this wine has good legs"), the term is largely meaningless when it comes to sensory evaluation.

LEWIS BAG

(n.) This sturdy canvas bag, originally intended for use by banks as a coin bag, has been repurposed as a tool to crush ice. To use, place ice cubes inside the bag, then lay it on a counter or other sturdy surface and beat with a mallet until the ice is the desired size. The canvas bag wicks away excess water and helps to keep the ice dry, which results in cocktails that are less diluted.

LIEU-DIT

(n.) Literally meaning "place-called" in French, this wine term refers to a

bounded geographical designation, such as a vineyard, that is not legally recognized by the appellation system. Though these sites lack official recognition, many have a good reputation for quality.

LIGHT BEER

(n.) A beer that is lower in alcohol and calories than regular beer. For example, Budweiser has an ABV of 4.9 percent and 143 calories per 12-ounce beer, while Bud Light is 4.2 percent ABV and has 110 calories.

LIGHT RUM

(n.) Also known as "silver" or "white" rum, light rum is clear or very pale in color and may be bottled aged or unaged. The flavor profile is often bright and mild, sometimes with the impression of sweetness, and as such it makes a good candidate for inclusion in mixed drinks and cocktails. Though this category has a reputation for being of lower quality than darker aged versions, some producers are crafting more intriguing clear

rums. Try bottlings from Flor de Caña or Cruzan.

LILLET

(n.) A brand of French apéritif wines that comes in both a Blanc version (made from the white Bordeaux grapes Sauvignon Blanc, Sémillon, and Muscadelle) and a Rouge (made from the red Bordeaux grapes Merlot and Cabernet Sauvignon). The Blanc was first made in Bordeaux in the late nineteenth century by two brothers, Paul and Raymond Lillet (at the time it was called Kina Lillet). The pair opened a distillery to make fruit-based eau de vie, but they also made a tonic wine using local wines, eau de vie, and quinine, which was fashionable at the time. In the late 1960s the company began to produce Lillet Rouge as well. The formula for Lillet Blanc and Rouge have been changed several times to decrease the bitterness, which can be problematic when trying to faithfully re-create historical recipes such as the Corpse Reviver #2 or the Vesper, but cocktail historians have suggested

work-arounds, such as adding quinine powder to the drinks.

LIMONCELLO

(n.) An Italian lemon liqueur made from a neutral spirit, lemon zest, and sugar. Popular in citrus-growing regions of southern Italy, such as the Amalfi Coast and Sardinia, this sweet-tart spirit is most often consumed chilled as a digestif. Versions made in Italy tend to use the Femminello Santa Teresa variety of lemon, but less traditional types use other lemons or citrus fruits. Because it is easy to make—you soak lemon zest in a neutral spirit for a few weeks, then strain it and add simple syrup—it is an ideal candidate for making at home.

LINCOLN COUNTY PROCESS

(n.) A technique used to make some Tennessee whiskeys in which the whiskey goes through charcoal filtration before being aged in barrels. Some say this benefits the whiskey by mellowing it, while others claim it strips away flavor.

LIQUEUR

(n.) Liqueurs, flavored spirits sweetened with a sugar product, have a long and tangled history, probably dating back to at least thirteenth-century Europe, when alcohol infused with herbs was used as a medicinal tonic. Today almost every alcohol-producing country makes a liqueur. By U.S. law, they must contain at least 2½ percent sugar but many contain much more. From there, the gates are wide open: any base spirit may be used, along with any combination of herbs, fruits, spices, creams, or flowers, and they can range from 15 percent to 55 percent ABV. The flavoring agents can be added by a number of methods: infusion, percolation, or distillation. Famous examples include sloe gin, pastis, Chartreuse, and triple sec.

L

LONG ISLAND ICED TEA

BALANCE and restraint are two adjectives one will never hear applied to this flamboyant sorority standard, with its five (five!) shots of alcohol tempered only by a splash of sour mix and cola. Long Island bartender Robert "Rosebud" Butt takes credit for coming up with the formidable combo in the early 1970s as part of a contest to design cocktails that featured triple sec. In a 2013 PBS interview, Butt explained how he designed the recipe by putting in a shot of "everything white at the bartender station." The cola? Something of a liquid garnish, he says, "just to make the color."

Serves 1

½ ounce vodka
½ ounce gin
½ ounce tequila
½ ounce light rum
¾ ounce lemon juice
¾ ounce simple syrup
   (1:1, sugar:water)
Splash Coca-Cola

Garnish: lemon wedge

Glassware: Collins

Add all ingredients (except Coca-Cola) to a cocktail shaker. Add ice and shake until chilled. Strain over ice into a Collins glass. Top with a splash of Coca-Cola and garnish with a lemon wedge.

LIQUOR

(n.) An alcoholic beverage produced by the distillation of any fermented product, including fruits, grains, and vegetables. The alcohol content of liquor is typically higher than it is for wine or beer.

LONDON GIN

(n.) Also known as London dry, this crisp, classic style is made around the world. The style evolved in the nineteenth century as a restrained opposition to the sweeter and more flamboyant Old Tom and genever gins. Legally, the gin cannot contain any artificial flavors and must be distilled to at least 70 percent alcohol before being mixed with water and, optionally, a tiny amount of sugar. The clean profile makes this style a good choice for lighter cocktails such as the gin and tonic.

LOWBALL

(n.) An umbrella term for any drink served in a lowball glass, otherwise known as an old fashioned or rocks glass. This sweeping category encompasses cocktails served with ice or neat, shaken or built, with mixers or without.

LOWLANDS

(n.) A Scotch-producing region in Scotland that has a tradition of producing a light style of Scotch. Only a handful of producers still remain.

LUMP ICE

(n.) A chunk of ice made by cracking apart an ice block. Though it has aesthetic charm when served in a drink, lump ice is often broken down further into crushed ice. Note that many old cocktail books call for lump ice in their recipes, though it is unclear what dimensions the ice should be.

MADEIRA

(n.) A fortified wine made on the Portuguese island of Madeira, located off the coast of Morocco. Production can be traced to at least the sixteenth century and the wines were popular around the world in the seventeenth and eighteenth centuries as the island served as one of the stops for ships headed out to colonies around the world. After discovering that the wines would spoil on these long voyages, producers began to fortify their wines with spirits, as done with port. The heat and movement from the ships also added a distinct flavor to the wines, which would come to be known as "maderized," and examples that had made a round trip on the ships were especially prized. The advent of a phylloxera epidemic in the late nineteenth century, which caused a grape blight in Europe, and Prohibition in the United States, which stifled demand, crippled production and the wines fell out of favor. In the 2000s, the wine has found some renewed popularity among a certain set of trendsetting bartenders and sommeliers, who have begun to place quality aged versions on their lists and shelves.

Like port, Madeira is made in a range of styles. Post-phylloxera, most of the island's vineyards were replanted with American hybrid grape varieties, which now end up in cheaper and lower-quality bottlings. Wines made with more than 85 percent of the original noble grapes may bear a grape label, which correlates to an eponymous style: Sercial is the driest and is commonly served as an apéritif; Verdelho comes in a medium-dry style and often has fruity aromatics; Boal (or Bual) is medium-sweet; Malvasia (Malmsey) is the sweetest.

Modern Madeiras undergo an aging process that approximates the sea voyage that would give the wines their special burnt-sugar character. The best are left to age naturally in casks in hot lofts, attics, or outdoors in the sun (the canteiros method) for a minimum of two years; vintage Madeiras can undergo this aging process for at least twenty years, with some notching upwards of one hundred years. Lower-quality versions are heated to between 113°F and 122°F in stainless steel tanks for a minimum of three months (estufagem process) before being transferred to casks to age. There are five tiers of aging: Finest (at least three years in oak casks), Reserve (five years), Special Reserve (ten years), Extra Reserve (fifteen years), and Vintage (made in one year from noble grape varieties). Vintage Madeira (those that bear a vintage date on the label) can age for decades, and it is not uncommon for bottles uncorked after a hundred or more years to still taste fresh on account of the wine's high acidity levels.

MAGNUM

(n.) A wine bottle containing 1.5 liters, or double the standard bottle.

MAILING LIST

(n.) A method of distributing wines directly to consumers from the winery. Consumers who sign up for the mailing list get the opportunity to buy an allocated number of wines each year, with newer customers usually receiving fewer than older ones. In practice, this is not dissimilar from a wine club, in which members receive a shipment of wines at set points throughout the year, but mailing list

MAI TAI

THE credit for this iconic 1940s drink is usually given to venerable tiki bar Trader Vic's, with the name a nod to the Tahitian *"maita'i,"* which means "good." Buoyed by the rise of tiki culture and some big celebrity endorsements (think Elvis in *Blue Hawaii*), this rum-based umbrella drink became cemented in the public imagination as a tropical must-have. The classic components of tiki are all here: a mix of rums, a citrus component, and a hint of exotica with the addition of orgeat (an almond syrup). But don't look to this drink for kitsch factor alone: when done up right, this cocktail is seriously good.

Serves 1

¾ ounce light rum
¾ ounce dark rum
1 ounce aged rum
⅛ ounce curaçao
¾ ounce pineapple juice
¾ ounce orange juice
¾ ounce lime juice
½ ounce orgeat

Garnish: umbrella, lime wheel, and a sprig of mint (optional)

Glassware: rocks

Add all ingredients to a cocktail shaker. Add ice and shake until chilled. Strain over ice into a rocks glass. Garnish with an umbrella, a lime wheel, and a sprig of mint.

Note: *Using good orgeat is key to any decent Mai Tai. Beware anything with weird ingredients.*

subscribers may choose to pass on their allocations in any given period, allowing newer members to purchase more. In the 1990s, many cult California wineries, such as Screaming Eagle and Harlan Estate, had capped mailing lists that were difficult to get onto.

MALT

(n. or v.) A term referring to either grains that have been sprouted then dried, or the process of drying these germinated grains. This practice helps to convert the starches in the grain to sugar, which the yeast consumes during fermentation, making the process more efficient. Barley is the most common grain that gets malted, though wheat, rye, and other grains sometimes undergo this process as well. Grains may be dried in kilns or ovens, and the timing and temperature of the roast can alter the flavor. When dried over an open flame, malted barley tends to take on a smoky character, which results in the distinctive flavor of certain Scotches and Rauchbier.

MALT EXTRACT

(n.) An ingredient used in making beer, this product, either a syrup or a powder made from concentrating the sugary liquid strained from boiled malted grains (the wort), is used as a shortcut (both financial and temporal) for making beer from grains.

MALT LIQUOR

(n.) Not actually a liquor, but rather a beer with an ABV above 5 percent and with a reputation for being cheaply made. To achieve higher alcohol levels, producers forgo the more expensive grain options, opting for fermentable fillers, such as sugar or corn.

Invented in the 1930s, malt liquor got a boost during World War II, when grains were expensive and scarce. By the 1960s, producers began to market it to inner-city communities as a high-alcohol product sold in 40-ounce bottles nicknamed "forties."

Many craft beers regularly surpass 5 percent ABV, but some producers,

MANHATTAN

ONE of the enduring heavyweights in the cocktail world, the Manhattan is something of a twist on the Old Fashioned, most likely spurred by the arrival of sweet vermouth in the United States in the latter part of the nineteenth century. The too-good-to-be-true story surrounding this drink's origins—that it was invented at the Manhattan Club for an event with Winston Churchill's mother as hostess—is just that: a tall tale. Although cocktail historians are still debating the subject, current theories favor either the Manhattan Club (though for an occasion not involving a British political figure) or a waiter named Black who worked in lower Manhattan in the 1870s as the source for the original recipe. There are other cocktails named for each of New York's boroughs, but none are as popular as the Manhattan.

Serves 1

2 ounces rye or bourbon
1 ounce sweet vermouth
2 dashes Angostura bitters

Garnish: brandied cherry or a lemon twist

Glassware: cocktail or coupe

Add all ingredients to a mixing glass. Add ice and stir well. Strain into a chilled cocktail or coupe glass. Garnish with a brandied cherry or a lemon twist.

MARGARITA

TALLY up another fine cocktail whose reputation has been ruined by the use of bottled sour mix: the true Margarita—a potent blend of fresh lime juice, tequila, and orange liqueur with an optional sweetener—is a respectable member of the cocktail canon. Plenty claim credit for its invention, including a restaurateur south of Tijuana in the 1930s and a socialite in Acapulco in the 1940s. Others believe it evolved as a south-of-the-border twist on the then-popular daisy, dreamed up during Prohibition, when Americans would travel abroad to drink. The Margarita was named *Esquire*'s cocktail of the month in December 1953, and it has hardly flagged in popularity since.

Serves 1

1½ ounces blanco tequila
¾ ounce orange liqueur
    (preferably Cointreau)
¾ ounce lime juice
1 teaspoon agave nectar

Garnish: salt for rimming
(optional) and a lime wedge

Glassware: cocktail, coupe, or
rocks

Prepare a cocktail, coupe, or rocks glass with a salted rim. Add all ingredients to a cocktail shaker. Add ice and shake until chilled. Strain into the prepared glass, or over ice into prepared rocks glass. Garnish with a lime wedge.

Note: *If using an orange liqueur other than Cointreau, like Combier, adjust the lime juice up or down according to the liqueur's sweetness. Some like salt on a Margarita; some don't. To make everyone happy, salt just one half of the glass. On the rocks, or up—it's up to you.*

such as Dogfish Head and Elysian Brewing, sell a malt liquor product, usually made from all grain, in 40-ounce containers as an ironic wink at the category.

MALVASIA

(n.) Also known as Malmsey, this is the sweetest style of classified Madeira wine, made from the Malvasia grape. The wine will have at least 4 percent residual sugar and notes of chocolate, nuts, and citrus. It is most often served as a dessert wine.

MANZANILLA

(n.) A fino-style sherry made in the seaside town of Sanlúcar de Barrameda, Spain. As with fino, a layer of flor (yeast) is allowed to develop over the sherry as it ages in casks, which protects it from oxidation, but the humidity in the region allows for a thicker layer of flor, offering more insulation. The resulting light, crisp style, often said to have a salty character on account of the proximity to the ocean, is best served chilled.

MARC

(n.) A French brandy made from grape pomace, the leftover skins and seeds of pressed grapes. Though similar in some ways to Italian grappa, marc must be aged in oak barrels, which impart a brown tinge and wood flavor (with the exception of marc de Gewürtztraminer, which may be clear). Marc de Bourgogne, from the Burgundy region, is generally considered to be superior. It is usually served neat as an after-dinner drink, similar to Cognac or Armagnac.

MARGARITA GLASS

(n.) A riff on the cocktail glass, with a similarly wide mouth but rounded edges and generally two tiers of bowls, a larger one atop a smaller one. The glass, whose design is more fanciful than useful, tends to be employed for frozen Margaritas and other blended cocktails. A coupe or rocks glass, however, works well for unfrozen versions of the cocktail.

MARTINI & ROSSI

(n.) Based in Turin, Italy, this company, which produces a variety of vermouths and sparkling wines, is most famous for their Rosso, a sweet Italian-style vermouth. Formed by wine merchant Alessandro Martini and herbalist Luigi Rossi in 1863, the outfit found great success with their proprietary recipe for Rosso, which was imported in the United States beginning in the mid-nineteenth century. The Rosso bottling, which is made from mix of wine, spirits, herbs, spices, flowers, roots, bark, sugar, and caramel for coloring, has a sweet, floral, spicy profile. The company, which is now owned by Bacardi, also produces an extra-dry vermouth, a rosato vermouth (made from red and white wine), and a number of other bottlings.

MASH

(n.) A mixture of grains and water heated to encourage the extraction of the grains' fermentable sugars. Cereal grains, including barley, corn, rye, and wheat, contain complex carbohydrates that can be converted into sugar that yeast can consume, leaving a by-product of alcohol and carbon dioxide.

To create a mash, the grain bill (the combination of cereal grains) is usually lightly milled to remove the husk from the seed, which allows better access to the grains' starch. The milled grain is then poured into warm water and kept warm until the grains' sugars are released. The mixture is usually then reheated to almost boiling, then strained. The strained liquid will then contain enough sugars for fermentation to take place.

In the production of bourbon and Tennessee whiskey, the term "sour mash" is used to indicate that some of the distilled mash from a previous batch is added to the current batch, which helps to protect the mix from bacteria and adds a distinctive flavor. Some producers, notably Woodford Reserve, have recently introduced a sweet mash line, which skips this step.

MARTINEZ

CONSIDERED by some to be the antecedent, or a least contemporary, of the Martini, the Martinez is a sweet spin on the vermouth cocktails popularized in the late nineteenth century. Made with Old Tom gin (a sweetened gin), sweet vermouth, and maraschino liqueur, the drink does skew saccharine, especially in comparison to a dry Martini, but looking at the proportions, it's easy to see the similarities between the two drinks. Historians tend to squabble about the drink's origins. Some say it's from a bar in the city of Martinez, California, while others credit bartender Jerry Thomas, saying he made it for a traveler headed to Martinez. The first known published recipe, however, is in *The Modern Bartenders' Guide*, by O. H. Bryon.

Serves 1

1 ounce gin
1½ ounces sweet vermouth
1 teaspoon maraschino liqueur
2 dashes Angostura bitters

Garnish: orange or lemon peel

Glassware: cocktail or coupe

Add all ingredients to a mixing glass. Add ice and stir until chilled. Strain into a chilled cocktail or coupe glass. Garnish with an orange or lemon peel.

MARTINI

DESPITE all the sleuthing done by cocktail historians in recent years, no one seems to have turned up a credible story for the birth of the Martini. Certain facts, however, can be established: it postdated the Manhattan and likely evolved from a mix of sweet vermouth and sweet gin when drier versions of those alcohols became popular at the turn of the twentieth century. The first printed versions of the Martini recipe are similar to the one below. Over time, however, the bitters fell out of fashion, then too did the vermouth, and the ratio between the two liquors tilted strongly toward gin. There now exists a world of permutations that require you to decide on the ratio of vermouth to gin, whether to garnish the drink with an olive or a twist, and even, yes, whether it is shaken or stirred (answers: your choice, your choice, stirred). Still, there are some points of agreement: a Martini must be made with gin, not vodka, and it must be mixed with vermouth; otherwise, one is simply drinking straight liquor. And finally, this caveat: While Martinis may be served in cocktail glasses, not everything served in a cocktail glass may be called a Martini.

Serves 1

2 ounces gin
1 ounce dry vermouth
   (preferably Dolin)
2 dashes orange bitters

Garnish: lemon peel

Glassware: cocktail or coupe

Add all ingredients to a mixing glass. Add ice and stir until chilled. Strain into a chilled cocktail or coupe glass. Garnish with an lemon peel.

Note: *Should you prefer a drier Martini, try a 4:1 ratio of gin to vermouth. A Dirty Martini simply requires a splash of olive juice and a substitution of a good, dry olive (or two) for garnish.*

M

MATURE

(adj.) A description for an aged wine that is ready to drink and will not benefit from any further aging.

MEAD

(n.) This alcoholic beverage made from honey rivals beer for the distinction of oldest alcoholic beverage, with archaeological evidence showing production in India, China, and Europe well over two thousand years ago. Made from fermenting a water-honey solution, mead is often called a "wine" because the process is similar.

Although traditionally a honey-water mix was left in the open air to be fermented by wild yeasts, today cultivated strains of yeast are available to the modern mead maker. Most mead takes at least three years of aging to turn to a drinkable product. This can be done in stainless steel tanks or barrels. The style of honey will affect the flavor of the mead; lighter, more delicate honeys will yield light mead, while darker honeys will produce more caramelized flavors.

There are different schools of thought as to why mead fell out of favor after the Middle Ages: some cite the rise of beer and wine, others the rise of sugar as the world's preferred sweetener. Today, though, things are changing: Once known as a lowly denizen of Renaissance fairs and historical reenactments, mead too has been swept up by the craft spirits craze. New artisanal distilleries are opening apace, and bartenders are working it into cocktails. The offerings come in a range of styles borrowed from other spirit categories: hop-flavored and dry, carbonated, oak-aged, and infused with herbs or fruits. Producers worth seeking out include B. Nektar and Kuhnhenn.

MERITAGE

(n.) A trademarked name for an American wine made from a blend of approved Bordeaux grape varieties, both red and white. Acceptable varieties include Cabernet Sauvignon, Merlot, Cabernet Franc, Mal-

bec, Petit Verdot, St. Macaire, Gros Verdot, and Carménère for red wines, and Sauvignon Blanc, Sémillon, and Muscadelle du Bordelais for white.

The name is a combination of "merit" and "heritage" and rhymes with the latter. The Meritage Alliance, which monitors the trademark, was founded in 1988 to provide wine makers with an official label for blended wines. If a wine made in the United States contains fewer than 75 percent of one type of grape, it must be labeled table wine. The Meritage label means the wine makers do not have to revert to the generic table wine designation.

MERLOT

(n.) A red grape variety commonly used to make red or rosé wines. When produced well, red wines made from the grape exhibit a smooth, velvety texture, have medium body, and carry notes of ripe red berries and plums. Although the grape is now widely grown throughout the world, production areas to note include the right bank of Bordeaux in France,

Napa Valley in California, and Washington State. In Bordeaux, the grape's spiritual homeland, the grape is one of five commonly included in a blend to make the region's famous (and often pricey) red wines. California producers found great commercial success with the grape in the 1980s and 1990s, which led to overplanting and overproduction, followed by a backlash from the public spurred by the success of the 2004 movie *Sideways*. A refocus on quality and better viticultural practices has led to some better choices from the state available on the market.

METAXA

(n.) A Greek brand of flavored brandy. Created in 1888, the proprietary recipe contains grape brandy, Muscat wine, and botanicals. The sweet brandy has notes of citrus, honey, caramel, and herbs. It is categorized according to how long it has been aged in French oak barrels (three, five, and seven years are the most common versions). Younger bottlings are best served with juice

MEXICAN FIRING SQUAD

GLOBE-TROTTING cocktail writer Charles H. Baker discovered this summer-perfect pink cocktail at a Mexico City bar in 1937, and two years later he included it in his book *Gentleman's Companion, Volume II: Jigger, Beaker and Flask*. For all the titular bluster, the drink—a mix of tequila, grenadine, lime juice, and a hit of Angostura bitters—is a genial balance of sour, sweet, and boozy. Serve it short, as Baker recommended, with a fruit salad of a garnish, comprised of pineapple and orange slices and topped with a cherry. Or, for a more contemporary feel, add soda water, turning the drink into a tall cooler.

Serves 1

2 ounces tequila
¾ ounce lime juice
¾ ounce grenadine
5 dashes Angostura bitters

Garnish: lime wheel

Glassware: rocks

Add all ingredients to a cocktail shaker. Add ice and shake until chilled. Strain into a rocks glass over ice. Garnish with a lime wheel.

or soda or mixed into cocktails, while older versions work well neat or on the rocks.

MEZCAL

....

(n.) A Mexican spirit distilled from the agave plant with a distinctive smoky character (technically, tequila is a type of mezcal). In the sixteenth century, Spanish conquistadors began distilling mezcal from pulque, an agave-based fermented beverage created by the Aztecs. Tequila was later refined in the eighteenth century to be only from blue agave plants grown in Jalisco and the surrounding states. Today mezcal is made in seven states in central and southern Mexico, with production centered in Oaxaca.

As is tequila, mezcal is made from the hearts of the agave plant (*piña*), but differences between the two begin with the plant selection. Whereas tequila can be made only from blue agave, mezcal can be made from a greater variety of plants in the agave family; the most popular variety is the *espadin* plant. The hearts

are roasted in underground pits filled with hot rocks and wood, which gives the spirit its characteristic smokiness. Many small producers double distill the liquid in copper stills instead of using more industrial column stills. The climate in which the agave is grown plays a factor in the spirit's flavor: highland plants tend to yield larger hearts, which lend a fruitier edge, while lowland plants have smaller hearts, which skews earthier. That there are distinctions in terroir for mezcal, much like there are for wine, is a driving force behind growing interest in the product.

Mezcal is sold in tiers similar to those for tequila: 100 percent agave and mixto, which must be at least 80 percent agave. Producers have been experimenting with oak aging to varying effect. Aging breaks down into three categories: unaged white; reposado, which must see two to nine months in barrel; and añejo, which must be barrel-aged for more than twelve months.

Because of its rustic and decentralized production, most mezcal that makes it to the United States tends to

MICHELADA

A **LL** great cocktails are greater than the sum of their parts, and perhaps no drink illustrates this better than the Michelada, a Mexican beer cocktail in which an otherwise unremarkable light beer gets doctored up with a kitchen sink's worth of condiments and is transformed into an essential hot-weather refresher. As a general concept, think of this as a Bloody Mary, but with beer instead of vodka. And, as when making a Bloody Mary, the condiments are key. Common additions include Worcestershire sauce, soy sauce, lime juice, hot sauce, tomato juice, celery salt, Maggi seasoning, or any combination thereof. Whichever you might add, remember that you're looking for something spicy, tangy, savory, slightly effervescent, and super-refreshing.

Serves 1

1 ounce lime juice
5–6 dashes hot sauce
3 ounces tomato juice
Salt and pepper
1 mexican beer

Garnish: salt and pepper for rimming (optional, *see:* Margarita)

Glassware: pint glass

Rim a pint glass with salt and pepper and fill it with ice. Add lime juice, hot sauce, tomato juice, and salt and pepper to the prepared pint glass and top with beer.

be artisanal and pricey, though look for bigger companies to capitalize as the demand grows stronger. Traditionally consumed neat, the smoky liquor also makes an interesting addition to cocktails. Brands to look out for include Sombra, Del Maguey, Ilegal, and Pierde Almas.

MICROBREWERY

(n.) A term, popular in the 1980s and 1990s, to describe small, independently owned breweries. Recently the word has largely been supplanted by the term "craft brewery."

MILD

(n.) The earliest mentions of mild beers date to seventh-century England, referring to an unhopped newly fermented beer. The term gained popularity in the eighteenth century, when it was commonly used to describe young, fresh versions of beer styles (mild stout or mild ale) that were meant to be consumed soon after brewing. The beer's short intended shelf life meant that brew-ers could use a smaller quantity of hops, which act as a preservative. In the nineteenth century, brewers often made several versions of milds, which were categorized by their alcohol content or color. In the mid-twentieth century, milds, by this time defined as dark ales that were somewhat sweet and low in alcohol, were England's most popular beer, but demand waned considerably after World War II as consumers gravitated toward bitter ales. The rise of craft brewing in the late twentieth century has helped to revive the style.

MILK PUNCH

(n.) This mixture of milk, liquor (usually bourbon or whiskey), sugar, and baking spices, served cold, was popular during the U.S. colonial era but dropped from the cultural radar after World War II, except in New Orleans and its environs, where it has continued to rate as party-worthy for holidays, special occasions, and brunch. Forward-thinking bartenders have revived the style for the contemporary audience.

MINT JULEP

ESSENTIALLY sweetened bourbon over ice with some mint for aromatics, the Mint Julep is one of the more powerful cocktails to be associated with daytime drinking—the association, of course, owing much to the Kentucky Derby, at which 120,000 juleps are said to be sold every year. Get past the fancy trappings, though, and you'll find an all-American drink with roots dating to before the Civil War. In *Straight Up or On the Rocks*, William Grimes traces the first mention of the julep to 1878 in Virginia. The drink was called a julap (the Arabic word for rosewater) and called for rum, water and sugar. The julep as we know it—crushed ice, mint, brandy or whiskey—became the "Coca-Cola of its time," as Grimes calls it, beginning in the 1820s. The gospel of the julep was further spread when Kentucky senator Henry Clay brought the recipe with him to Washington, D.C., in the early 1800s.

Serves 1

---

1 large mint sprig
2½ ounces bourbon
¾ ounce simple syrup
　(1:1, sugar:water)

Garnish: bouquet of mint

Glassware: julep tin or rocks

In a julep tin or rocks glass, muddle the mint sprig with simple syrup by gently pressing to release the oils. Pack the glass with finely crushed ice. Pour bourbon over ice, and mound more ice into the top of the glass. Garnish with a bouquet of spanked mint.

Note: *This is a strong drink, so pouring the bourbon over the ice makes for greater dilution. Speaking of ice, the finely crushed variety is key to any julep.*

MILK STOUT

(n.) A stout made with added lactose, which does not ferment and contributes sweet flavor, smooth texture, and added body. Also known as sweet stout or cream stout, this style of beer was developed in early twentieth-century England as an offshoot of mild stout, a sweet, young style of stout that was popular in the prior century. In 1946 the British government prohibited the use of the word "milk" on beer labels, but the style persisted under a variety of brand names. According to historian Martyn Cornell, milk stout, with its low alcohol content and sweet profile, came to be associated with a demographic of older working-class women.

MIMOSA

(n.) A mixed drink consisting of equal parts orange juice and sparkling wine that has become a signature of brunch, first-class airline freebies, and bridal showers. Historic recipes sometimes call for ½ ounce of triple sec or curaçao for an additional layer of orange flavor.

MIRABELLE

(n.) A French eau de vie made from distilling yellow plums, usually served chilled as an after-dinner drink.

MIS EN BOUTEILLE

(phrase) A French term that translates to "put in the bottle," it is used to describe whether the wine was bottled at the domaine or château (*au château* or *au domaine*) or by a third party (*par*).

MIST

(n.) Similar to "on the rocks," this drink order is a request for a spirit or liqueur to be poured over shaved or crushed ice.

MISSISSIPPI PUNCH

KEEP track of how many of these you've had: this recipe calls for a formidable 4 ounces of liquor, tempered only by a smidge of lemon juice and sugar. First recorded in Jerry Thomas's 1862 edition of *How to Mix Drinks*, the drink may have a Southern name, but it has international flavor in the combination of French Cognac, Caribbean rum, and American bourbon—a mix that works better in practice than it looks on paper.

Serves 1

2 ounces Cognac
1 ounce bourbon
1 ounce dark rum
½ ounce simple syrup
   (1:1, sugar:water)
¾ ounce lemon juice

Garnish: seasonal berries and citrus

Glassware: Collins

Add ingredients to a cocktail shaker. Add ice and shake until chilled. Strain into a Collins glass over crushed ice. Add more crushed ice and then garnish with seasonal berries and citrus.

M

MIXED DRINK

(n.) A drink with two or more ingredients, usually used in reference to drinks made with a liquor base and a nonalcoholic mixer, such as a Screwdriver (vodka and orange juice).

MIXER

(n.) Any nonalcoholic component of cocktail or mixed drink, most frequently soda or juice.

MIXTO

1. *(n.)* A designation for tequilas distilled from less than 100 percent but more than 51 percent blue agave; generally considered inferior to tequilas made from 100 percent blue agave.

2. *(n.)* A designation for mezcals distilled from less than 100 percent but more than 80 percent agave; generally considered inferior to mezcals made from 100 percent agave.

MIXOLOGIST

(n.) A somewhat pretentious term that rose in popularity during the cocktail renaissance of the 2000s for someone who makes and serves drinks.

MOCKTAIL

(n.) A portmanteau of "mock" and "cocktail," used to designate a cocktail that contains no alcohol. Although this term can and does overlap with "virgin," the word "virgin" should be used when the alcohol is omitted from an existing cocktail (e.g., a virgin Piña Colada), while "mocktail" is a better descriptor for a unique recipe. Nonalcoholic cocktails are a growing trend in the United States, with top bars and restaurants developing serious mocktails for their beverage programs.

MODIFIER

(n.) A cocktail-making term used to indicate the addition of an ingredient that modifies the base spirit.

MOJITO

A DESCENDANT of the Draque, an old Cuban concoction of unrefined rum, cane sugar, and lime juice, the Mojito was most likely invented when more delicate light rums entered the U.S. market in the mid to late nineteenth century. The first printed recipes for a Mojito as we would recognize it date to the 1930s, and there are boundless theories about how the drink got its name: maybe it's a reference to the Cuban lime seasoning, *mojo*, or a play on the Spanish for "wet," *mojado*. The drink enjoyed a recent surge of popularity in the United States in the early 2000s. The drink is a curse when made poorly, with small forests of mint bruised by overeager muddling, but a blessing when made properly, not too sweet and with mint—just a few sprigs—lightly pressed.

Serves 1

2 mint sprigs
2 teaspoons sugar
1 lime, quartered
2 ounces light rum
Soda water

Garnish: mint sprig and lime wheel

Glassware: Collins

In a Collins glass, add the mint sprigs and sugar. Muddle the mint by pressing it lightly with a muddler to release the oils. Drop in lime pieces and muddle to release juice. Add rum, stir, and add ice. Top with soda water. Garnish with a mint sprig and a lime wheel.

Cocktail writers and makers disagree about the exact boundaries of what can be considered a modifier; some count fortified wines, liqueurs, fruit juices, eggs, and dairy ingredients, while others draw the line at including liqueurs or fruit juices. More generally, it can be thought of as the largest ingredient in the cocktail by volume (disregarding the base spirit), while other ingredients used in small quantities, such as bitters or syrups, can be considered "accents."

MOLASSES

(n.) The by-product of processing raw sugar into white granulated sugar, this dark, sweet syrup has long found a home in baked goods, but it can be used in cocktails as well. Often it is thinned with water before using so it can be more easily incorporated into drinks.

MOONSHINE

(n.) A spirit produced illegally in the United States, true moonshine can be distilled from any fruit, grain, or sugar. The common factor is the illegality of the production, with the name thought to be a reference to something done in the cover of night by the light of the moon. In general, most moonshine is high-proof and unaged. Some commercial distillers have recently found success marketing white whiskey (unaged whiskey) as moonshine, though the term on the label carries no real legal meaning.

The roots of moonshine stretch back to the era of the American Revolution, when the federal government enacted a tax on liquor to recoup the costs for war with the British. Resentment built, and many small backyard producers and farmers continued making their own spirits, battling the "revenuers," or federal agents sent to collect taxes. Pittsburgh's Whiskey Rebellion in 1794 marked a high point of conflict between the factions, but illegal production of alcohol continued apace. In the 1920s and 1930s, Prohibition also had the unintended effect of spurring moonshine production, and as demand increased, cheaper and cruder versions filled the

MONKEY GLAND

LET'S get this out of the way first: yes, in a headline-grabbing move, this cocktail was named for a nineteenth-century surgical procedure that involved grafting monkey testicles into men to increase their sex drive. The nudge-nudge-wink-wink name plus the addition of illicit absinthe to an otherwise vanilla combo of gin and orange juice made this vivid orange-red cocktail a popular order in Paris in the 1920s, from which it spread to London and the United States. Other anise-flavored spirits filled the void when absinthe was banned, but now you can make one as it was meant to be.

Serves 1

1½ ounces gin
1½ ounces fresh orange juice
1 teaspoon grenadine
1 teaspoon simple syrup
   (1:1, sugar:water)
1 teaspoon absinthe

Glassware: coupe

Add all ingredients to a shaker, add ice, and shake. Strain into a coupe glass.

MORNING GLORY FIZZ

AS with the Blood and Sand and Rob Roy, this is one of the rare cocktails to use Scotch. But instead of the elegant night-on-the-town vibe those brown liquor–based cocktails exude, the Morning Glory Fizz, as the name would imply, was meant to be taken as a morning-after cure. The recipe works well, however, any time of the day: the eye-brightening citrus juice and the herbaceous absinthe are countered by the rich, silky texture of the egg whites and just enough sweetness from the sugar to make the drink go down easy. The earliest references to the drink date to 1882, when the author Harry Johnson suggested the drink was "an excellent one for a morning beverage, which will give a good appetite and quiet the nerves."

Serves 1

2 ounces blended Scotch
½ ounce lemon juice
½ ounce lime juice
½ ounce simple syrup
   (1:1, sugar:water)
1 egg white
3–4 dashes absinthe

Garnish: orange peel or orange wheel

Glassware: fizz or rocks

Add all ingredients but the soda water to a cocktail shaker, and dry shake. Add ice to shaker, and shake well. Strain into a fizz or rocks glass and garnish with an orange peel or orange wheel.

MOSCOW MULE

BORN from a long lineage of ginger beer–based cocktails known as "bucks," this drink featuring vodka, ginger beer, and lime juice was created in the early 1940s. Although the exact origins of the recipe are disputed, most accounts credit an alcohol-fueled meeting between John G. Martin, an executive at the company that bottled the then-unknown Smirnoff, and Jack Morgan, owner of the Cock 'n Bull bar in Hollywood and a producer of ginger beer. Together the pair dreamed up an easy-to-make drink using their underperforming products and gave it a funny name to make it easier to sell ("Moscow" is a nod to vodka's Russian roots). After a lull in its popularity during World War II, ads for "Mule Parties" featuring celebrities such as Woody Allen helped raise the profile of this drink in the 1960s—as well as that of vodka, which would go on to supplant gin and whiskey as the country's most popular spirit. Tradition dictates that this drink should be served in a copper mug (some origin myths account for a third friend who needed to offload said mugs), though highballs or Collins glasses are suitable substitutions.

Serves 1

2 ounces vodka
¾ ounce lime juice
4 ounces ginger beer

Garnish: lime wheel

Glassware: Collins, highball, or copper mule mug

Add vodka and lime juice to a Collins, highball, or copper mule mug (if you're fancy enough to own one). Top with crushed or cracked ice. Top with ginger beer and swizzle gently to mix. Garnish with a lime wheel.

underground market. After Prohibition, the popularity of moonshine subsided somewhat, as cheap liquor became more available. Today the DIY movement has fueled a small revival of home-distilled moonshine.

MOSCATEL

(n.) A dessert-wine style of sherry made from Moscatel grapes that have been allowed to dry and raisin in the sun, which concentrates the sugars. After fermentation it is aged, resulting in a sweet, viscous, nutty wine.

MOSTO VERDE

(n.) A relatively new style of Peruvian pisco made from distilling grapes that have been partially fermented.

MOUSSE

(n.) A wine term that describes the foamy head on a glass of sparkling wine. A delicate mousse, for instance, which consists of tiny bubbles, is usually considered a desirable trait for sparkling wines. Other common ways the mousse may be described are as "creamy" and "aggressive."

MUDDLE

(v.) A bartending technique in which a long blunt instrument is used to mash fruits, herbs, sugar, or spices. Depending on what is being muddled, the action performs different things: releasing the oils in citrus peels or herbs, speeding the rate that sugar will dissolve in liquids, or extracting juice from berries or citrus pulp. The force with which an ingredient is muddled should be based on the qualities of the ingredient. While citrus pulp may need a more intense pressing, delicate herbs such as mint may need only a light crushing.

MUDDLER

(n.) A bartending tool used to muddle cocktail ingredients. A long-handled rod with a blunt end, usually made from wood, a muddler may also have indentations on the blunt head

to better press or puncture ingredients, but any long instrument with a flat edge, such as a wooden spoon, may be used. It should be long enough that you can keep a good grip on it while performing the muddling action, and it shouldn't be made of a reactive metal or have any varnish that could fall into the cocktail.

MULL

(v.) To add spices, sugar, and fruit to a heated beverage, usually wine.

Common mulling spices include cinnamon, cloves, and citrus peel. This tradition, often associated with winter holidays, has long roots in Europe, where many cultures have their own version of mulled wine, including *Glühwein* in Germany, *glögg* in Norway, and *vin chaud* in France.

MUST

(n.) The pressed or extracted grape juice that will be fermented into wine.

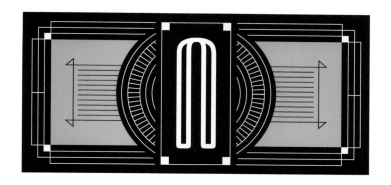

NAMASAKE

(n.) A label indication that a sake is unpasteurized. Sake is usually pasteurized twice, once after brewing and again after a maturation period. Namasake is not pasteurized at all, resulting in a fresher and brighter profile. Whether that makes the sake better is a matter of debate: detractors say the fresh flavors can obscure the true character of the sake. Because the sake is less stable, it must be carefully refrigerated to keep it from developing off flavors or oxidizing. Within this category are two subtypes: nama-chozo, which means the sake has been pasteurized once after maturation but not after brewing, and its converse, nama-zume, which means the sake has been pasteurized after brewing but not after maturation. All grades of sake can be made in the namasake style.

NATURAL WINE

(n.) A term that generally refers to wines made with a minimal amount of human manipulation. Though no legal definition or certification exists, natural wines tend to be made with grapes that have been grown organically or without industrial inputs, use ambient yeast only, and contain little to no sulfur dioxide to stabilize the

product. The "natural" designation has been a source of much contention in the wine world. A continuing debate among the natural wine community involves how much, if any, sulfur (a common stabilizing agent) may be used and whether introducing yeast strains rather than using ambient yeast alone is acceptable. Detractors of the category as a whole object to the use of the word "natural," which suggest that other wines are "unnatural," as well as the nebulous definition of the term, and they also point out that some natural wines become spoiled from the lack of sulfur.

NATURAL YEAST

(*n.*) The strains of yeast ambiently present in a vineyard, winery, or brewing environment; also referred to as indigenous yeast. Most brewers and wine makers select strains of yeast that have been cultivated for particular traits to ferment their products. Others allow the yeast that is ambient in the environment to perform the fermentation. There are risks involved with using natural yeast,

such as a greater chance of bacterial contamination or an incomplete fermentation, but some say natural yeasts add a greater complexity.

NEAT

(*adj.*) A drink order requesting that a spirit be served unchilled without ice or water, most frequently associated with spirits in the whiskey family.

NÉGOCIANT

(*n.*) A French term for a merchant who buys either grapes or wine, then makes or blends a wine and bottles it under his or her own label. This practice was and continues to be common in France, especially in regions like Burgundy and Champagne, where many smaller grape-growing estates sell their fruit to well-known *négociants* such as Louis Jadot or Joseph Drouhin.

NEUTRAL SPIRIT

(*n.*) A clear, odorless spirit of nearly 100 percent ethanol. Produced in a

NEGRONI

LIKE all good stories should, the one about the Negroni's origin involves rakish Italian nobility. Most accounts credit the recipe to one Count Negroni, a swashbuckling proto-boho who reportedly spent time as a rodeo cowboy in the United States. An illustration of his wild ways, legend has it that at a bar in Italy in 1919, he asked for a something like an Americano, but boozier. Swap gin for soda water, and presto, the Negroni. Navigating between bitter and sweet, this powerful drink—a study in balance—has become one of the cornerstones of the classic cocktail revival.

Serves 1

1 ounce gin
1 ounce Campari
1 ounce sweet vermouth

Garnish: orange or lemon peel

Glassware: rocks, cocktail, or coupe

Add all ingredients to a mixing glass. Add ice and stir until chilled. If serving on the rocks, strain over ice into a rocks glass. If serving up, strain into a chilled cocktail or coupe glass. Garnish with an orange or lemon peel.

NEGRONI SBAGLIATO

T HE word *sbagliato*, appended here to the name of a classic cocktail, translates to "incorrect" or "mistaken." Not so. With prosecco in place of the Negroni's traditional gin, this spritzy beverage makes for a buoyantly bitter Italian aperitivo.

Serves 1

1 ounce Campari
1 ounce sweet vermouth
Prosecco (or any dry
　sparkling wine)

Garnish: orange peel

Glassware: rocks or lowball

In a rocks or lowball glass, add Campari, sweet vermouth and ice. Top with prosecco or sparkling wine and stir gently to combine. Garnish with an orange peel.

column still from any type of sugar, this flavorless product forms the base for many vodkas, gins, and liqueurs. If made from grain, it may be called "neutral grain spirit."

NEW MAKE

(n.) An unofficial term for spirits that have just been made, usually used to refer to whiskey. The spirit should be undiluted and clear, as it will not yet have undergone the barrel-aging process, which can add brown color.

NEW WORLD

(adj.) A wine term indicating that a wine has been made in any country outside Europe. New World wines are often considered to be bolder and fruitier than their Old World counterparts, although this is not always true. This distinction, however, is rapidly losing currency as European wine makers adopt techniques popularized by New World wine makers and vice versa. The term can be bent to refer to wines made in a "New World" style—that is, fruity and bold—regardless of their geographical origin.

NIGHTCAP

(n.) An alcoholic beverage consumed before going to sleep, a nightcap is different from a digestif, as it is not necessarily associated with the end of a meal, though the categories sometimes overlap. Individual preferences will dictate the alcohol, though it is usually a single spirit served neat. This practice evolved because alcohol was thought to improve sleep, though several recent scientific studies dispute this theory.

NIGORI

(n.) A type of sake that is unfiltered. Most sakes are filtered after the brewing process to remove unfermented rice solids, enhancing their clarity. Nigori sakes, however, skip this step, resulting in a cloudy product. The quantity of particles can vary, resulting in anything from a light milkiness

NEW YORK SOUR

NEW York has a knack for adopting everything from fashion to food to people, molding each into its own particular blend of outrageous, sophisticated, and neurotic. Such is the case with the New Your sour, a relatively common variation on the frothy whiskey classic that, up until the early twentieth century, flew under several aliases, including the Continental Sour and the Southern Whiskey Sour. What separates this drink from a regular sour is the addition of a red wine float, which transforms the unassuming sour into this Technicolor foglifter of a cocktail.

Serves 1

2 ounces rye or bourbon
1 ounce lemon juice
1 ounce simple syrup
　(1:1, sugar:water)
¼ ounce red wine

Glassware: rocks

Add whiskey, lemon juice, and simple syrup to a cocktail shaker. Add ice and shake until chilled. Strain over ice into a rocks glass. Gently drizzle red wine over the back of a bar spoon to create a float atop the cocktail.

to an opaque richness, and the flavor tends to be fruity and mild. This type of sake benefits from being served chilled. Note: The particles sometimes settle at the bottom of the bottle, necessitating a quick shake to return the sake to a uniform cloudiness.

NOBLE ROT

(n.) A type of fungus that can grow on grapes. Although fungus and mold are usually considered things to avoid in the vineyard, as they can negatively affect grapes, under certain conditions ripe grapes may become infected with noble rot, also known as the *Botrytis cinerea* fungus. The resulting grapes may be used to make particularly good sweet wines, such as Sauternes, Tokaji, and some sweet German and Austrian wines, among others.

NOG

(n.) Though the term referred to a type of English ale in the 1700s, it evolved to describe a cocktail made with eggs, the most famous example being eggnog.

NOILLY PRAT

(n.) A brand of dry vermouth made in Marseille, France. First formulated by Frenchman Joseph Noilly in 1813, this vermouth is thought to be the first commercially produced dry vermouth; the dry style would eventually become known as "French" vermouth, as opposed to the red sweet vermouth from Italy. The base wine is made from a blend of white Picpoul and Clairette grapes, to which a blend of partially fermented sweet Muscat grape juice, beet sugar spirit, and twenty herbs and spices, including chamomile, nutmeg, and gentian, are added. The brand produces four labels of vermouth: Original Dry (which may be mixed in cocktails or sipped neat), Extra Dry (a special formulation for the U.S. market designed to be a mixer), Rouge (a red sweet style introduced in 1956), and Ambre (a limited production sweet vermouth).

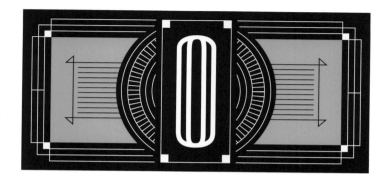

OAKY

(adj.) A flavor descriptor applied to wines, beers, and spirits that have been aged in wood barrels or casks. Typical flavors associated with oak include vanilla, spice, smoke, toast, and char. Some consider these characteristics to be positive, while others find them overpowering.

OFF PREMISE

(phrase) A place of business at which alcohol may be sold for consumption off-site, such as liquor stores and wine shops.

OKTOBERFEST

1. *(n.)* A style of German amber lager traditionally brewed in the spring, aged through the summer, and served at harvest festivities in the fall. Modern versions are typically medium-bodied with a deep gold to amber color. Smooth in character, the beers usually have very little hop character.

2. *(n.)* A German festival that began in Munich in 1810 to celebrate a royal marriage. Though Munich remains the epicenter for this sixteen-day celebration at the end of September, which attracts more than six million revelers every year, the

OLD CUBAN

CREATED by Pegu Club founder Audrey Saunders in 2004, the Old Cuban is something of a fresh take on the Mojito, with Champagne substituted for the soda water and a dash of bitters added. The sparkling wine adds a glittery night-on-the-town finish to the warm weather–ready mint-spiked cooler, making it appropriate for celebrations both high (New Year's Eve) and low (weekday nights).

Serves 1

1½ ounces 12-year-old Appleton Estate Jamaican rum
1 ounce 1:1 simple syrup
¾ ounce lime juice
6 mint leaves
2 dashes Angostura bitters
2 ounces chilled Champagne or dry sparkling wine

Garnish: mint sprig

Glassware: cocktail

Shake all ingredients—save for the Champagne—with ice in a cocktail shaker. Double strain into a chilled cocktail glass and top with 2 ounces of Champagne. Garnish with a small mint sprig.

OLD FASHIONED

NEARLY stomped out of existence by its fruity mid-twentieth-century incarnations the original Old Fashioned is as traditional a cocktail as they come: it's a simple mix of spirits, sugar, bitters, and water that first appeared in print in 1806, making it the first printed recipe for a cocktail. Other alcohols were permitted, but the whiskey or rye version of this drink, served over ice, is what we now know as the Old Fashioned, which is thought to be named later that century after more elaborate newfangled cocktails entered the canon. During Prohibition the recipe veered into odd territory, with fruit and cherries added to distract from the crude spirits that were available then. After repeal, it was the imposter version that stuck until the recent cocktail revival brought the original recipe back from the brink of extinction.

Serves 1

1 sugar cube (see note)
Splash soda water if using sugar cube or sugar
2–3 dashes Angostura bitters if using simple syrup
2 ounces rye or bourbon

Garnish: lemon or orange peel

Glassware: double rocks

In a double rocks glass, muddle the sugar cube or sugar with Angostura bitters and a small splash of soda water until dissolved. If using simple syrup, swirl with bitters in a double rocks glass. Add whiskey and ice (preferably an oversized cube) and stir well. Garnish with a lemon or orange peel.

Note: *If you don't have sugar cubes on hand, a teaspoon of sugar or a generous ¼ ounce of simple syrup will do the trick.*

OLD PAL

THIS cocktail is born from the Negroni family tree, with rye for gin and dry vermouth instead of sweet. It first appeared in print in Harry MacElhone's 1922 edition of *ABC of Mixing Cocktails*, where the famed bartender-turned-author credits William "Sparrow" Roberts, *New York Herald* sports editor (and frequent patron at his Paris bar), for the recipe. Interestingly, the key change-up in the drink is not swapping the base spirit of spicy rye for gin (which makes the drink kissing cousin of the Boulevardier, a Negroni made with bourbon), but the use of dry vermouth instead of sweet, which makes for a much leaner, drier profile.

Serves 1

1 ounce rye
1 ounce Campari
1 ounce dry vermouth

Garnish: orange or lemon peel

Glassware: cocktail or coupe

Add all ingredients to a mixing glass. Add ice and stir until chilled. Strain into a chilled cocktail or coupe glass. Garnish with a lemon or an orange peel.

often beer-heavy festivities have spread globally, with many bars and breweries around the world marking the occasion.

OLD FASHIONED GLASS

(n.) Also known as a rocks or low-ball glass, this small tumbler holds 6 to 10 ounces of liquid. It usually has a wide mouth and a sturdy base designed to withstand muddling. A double old fashioned glass holds 12 to 16 ounces and is suitable for lowball drinks with more ingredients or larger amounts of ice.

OLD VINES

(n.) A nebulously defined wine term that generally indicates that the grapes for a wine have come from vines that are not newly planted. There is no legal standard for how old vines must be to be classified this way—some say twenty-five years, others more than one hundred—or whether new cuttings grafted onto old rootstock may be classified as "old," but "old vines" are generally

perceived as superior in the consumer marketplace, and such wines often fetch a higher price. Old vines generally yield fewer grapes than younger ones, which results in more complexly flavored grapes, and they also have a well-developed root system that will not be overwhelmed in times of rain or drought. Whether these traits translate to a better wine is a matter of personal preference and perception. In French, the term for old vines is "*viellies vignes.*"

OLD WORLD

(adj.) A wine term indicating a wine has been made in Europe. Old World wines are considered to be earthier and subtler than their New World counterparts, though this does not always hold true. Wines made outside Europe that embody these characteristics may be described as made in the "Old World" style, regardless of their geographic origin.

OLEO SACCHARUM

(n.) A syrup made from sugar (*saccharum*) and oil (*oleo*), most often the oil from citrus peels. Commonly used in nineteenth-century punches, this alcohol-free mixer has regained traction in the cocktail renaissance of the 2000s, with many bars and restaurants making the ingredient in-house to use in punches and other nineteenth century–era drinks.

OLOROSO

(n.) A dry style of sherry allowed to age in the barrel without the protective layer of flor (yeast), which yields a nutty, deep brown oxidative wine that is best served slightly chilled.

ON PREMISE

(phrase) A place of business at which alcohol may be sold for consumption on site, such as bars and restaurants.

ON THE ROCKS

(phrase) A drink order requesting that a spirit or cocktail be served over ice cubes, or "rocks."

ORANGE BLOSSOM WATER

(n.) Water infused with orange flowers, primarily for fragrance. Commonly used in traditional Moroccan and Mediterranean baking, this non-alcoholic liquid also makes an appearance in cocktails such as the Ramos Gin Fizz.

ORANGE WINE

(n.) A style of wine made from white grapes that have been left to ferment or macerate on their skins; the contact with the skins can give the wine an orange or pink tinge, as well as transfer some of the tannins and phenols in the skins to the wine. The process for making orange wine is similar to that for making rosé wines, which use red grapes instead. Some producers choose to make orange wines in an oxidative style, using bar-

O

rels or amphorae to age the wine, but that is not a requirement of the style. The epicenter for orange wine production is the Friuli-Venezia Giulia region of Italy, but good examples can be found from Slovenia, France, California, and the rest of the world.

ORGEAT

(n.) A sweet almond-based syrup flavored with orange flower water. French in origin, it is used as a cocktail mixer in many classic drinks, such as the Mai Tai, the Scorpion, and the Japanese Cocktail. As commercial versions can be laden with high-fructose corn syrup and lack the slightly creamy texture of the best versions, some forward-thinking bars and restaurants are making this syrup in-house and coming up with creative variations based on other nuts. When purchasing a bottle, brands to try include Small Hand Foods and Sonoma Syrup.

OUDE

(n.) One of the original styles of genever gin, which tends to be maltier, sweeter, and more aromatic than others.

OUZO

(n.) Ouzo is the Greek member of a loose-knit family of anise-flavored spirits from the Mediterranean, a group that also includes raki (Turkey), arak (Lebanon), and sambuca (Italy). The best examples of the category are distilled in copper stills from grape pomace (the leftover skins and seeds from the wine making process) and anise plus a slate of spices, including coriander, star anise, and cinnamon. The results are then diluted to proof using water. Cheaper versions infuse neutral spirits with a spice mix.

Ouzo is typically consumed as an apéritif, either chilled or neat, or by adding room-temperature water slowly, then adding ice once it turns from clear to milky white, and serving it alongside salty appetizers, such

O

as olives or sardines. Brands to look out for include Plomari and Tsilili.

OVERPROOF RUM

(n.) These super-alcoholic rums usually have an ABV of 60 percent or higher and are particularly popular for floating on top of tropical or tiki drinks or using in cocktails that are set on fire.

OXIDIZED

(adj.) When a wine becomes exposed to oxygen, it develops a darker color and the flavor of browned apples. The wine is then referred to as "oxidized" or, less commonly, "maderized." Some producers induce this in their wines deliberately, especially in fortified wines such as sherry or Madeira.

PALE ALE

(n.) A generic term for a golden-colored ale with a moderate to high hop profile. Popularized in eighteenth- and nineteenth-century England, the drink has a lighter color (achieved by brewing beer from lighter-colored malts) that stands in contrast to darker porters, stouts, and milds. With a higher or more apparent hop content from the lack of dark roasted malt flavor, the style came to be known as "bitters," and the pale ale family tree would branch out into East India pale ales, American pale ales, extra special bitters, and more. Regional styles, such as American pale ales from the West Coast or bitters from England, tend to gain character from the local or traditional hop varieties used in brewing.

PALO CORTADO

(n.) A hybrid style of sherry that begins the aging process with a layer of flor (yeast) that protects the wine from oxidation. However, when the flor accidentally dies off, the wine begins to age like an oloroso. The style varies greatly from bodega to bodega, but it generally has a nutty, raisiny aroma and a crisp, light body.

PAINKILLER

WITH coconut cream, pineapple juice, orange juice, and a Virgin Islands birthplace, this rum-based cocktail is a tropical drink to the core. There's some dispute over which bartender created this twist on the Piña Colada sometime in the 1970s (generally, the credit goes to Daphne Henderson of the Soggy Dollar Bar), but there's no question as to who owns it: Pusser's Rum, which trademarked the Painkiller name in the 1990s.

Serves 1

1½ ounces dark rum
1½ ounces fresh pineapple juice
½ ounce fresh orange juice
¾ ounce cream of coconut

Garnish: freshly grated nutmeg

Glassware: snifter

Add all ingredients to a cocktail shaker. Do not add ice, but shake well. Pour into a snifter and top with crushed ice. Garnish generously with grated nutmeg.

PAN AMERICAN CLIPPER

THIS rosy pink cocktail named for a luxury plane first appeared in Charles H. Baker's *The Gentleman's Companion*, his 1939 account of drink recipes gathered from his world travels. Baker reportedly took this recipe from a pilot friend, explaining the nod to the airline. Furthering the notion of travel, the ingredients have a French accent, with Calvados, a French apple brandy, and grenadine tempered by a few shakes of absinthe for an herbal exoticism.

Serves 1

2 ounces Calvados
¾ ounce fresh lime juice
½ ounce grenadine
½ teaspoon absinthe

Garnish: lime peel

Glassware: coupe

Add all ingredients to a shaker, add ice, and shake. Strain into a chilled coupe glass. Garnish with a lime peel.

P

PARING KNIFE

(n.) A small kitchen knife with a straight blade of three to four inches that is useful for making cocktail garnishes, such as by peeling or slicing citrus fruit.

PASTIS

(n.) An anise-flavored liqueur developed by Pernod as a replacement for absinthe, which was banned in France in 1915 for its supposed hallucinogenic properties. The formula for pastis borrows many of its predecessor's flavorings, minus the wormwood. Star anise is the dominant flavoring, but secondary herbal accents vary from brand to brand. Pastis usually carries a note of licorice, whereas absinthe does not, and it is also bottled with sugar, making it a liqueur.

Although pastis is usually yellow or brownish in color, the Pernod brand is an outlier, with its striking green color. Today production methods vary: some brands of pastis are made using the traditional method, with the herbal flavors developed during distillation, but cheaper versions tend to add flavor and color to a base spirit.

In France, pastis is considered an apéritif and is commonly served either mixed with chilled water at a ratio of 1:5, or neat with chilled water on the side so it can be mixed to the consumer's taste. When water is added, the liqueur will turn cloudy. Ice may be added after the water is mixed in, though it is not necessary. Pastis also makes an appearance in many cocktails and may be substituted in drinks that call for absinthe. The most recognizable brands include Ricard and Pernod (preferred in the south of France and Paris and beyond France, respectively), but artisanal brands are making a splash too, as are brands from outside France. Look for Henri Bardouin or Charbay, from Napa Valley.

PEATED

(n.) A descriptor for smoky flavors in Scotch that result from being made from grains that were dried over fires fueled by peat (soil matter

PEGU CLUB

As the British colonized their way across Asia in the nineteenth century, they set up outposts for their empire's wayward explorers in an effort to provide a civilized gathering place after a long day of conquering. Each of these boys' clubs had their own rituals and drinking rites, and the Pegu Club, located in Yangon, Myanmar, found itself at the center of British social life in 1920s. Its members, citizens of a bygone political era, knew the city as Rangoon, Burma, and this drink was their house cocktail. The Pegu Club eventually found its way into Harry's New York Bar owner Harry MacElhone's *Barflies and Cocktails* in 1927 and was further immortalized by Audrey Saunders's New York City bar of the same name.

Serves 1

2 ounces London dry gin
¾ ounce dry curaçao (preferably Pierre Ferrand)
¾ ounce lime juice
1 dash Angostura bitters
1 dash orange bitters

Garnish: lime or orange peel

Glassware: cocktail or coupe

Add all ingredients to a cocktail shaker. Add ice and shake until chilled. Strain into a chilled cocktail or coupe glass. Garnish with an orange or a lime peel.

Note: *The Pegu Club is an extremely dry cocktail. If a hint of sweetness is preferred, splash in a dash or two of simple syrup (1:1, sugar:water).*

from bogs). Certain regions of Scotland, such as Islay, are known for producing particularly peaty Scotches.

PEDRO XIMÉNEZ

(n.) A dessert-wine style of sherry made by fortifying and aging wine from Pedro Ximénez grapes that have been allowed to dry and raisin in the sun. The drying process concentrates the sugar in the grapes, resulting in a sweet wine.

PERCOLATION

(n.) A method of flavoring alcohol that borrows from the sous-vide cooking technique, in which ingredients are vacuum-sealed in a bag and then placed in warm water to cook. Cooking spirits to add flavor is generally frowned on because ethanol evaporates more quickly than water, but by using a sealed bag, no alcohol or other elements will be sacrificed to evaporation.

PERFECT

(adj.) A description for a vermouth cocktail in which the vermouth component is a mix of half sweet and half dry, usually applied to the Martini or the Manhattan.

PÉTILLANT

(adj.) A French term that describes a wine that is lightly sparkling.

PÉTILLANT NATUREL

(n.) Slangily known as pét-nat, these French sparkling wines are made by bottling wine during the first fermentation. Instead of waiting for the first fermentation to finish and then dosing the wine with extra yeast and sugar to achieve carbonation (as in the *méthode champenoise*), the wines are bottled while the first fermentation is taking place (known as the *méthode ancestrale*), which captures some of the escaping carbon dioxide from fermentation to create bubbles in the wine. The effect is somewhat unpredict-

P

able and can result in large differences in flavor and the quantity of bubbles from vintage to vintage and from bottle to bottle, but fans of the style appreciate the variance and the representation of terroir, as only native yeasts and the sugar from the grapes may be used.

PEYCHAUD'S

(n.) A type of bitters made from a family recipe of Antoine Amédée Peychaud, a Haitian apothecary who emigrated to New Orleans. Created around 1830, the product is somewhat comparable to Angostura but is generally considered to be lighter and sweeter. This is an essential component of the Sazerac, which was also invented in New Orleans.

PHYLLOXERA

(n.) A tiny aphid-like insect that kills certain grape vines. In the late nineteenth century, a plague of phylloxera caused great devastation to European vineyards, wiping out what some estimate as more than two-thirds of planted vines. Not only did this hamper wine production, but it also greatly impacted the amount of Cognac and other spirits made from a grape base that were produced, which in turn affected the composition of certain cocktails (*see:* Sidecar). A solution was found by grafting European vines onto rootstock native to the United States, which was naturally resistant to the pest.

PILSNER

(n.) This style of pale lager hails from the now-Czech, once-Bohemian town of Pilsen, where it is thought to have been first brewed in the mid-nineteenth century. The beers are typically a light golden color and skew rather crisp and bitter rather than fruity, with a spicy hop profile.

PILSNER GLASS

(n.) A tall conical glass used to serve pilsners and other light styles of beer; it usually holds from 8 to 16 ounces.

PHILADELPHIA FISH HOUSE PUNCH

DRINK as the forefathers of the United States did with this high-octane punch made from a base of Cognac, rum, and peach brandy. The "fish" in the title is not an ingredient but a reference to the Schuylkill Fishing Company, an eighteenth-century residence/private club located in what is now Pennsylvania, where members would gather to eat, fish, and drink prodigious amounts. George Washington was reportedly a fan of the club's signature concoction, which cocktail writer Jerry Thomas would later include in his *How to Mix Drinks*.

Serves 18–20

1 cup sugar
4 lemons, peeled and peels reserved
4 cups warm black tea (or water)
1 cup lemon juice
4 cups Jamaican rum
2 cups Cognac
½ cup peach brandy

Garnish: lemon wheels and freshly grated nutmeg

Glassware: rocks

In a large bowl, add sugar and lemon peels and rub together to release the citrus oils into the sugar. (This is called oleo-saccharum). Allow oleo-saccharum to infuse for at least 30 minutes. Dissolve sugar with warm tea. Add lemon juice, rum, Cognac, and peach brandy and stir to mix. Add a block of ice to chill, and continue to add smaller pieces of ice for desired dilution (see note). Garnish with lemon wheels and freshly grated nutmeg. Ladle into individual rocks glasses.

Note: *Freezing a Bundt pan or large bowl of water overnight is the go-to shortcut for creating a block of ice.*

P

PIMM'S NO. 1

(*n.*) A gin-based liqueur created by English bar owner James Pimm in the mid-nineteenth century. The recipe for the reddish-brown spirit contains a proprietary mixture of herbs and spices, leading to a sweet and spicy profile. Pimm originally bottled six different types of liqueurs based on different spirits, including brandy, rum, and vodka, but the first was and remains the most popular. The liqueur is most often used in the Pimm's Cup cocktail, a highball made with lemonade or ginger ale, served over ice in a tall glass and garnished with cucumber.

PINOT GRIS/GRIGIO

(*n.*) A white grape variety used to make dry and sweet white wines. Thought to have originated in France, the grape gets its name, "gris," from the French word for "gray" on account of its skin's grayish-red tinge. When made into wine, Pinot Gris can be a bit of a shapeshifter depending on regional styles and wine maker preferences. In Italy, where the grape is known as Pinot Grigio, cheaply produced wines made with the grape are generally light and crisp but somewhat unremarkable. Producers in the northeast of Italy, and in Alto Adige in particular, tend to place a higher emphasis on quality, making wines with aromatic qualities and depth of flavor. Some vinify the grape on its skins in a manner similar to rosés (which are made from red grapes) to make so-called orange wines, which typically have more body and tannins than white wines made with the grape. In Alsace, France, still wines made from the grapes take on tropical fruit aromas and a rich texture, while dessert wines (*vendange tardives*), often with a tinge of botrytis, strike a balance between acidic and sweet. The grape has also found success in Oregon, Australia, and California, where the wines tend to exhibit more fruit-forward characteristics and a medium body.

PIMM'S CUP

WHEN Englishman James Pimm invented this crisp sling based on his eponymous gin-based liqueur and served it at his London oyster bar in the mid-nineteenth century, surely he could not have imagined that it would become the official cocktail of Wimbledon. Yet today this simple cooler is second only to strawberries and cream in iconic-ness at the tony annual tennis event, the U.K.'s answer to the Mint Julep traditionally served at the Kentucky Derby. Typically garnished with cucumber spears or slices and a mix of oranges or strawberries, this summer-ready drink is an ideal candidate for preparing in a large batch and serving from a pitcher.

Serves 1

2 ounces Pimm's No. 1
½ ounce lemon juice
¼ ounce simple syrup (1:1,
    sugar:water)
Soda water
2 dashes Angostura bitters

Garnish: cucumber spear or
slice, mint sprig, seasonal berries
and citrus (optional)

Glassware: Collins

In a Collins glass, add Pimm's, lemon juice, and simple syrup and stir. Add ice, top with soda water and bitters, and stir gently to mix. Garnish lavishly like a flower arrangement with a cucumber slice, fresh mint sprig, berries, citrus, and a pocket square.

Note: *Bitters are not part of the original formula, but they add a little kick and complexity to the Pimm's spiced mix.*

PIÑA COLADA

BASED on a Cuban recipe for a nonalcoholic pineapple slushy (a *piña fria*) that was popular in the early 1900s, this frozen beverage evolved to include cream of coconut and rum. The Puerto Rican Hilton claims to have invented the recipe in 1954, but the first known mention of what we know as the Piña Colada appeared in the *New York Times* in 1950, which attributed the drink to Cuba. Immortalized in song by Warren Zevon's "Werewolves of London" ("I saw a werewolf drinking a Piña Colada at Trader Vic's") in 1978 and then again in 1979 with the number-one single "Escape (The Piña Colada song)" by Rupert Holmes, the Piña Colada clearly held a place in the public imagination as a fanciful, otherworldly umbrella drink.

Serves 1

2 ounces rum, white or golden
½ ounce lime juice
1 ounce pineapple juice
1 ounce cream of coconut
1 ounce coconut milk
1 cup ice

Garnish: pineapple wedge and a cocktail umbrella

Glassware: Collins or hurricane

Add all ingredients to a blender. Blend on high until smooth. Pour into a Collins or hurricane glass (or a hollowed out, frozen pineapple if you're feeling kitschy). Garnish with a pineapple wedge and an umbrella.

PINK LADY

ESSENTIALLY a Gin Sour colored with grenadine and fortified with applejack, the Pink Lady tends to get noticed for two things: its pinkness and its gendered name. But here's what you need to know: thought to be invented in the 1930s during Prohibition, the drink probably included grenadine to mask the flavor of poor-quality gin. It is nearly identical to the Clover Club, a cocktail from the same era, save for the addition of applejack, a dry domestic brandy made from apples. The result is tart, fairly dry, seriously strong, and fit for any gender.

Serves 1

1½ ounces London dry gin
½ ounce applejack
½ ounce fresh lemon juice
1 small egg white
2 dashes grenadine

Garnish: brandied cherry

Glassware: coupe

Add all ingredients to a shaker and dry shake. Add ice to shaker and shake well. Strain into a chilled coupe glass and garnish with a brandied cherry.

PISCO SOUR

T**HIS** frothy spur off the sour family tree made with pisco, lemon juice, simple syrup, and egg whites has roots in both America and Peru. The story goes that American-born Victor Morris moved to Peru in the early twentieth century to work on the railroads but ended up opening a bar instead. He supposedly fashioned an antecedent of what we know as the Pisco Sour using Peru's local liquor and the sour template. Although extremely popular in Chile and Peru today, this cocktail is only beginning to make inroads in the United States, rising with the tide of new quality pisco imports.

Serves 1

2 ounces pisco
¾ ounce lemon juice
½ ounce simple syrup
    (1:1, sugar:water)
½ large or 1 small egg white

Garnish: Angostura bitters

Glassware: cocktail or coupe

Add all ingredients to a cocktail shaker and dry shake. Add ice to the shaker and shake well. Strain into a chilled cocktail or coupe glass. Garnish with 2 or 3 dashes of Angostura bitters.

P

PINT

(n.) A unit of measurement equaling 16 fluid ounces in the United States or 20 fluid ounces in England; commonly used as a serving of draft beer.

PINT GLASS

(n.) A tumbler that holds a liquid pint, which is either 16 fluid ounces (in the United States) or 20 ounces (in the United Kingdom). The pint glass is a standard bar item that is usually used to serve beer or soda, but it may also be used as a mixing glass for making cocktails, or as one half of a Boston shaker.

PISCO

(n.) Chile and Peru both lay claim to inventing this grape brandy, thought to be created some four hundred years ago. There are variations, but most pisco is distilled from fermented grapes in copper pot stills and bottled young; it is clear or light yellow in color, with flavors that range from nearly neutral, like vodka,

to fruity and nutty. Best known in the United States as the base alcohol for Pisco Punch and the Pisco Sour, the spirit was very popular in Gold Rush–era San Francisco, in the mid-nineteenth century, but its popularity faded during Prohibition.

Recently, a shift toward quality distillation is helping pisco shed its rustic image, and the liquor is gaining mainstream traction. The best are made from first-press grape juice, while industrial versions often use grape must, the skins, seeds, and stems of the fruit, as well. Peruvian offerings face more regulations than Chilean ones: No additives (water or sugar) are allowed, the grapes must be grown in designated areas, and the pisco must be made from one or a combination of up to eight allowed grape varieties. If the pisco is made from one grape variety, it may bear the label "puro," while others will use "acholado" (a blend) or "aromatico," if only aromatic grape varieties are used. A new category is "mosto verde," in which pisco is distilled from grapes that have not been fully fermented. Chilean laws are less strict

PLANTER'S PUNCH

T HOUGHT to be born in Jamaica in the nineteenth century, this dark rum–based drink has a simple template—essentially fruit juice, a sweetener, and rum served over ice—that makes for a good jumping-off point from which you can tailor the recipe to your taste. And you would have historical precedent: with a proliferation of recipes over the past century and a half, this punch is really more of concept than an exact formula. Some add sliced tropical fruit to a minimalist base, while others go big with an array of fruit juices and liqueurs.

Serves 1

3 ounces dark rum
1 ounce lime juice
½ ounce grenadine
½ ounce simple syrup
2–3 dashes Angostura bitters

Garnish: mint sprig and/or citrus wheel of choice

Glassware: Collins

Add all ingredients to a Collins glass. Fill with crushed ice. Swizzle with a swizzle stick or bar-spoon, until glass is frosted over. Add more crushed ice and garnish with a mint sprig, a citrus wheel, and a straw.

P

and the offerings are generally less expensive; sugar and water may be added and oak aging is permitted, which can add a caramel color and vanilla flavors.

PLYMOUTH GIN

(n.) This type of gin is defined by its geographic origins: it must be made in Plymouth, England. Coates & Co. gin, made in Plymouth at the Black Friars Distillery, was popular with the British navy in the late nineteenth century and received a geographical designation for gin from the area from the government. Today, however, Black Friars is the only distillery left in Plymouth, making the gin produced there the only Plymouth gin. The style comes closest to London dry, but with a fuller body and a more fruit-forward, earthy botanical mix. Some consider this gin to be the ideal choice for a Martini, but it is also closely associated with certain other cocktail recipes, such as the Pink Gin.

POIRE WILLIAMS

(n.) A French eau de vie made from distilling Williams pears (known as Bartlett pears in the United States) that is most often served chilled as an after-dinner drink. Some producers bottle their product with a pear inside the bottle; this is achieved by placing the bottle around the bud on a tree and letting the pear grow inside the bottle.

POMACE

(n.) The seeds, skins, pulp, and stems of grapes left after pressing the grapes for juice.

PONY

1. *(n.)* A small tulip-shaped glass that holds 1 fluid ounce, commonly used in historic cocktail recipes and considered to be the predecessor of the shot glass. Today, a pony shot refers to a small shot of 1 ounce.

2. *(n.)* A small bottle of beer that holds 7 ounces, compared to the

P

standard 12 ounces (also known as a "nip").

3. *(n.)* A small beer keg that holds 7.75 gallons, compared to the standard 15.5 gallons.

PORT

(n.) A sweet fortified wine from the Douro Valley of Portugal invented in the seventeenth century to preserve wines traveling to England by ship. Port is made by adding grape brandy to wine during the fermentation process. The high alcohol content of the brandy kills the yeast, which had been converting sugar to alcohol. The result has a residual sweetness and a higher alcohol content than wine, both signatures that help preserve the wine.

There are numerous classifications for port, largely having to do with how it is aged. Vintage port, prized among wine collectors, is made only during the best years and is aged for two years in oak casks before it is bottled with little exposure to oxidation. With a deep-red color and fruity flavor, it is meant for aging in the bottle for many years and often commands a hefty price tag. Tawny port is made from a blend of vintages that have been aged in oak casks between ten and forty years. During the aging process it gains some exposure to oxygen, which lends it a nutty flavor and brownish-red color. Colheita port is a tawny port made from a single vintage and aged for at least seven years. Ruby port is the youngest and simplest, made from a blend of vintages aged two or more years in stainless steel or neutral oak casks and meant to be drunk young.

While port is largely anchored in the wine world, it has a long history in cocktails as well, and it is used frequently in historic punches such as the St. Charles Punch or the port wine sangaree. When using it in mixed drinks, ruby port is usually your best choice.

PORTER

(*n.*) A dark, malty, moderately hopped style of beer. Porter was developed in eighteenth-century London as an aged, stronger version of brown ale, and it quickly became popular with the city's river and street porters (from which the beer took its name). Stout, which at the time referred to a stronger type of beer (a particularly strong porter would be sold as "stout porter"), would become its own category of dark, more alcoholic beer, whereas porter came to mean a weaker dark beer. Most modern porters reach 4 to 6 percent alcohol and have a medium body with an off-white or tan head. Some make the distinction that stouts are brewed with dark roasted malts, which give a deep, roasted character, whereas porters include those less frequently, but the difference is not always clear.

POUR SPOUT

(*n.*) This attachment with a spout that fits on or in the neck of a liquor bottle is usually made from metal and rubber or plastic. The device helps both encourage a cleaner pour and regulate the flow of liquid for ease of measuring. Some are fixed with a contraption that allows the pourer to dispense only 1 ounce at a time.

POUSSE-CAFÉ

(*n.*) Created in New Orleans in the mid-1800s, these elaborate after-dinner drinks consist of layers of colorful liquors and juices, which are served in a pousse-café glass, a narrow glass cylindrical tube atop a short stem.

POUSSE-CAFÉ GLASS

(*n.*) A narrow tulip-shaped, hourglass-shaped, or cylindrical liqueur glass on a stem used for serving layered pousse-café drinks. These small glasses usually hold around 1½ ounces.

PRESBYTERIAN

SINCE it has just two ingredients, Scotch and ginger ale (three if you count the soda water), it's likely that you've had this refreshing cocktail, even if you didn't know the proper name. The title is a puzzler, but it's reasonable to speculate that it was named for the dominant religion in Scotland, home to its base spirit. Regardless, the easy formula for this cocktail leaves room for experimentation: substitute bourbon or rye for the Scotch, or use varying amounts of ginger ale and soda.

Serves 1

2 ounces blended Scotch
Ginger ale
Soda water

Garnish: lemon peel

Glassware: Collins

Add Scotch to a Collins glass and add ice. Top with half ginger soda and half soda water. Garnish with a lemon peel.

P

POWDERED EGG WHITES

(n.) A cocktail ingredient made from dehydrated egg whites, used by some bars and restaurants in mixed drinks to avoid the threat of salmonella poisoning from raw egg whites. To rehydrate powdered egg whites, mix with water (usually 2 teaspoons of powder to 1 ounce of water for the equivalent of one egg white). They are a good alternative to using pricier pasteurized egg whites.

PROHIBITION

(n.) Many governments have enacted periods of prohibition, a law that forbids alcohol. In the United States, the term is most commonly associated with the period from 1920 to 1933, shortly after the federal government passed the Eighteenth Amendment, which banned the production, transportation, and sale of alcohol, and the Volstead Act, which enforced the amendment.

The temperance movement, which cited alcohol consumption as a root cause of social ills such as domestic violence, had been gaining popularity in religious and progressive circles since the late eighteenth century. The movement helped successfully pass nineteen statewide alcohol bans before the federal government enacted Prohibition. The push to ban alcohol nationally gathered momentum during World War I, as anti-German sentiment targeted breweries founded by Germans (which was most of them), agricultural products used for making alcohol were thought to be better used in support of the war, and the women's suffrage movement adopted the cause.

Alcohol production and consumption famously did not stop when the ban went into effect. It merely went underground, where a new black-market economy starring moonshine, bootleggers, and speakeasies sprang up to accommodate drinkers. With a thriving illegal market, however, also came violence. Homicide rates spiked, and gang wars threatened cities. The growing unpopularity of the law inspired President Franklin D. Roosevelt to sign the repeal of the Eighteenth Amendment in 1933.

P

Still, by the time of repeal great damage had already been inflicted on the once-thriving alcohol industry. Although there were 1,345 breweries in the United States in 1915, post-Prohibition the number dwindled to 776, and the number continued to fall thereafter, as operations consolidated to survive. The number of licensed distilleries topped out at eight thousand in 1896, but that number would drop to below one hundred after Prohibition and stay there for the next eighty years. In 2012, the American Distilling Institute reported that four hundred craft distilleries were operating in the United States.

PROOF

(n.) A unit of measure for alcohol strength calculated in the United States by doubling the percentage of alcohol by volume (ABV). For example, a spirit made of 40 percent alcohol is considered to be 80 proof.

The term is thought to originate from the eighteenth-century English practice of testing rum's strength by igniting liquor-soaked gunpowder to see if the alcohol was strong enough to catch fire. This experiment would work only if the rum was over 57.15 percent ABV, what was then termed 100 proof. Though the United States used a simplified version of this formula by doubling the percentage of alcohol to determine the proof, the English used this correlating ratio until 1980, when they began labeling liquor in terms of ABV. In the United States, the term is not required on bottle labels, though it is permitted.

PROSECCO

(n.) An Italian sparkling wine made in the Friuli-Venezia Giulia and Veneto regions. The wine must be made primarily from the Glera grape, which may be supplemented by other varieties such as Pinot Grigio or Verdiso. Unlike Champagne and Cava, which achieve carbonation through the *méthode champenoise*, or being bottled with extra sugar and yeast, most prosecco gets its bubbles from the Charmat method. After the first fermentation, the wine is moved into

P

a sealed tank with extra yeast and sugar, where it carbonates en masse before being bottled under pressure. Because the wine often doesn't come in contact with the yeast as much as Champagne or Cava does, the flavors tend toward the fresh, bright, and simple. The method for producing prosecco can be cheaper than that for producing Champagne, which means that prosecco can be considerably cheaper.

Though prosecco once had a reputation for being of poor quality, recently it has made great strides. Most bottles are made in the extra-dry or brut style, but sweeter versions, which are labeled "dry" or "demi-sec," also exist. The wine comes in two levels of carbonation: *frizzante* (lightly sparkling) and *spumante* (sparkling).

PULQUE

(n.) An alcoholic beverage made from fermenting the sap from the maguey (agave) plant. Historical records show that this beer- or wine-like beverage was being made as early as 1000 AD in pre-Hispanic Mexico, and it often featured in the religious ceremonies of the Aztec. The modern-day incarnation of the beverage is milky white, has a sour profile, and notches around 6 percent ABV. It is generally consumed while freshly fermented and unaged, though some versions are pasteurized and bottled.

PUNCH

(n.) Before the single-serve cocktail became popular, mixed drinks were made large-format style, called punch, and served in bowls. Classic examples of the category contain a variation on five ingredients: spirits, sugar, water, spice, and citrus. Some speculate that punch originated with expats in India as a way to mask the flavor of inferior spirits ("punch" is thought to be derived from the

P

Indian word for five, *panch*), and the trend spread via sailors to England and the Americas. However the drink originated, it was ubiquitous by the eighteenth century, when it was made of an assortment of liqueurs, juices, sugars, spices, and creams in a rainbow of variations. A quickly industrializing world, however, soon laid waste to the shared punch bowl, favoring individualized drinks instead. During the recent cocktail renaissance, many bartenders have attempted to revive the tradition for the modern audience. Popular examples of the category include gin punch and admiral's punch.

PUNCH CUP

(n.) A small glass, sometimes with a handle, that holds 6 to 8 ounces and is used to serve punch; usually part of a matching set that includes a punch bowl.

PUNT E MES

(n.) This brand of Italian vermouth has a sweet-bitter profile with notes of citrus and spice. The recipe for the dark-brown aromatized wine dates from the 1870s, when it was invented by the Carpano company, which also produced Carpano Antica up until it, along with Punt e Mes, was sold to Fratelli Branca in 2001) and contains a propriety blend of botanicals. Usually served as an apéritif or digestif with soda and a slice of orange, Punt e Mes may also be used wherever sweet vermouth is called for.

PURO

(n.) A Peruvian pisco made from one grape variety, commonly Quebranta.

QUINA

(n.) Also known as cinchona, quina is a family of trees and shrubs native to South America that are prized for their medicinal properties. The bark of the cinchona tree can be made into quinine, which can treat malaria. The ingredient became popular in Western countries in the seventeenth century as a way to combat malaria in colonial outposts such as India and northern Africa, after which it made its way into tonic water, as well as many liqueurs and fortified wines, including Kina Lillet, Bonal, and Fernet.

QUININE

(n.) An extract from the bark of the cinchona tree that, when ingested, can mitigate malaria symptoms. Discovered by the Peruvian Incas, this remedy was adopted in the seventeenth century by British colonialists in India, who mixed the bitter powder with sugar and soda water as an antimalarial tonic (and frequently served this with gin, creating the gin and tonic). An approximation of this would later be manufactured by Schweppes as tonic water. Modern mass-market tonic water contains synthetic quinine, but some boutique brands, like Fever-Tree and

Q

QUEEN'S PARK SWIZZLE

CREATED in Trinidad, this simple rum-based drink gets its name from a famous cricket field in the island's capital, Port of Spain. The traditional Demerara rum called for, however, is dark and heavy and comes from neighboring Guyana, which had a more established rum industry than Trinidad, which is now famed for a much lighter style. Containing few ingredients, this drink is distinguished by the swizzle technique used to make it, which calls for agitating the drink with a swizzle stick until frost forms on the glass.

Serves 1

1 large sprig mint
1 ounce simple syrup
  (1:1, sugar:water)
1 ounce lime juice
2 ounces Demerara rum
4 dashes Angostura bitters

Garnish: mint sprig

Glassware: Collins or hurricane

In a Collins or hurricane glass, gently muddle mint leaves with simple syrup to release the oils. Add lime juice, rum, and crushed ice. Swizzle with a straw or swizzle stick to mix. Add more crushed ice and dash Angostura bitters over top. Garnish with a mint sprig.

R

Tomr's, use the real deal. Bars and restaurants have also been experimenting with in-house versions.

RABARBARO

(n.) A bittersweet Italian amaro flavored with rhubarb that can be served with soda and lemon peel as an apéritif, or straight as a digestif. Zucca is the best-known brand.

RAMAZZOTTI

(n.) An Italian amaro with a bitter, sweet, herbal profile. This dark-brown liqueur was first formulated in 1815 in Milan, Italy, and the recipe has reportedly not changed since. Said to contain thirty-three ingredients, it is commonly described as having flavors of licorice, orange peel, and vanilla and as having an almost root beer–like character. At 60 percent ABV, Ramazzotti skews higher in alcohol than many of its peers.

RAUCHBIER

(n.) A smoky style of lager native to Bamberg, Germany. Thought to have been invented in the sixteenth century, Rauchbier (literally "smoke beer" in German) is made using malted barley that has been dried over a fire, which imparts a smoky, spiced flavor. Though it can be produced in a range of styles, from extremely smoky to more malty, the beers usually have a medium amber body and little hop influence. Rauchbier-like smoked beers are produced around the world.

RECTIFIER

(n.) Part of a patent still, this column condenses the alcohol vapor created by the analyzer into a liquid spirit.

REDUCED

(n.) A wine fault caused by the presence of volatile sulfur compounds, which leave a telltale sign of the smell of rotten eggs or burnt rubber. Many types of these compounds are made

REMEMBER THE MAINE

DESCRIBED first by spirits writer Charles H. Baker in his 1939 classic *The Gentleman's Companion,* this rye-based drink with an ingredient list that's part Sazerac, part Manhattan has a dramatic backstory. The USS *Maine,* a U.S. naval ship, was sitting off the coast of Havana in 1898 in a bout of saber rattling with Spain, which controlled Cuba at the time. When the ship mysteriously exploded and sank (some blame a coal fire), warmongering journalists used the phrase "Remember the Maine, to Hell with Spain" as a rallying cry that would jump-start the Spanish-American War, leading to Cuban independence. Baker, however, wrote about the drink in the context of the 1933 Cuban Revolution, when Baker happened to be in Havana during "the unpleasantness . . . when each swallow was punctuated with bombs going off on the Prado or the sound of 3-inch shells being fired at the Hotel Nacional."

Serves 1

1 dash absinthe
2 ounces rye
¾ ounce sweet vermouth
2 teaspoons Cherry Heering

Garnish: brandied cherry

Glassware: cocktail or coupe

In a chilled cocktail or coupe glass, add a dash of absinthe. Roll around to coat and discard excess. Add the remaining ingredients to a mixing glass. Add ice and stir well. Strain into prepared cocktail or coupe glass. Garnish with a brandied cherry.

R

during the wine making process; some reports count around one hundred, including mercaptan and hydrogen sulfide. Not all reductive flavors are considered a flaw—some, such as the aroma of flint or a struck match, are classic flavors in quality wines—but wine makers generally strive to avoid making wine with the less desirable aromas.

REPOSADO

(n.) Meaning "rested" in Spanish, this designation indicates that a tequila or mezcal has been aged for two to eleven months in wood barrels. Mezcal that bears the reposado label must be aged in wood barrels for two to nine months.

RESERVE/RISERVA/ RESERVA

(n.) A wine label term that can refer to legal requirements for how long the wine has been aged. In Rioja, for example, "reserva" means the wine has been aged for three years, with at least one of those in oak barrels.

In other wine-producing regions, such as California, the term is not legally regulated but is usually meant to imply a special—and often pricier—bottling.

RESIDUAL SUGAR

(n.) A measurement of how much sugar is left in an alcoholic product after undergoing fermentation, usually expressed in grams of sugar per liter. During the fermentation process, yeast cells convert sugar to alcohol and carbon dioxide. If the fermentation is not allowed to progress completely—whether this is done on purpose or is the result of something going wrong, like a bacterial infection—unconverted sugars will remain in the liquid. Note that residual sugar is not the same as perceptible sweetness. Other traits, such as the high acidity present in top sweet Rieslings, can mask or balance residual sugar, making the product seem less sweet than it is.

R

RICARD

(n.) A pastis from Marseille, France, that was invented in 1932 by Paul Ricard, a wine merchant's son. The proprietary formula for this anise-flavored liqueur includes licorice, aniseed extract, and a secret combination of herbs common in Provence. Although the pastis made by rival Pernod (initially made as a replacement for their popular absinthe when it was banned) would gain acclaim in Paris and abroad, Ricard became the favorite of southern France. The spirit is commonly mixed with cool water in a ratio of 1:5, with ice cubes added after mixing.

RICKEY

(n.) A subset of coolers made with liquor, seltzer, and lime over ice, but without any sweetener. The drink is named for Joe Rickey, the Southern lobbyist who popularized the whiskey version in Washington, D.C., in the late 1800s. The two most common versions are based on whiskey and gin.

RIM

(v.) This cocktail-making technique, most commonly performed when making Margaritas or Sidecars, involves dusting the rim of a serving glass with sugar or salt. To rim a glass, spread the salt or sugar on a small plate, moisten the lip of a glass with one of the liquids used in the cocktail (like citrus juice or a liqueur), and then dip the outer edge of the wet lip in the sugar or salt. Gently shake off any excess, then fill the glass with the cocktail and serve. Some bartenders are experimenting with other ingredients, such as cocoa powder, crushed chili powder, and flavored sugars. *See:* Frosted Glass.

RINSE

(v.) When a cocktail recipe requires a mere hint of an assertive liqueur or spirit, it will sometimes call for a rinse, which means that a small amount of the spirit is poured into the serving glass, swirled around, and then discarded, with the cocktail poured in afterward. The rinse

ROB ROY

THE first known mentions of the Rob Roy credit New York's Waldorf-Astoria Hotel for the 1897 recipe—essentially a Manhattan made with Scotch whisky. Cocktail historians figure the name was a nod to a play about the great Scotsman (hence the Scotch whisky), which had premiered three years earlier in Manhattan. The drink skews a touch leaner than its counterparts made with bourbon or rye, and since the Scotch gets doctored up with sweet vermouth and bitters, note that this cocktail is no place for your pricey single malts; choose blended Scotch instead.

Serves 1

2 ounces blended Scotch
1 ounce sweet vermouth
2 dashes Angostura bitters

Garnish: brandied cherry or a lemon twist

Glassware: cocktail or coupe

Add all ingredients to a mixing glass. Add ice and stir until chilled. Strain into a chilled cocktail or coupe glass. Garnish with a brandied cherry or a lemon twist.

should to reach all the way to the rim of the glass, so swirl somewhat deliberately. This technique is perhaps most famously seen in cocktails such as the Sazerac and Corpse Reviver #2, which need just a touch of the anise flavor of absinthe or Herbsaint to be complete.

ROSE'S SWEETENED LIME JUICE

(n.) Also known in England as "lime cordial," this brand of sweetened lime juice was created in 1867 as a way to preserve citrus without alcohol for long voyages at sea to prevent scurvy. The modern version has been reformulated and is made of water, high-fructose corn syrup, and lime juice. Many historical Gimlet recipes call for Rose's; whether you use the purchased product or make a homemade approximation is a matter of personal preference.

ROTOVAP (ROTARY EVAPORATOR)

(n.) A piece of high-tech scientific equipment used to make cocktail ingredients that extracts solvents from solids. Resembling a long tube with two bulbs attached, the machine works by lowering the pressure (creating a vacuum, essentially) in one bulb, causing certain compounds to evaporate and then condense back in the other bulb. The process mimics distillation, except by using lower temperatures, aromatic compounds that would normally be destroyed in a high-heat environment can be preserved. Bartenders are using the machine to infuse neutral spirits and vodka with spices and herbs, as well as extracting the essential oils and essences of solids (enabling them, for example, to extract the flavor of chiles, but without the heat) to flavor drinks.

ROYALE

(n.) A category of apéritif drinks consisting of a spirit, liqueur, or

R

cider topped with Champagne and served in a flute. The most famous example in this category is France's Kir Royale, a mix of black currant liqueur and Champagne.

RUBY PORT

(n.) A style of port made from a blend of vintages that have been aged in stainless steel tanks or neutral oak for two or more years. This style, which is often fruity and fresh, is intended to be drunk soon after purchase.

RUM

(n.) Rum is a spirit made from fermented sugar cane juice or any of its by-products, including molasses and syrup. It must be distilled at less than 190 proof and bottled at more than 80 proof. There are almost no legal categories for production methods, save for rhum agricole, an appellation of the French West Indies, which must be made from fermented fresh cane juice and is generally considered of a higher quality than most

other rums. The rest can be lumped into inexact categories: Light rum, generally clear and made in a dry style, is aged in neutral oak or stainless steel for short periods of time. Golden rum is light yellow or golden, its color gained from either the addition of caramel syrup or aging in oak casks, which imparts a vanilla or caramel flavor. Dark rums have been aged for longer or have more caramel added. Though most rums are made for mixing in cocktails, the category of aged rums meant for sipping is growing.

The production of rum is linked inextricably with early English and European colonies in the Americas, where cheap sugar grown with slave labor made for an economical spirit. It made up one of the legs of the infamous triangle trade that commercially linked the sale of West African slaves, Caribbean sugar, and New England rum in the fifteenth to eighteenth centuries, though some historians argue rum's importance in this triangle may be overstated.

Although rum was very popular in colonial America, two things happened that would cause whiskey to

RUSTY NAIL

FOR those loath to order Scotch neat, this drink is based on a simple formula: Scotch plus a Scotch-based liqueur over ice. The liqueur, traditionally in the form of Drambuie, an herbaceous concoction of Scotch and honey, wields a subtle influence, just enough to add some sweetness and spice. Cocktail historian David Wondrich has traced the origins of the combination to the 1930s, although it didn't become truly popular until the 1960s Rat Pack era.

Serves 1

2 ounces blended Scotch
1 ounce Drambuie

Glassware: double rocks

Add ingredients to a double rocks glass. Add ice and stir.

R

become the country's spirit of choice instead: the English severed the supply of cheap molasses to the United States after the Revolutionary War, and expansion into fertile territories made grain a more obvious choice for distilling rather than sugar. Rum would rise again with the advent of tiki culture and the clever Prohibition-era machinations of the Bacardi company, which lobbied to open distilleries in Puerto Rico just before repeal, so that the market could be flooded with rum once it became legal again.

RYE WHISKEY

(n.) Rye whiskey must be made from a grain bill of at least 51 percent rye, with the rest comprised of a mix of wheat, corn, and malted barley. When aged for at least two years in oak barrels, it may bear the label "straight." Like bourbon, it may not be distilled higher than 160 proof to preserve the character of the grain, and it must be bottled at more than 80 proof. Note that Canadian "rye" is not subject to the same labeling laws as those made in the United States, and it often contains very little to no rye.

Once the brightest star in the constellation of American spirits, rye whiskey dates back to the colonial era, and the spirit figured prominently in the drink recipes of the day. Prohibition, however, kneecapped production, and the category remained largely dormant for the next seventy years, until the dual fires of cocktail craze and the whiskey renaissance ignited interest again.

Rye has a spicier, sourer character than bourbon and forms the robust backbone to some of the most iconic American cocktails, including the Old Fashioned, the Manhattan, and the Sazerac. American brands to try include Rittenhouse, Old Potrero, Michter's, and Willett. Because rye was formerly out of favor in the United States, there are few aged versions available today, but expect that to change as distillers respond to increasing demand for the product.

SABER

(*v.*) The process of opening a bottle of sparkling wine by hitting a weak spot on the neck of the bottle's weak with a hard object, traditionally a saber or sword. Called *sabrage* in French, this theatrical presentation doesn't actually involve cutting the neck of the bottle with the sharp edge of a sword. Instead, the dull side of the sword (or the handle of a spoon, chef's knife, or butter knife) hits the lip of the opening, where the bottle's structure is weakest, causing the pressure from the carbonated contents of the bottle to push the entire top off the bottle. The practice reportedly orig-

inated with Napoleon's army, who would saber Champagne bottles at celebrations.

To saber a bottle, first chill a highly carbonated sparkling wine (or beer). Note that cheaper sparkling wines tend to not be carbonated to a high enough degree to pull this maneuver off; choose a heavy-bottled Champagne to be certain of success. Remove the wire cage from the cork, then locate the two seams that run up and down the sides of the bottle. Pointing the neck of the bottle away from you (and other people, windows, and breakable objects), hold the bottle at a 45-degree angle. Run the dull edge of your chosen saber or

S

saber-like object up the seam of the bottle toward the neck forcefully. When the knife blade hits the neck, the entire top ring should fly off. (You may need to try this two or three times for it to work.)

SAISON (FARMHOUSE ALE)

(n.) A French or Belgian style of ale that was traditionally brewed during the winter or spring for summer consumption by seasonal workers, who were known as *saisonaires*. Since production was so localized, the ale could vary widely from farm to farm, with the common characteristic being the timeframe in which the beer was brewed. Modern saisons, which are made around the world, tend to be pale gold to light amber in color, are medium-bodied, and often have a fruity or spicy character, with an ABV of 5 to 8 percent. The archetype of the style is Belgium's Saison Dupont, but many good examples can be found from breweries across the United States and Europe.

SAKE

(n.) References to sake, a Japanese alcoholic beverage made from rice, date back over a thousand years. The production of sake is similar to that of beer: rice grains are harvested, milled, and polished, then soaked and steamed. A cultivated fungus, koji, is introduced and the rice is simultaneously broken down into glucose and fermented for three to six weeks in large vats. The resulting liquid is then filtered and diluted with water to around 16 percent AVB.

Polishing the kernels of rice before fermentation results in several different quality levels of sake: junmai, made from rice whose hulls have been milled down by 30 percent at the more rustic end, and junmai ginjo (40 percent) and junmai daiginjo (50 percent) on the more refined side. The junmai designation indicates that no distilled alcohol has been added. There are also unfiltered sakes (nigori), aged sakes (koshu), and sparkling sakes.

Other factors affecting the quality include the water from the region

SATAN'S WHISKERS

DESPITE the titillating name, this classic 1930s-era cocktail runs relatively tame. First recorded in Harry Craddock's *Savoy Cocktail Book*, the recipe calls for equal parts gin and dry and sweet vermouths dressed up with a sunny dose of citrus in the form of Grand Marnier, orange juice, and orange bitters. A variation using curaçao instead of Grand Marnier is described as "curled" as opposed to "straight."

Serves 1

½ ounce gin
½ ounce sweet vermouth
½ ounce dry vermouth
¼ ounce Grand Marnier or
    orange curaçao
½ ounce fresh orange juice
3 dashes orange bitters

Garnish: orange peel

Glassware: cocktail or coupe

Add all ingredients to a cocktail shaker. Add ice and shake until chilled. Strain into a chilled cocktail or coupe glass. Garnish with an orange peel.

S

in which it is made, the temperature at the brewery (the colder the better), and the strains of yeast and rice used. Pairing sake with food can be an intricate game, but an easy rule of thumb is to match sakes with their regional cuisine, though there is plenty of room to match sakes with Western food.

The best sakes are served chilled or at room temperature, and good examples are increasingly showing up on the best wine lists in the world. Sake also makes a fine mixer for delicate cocktails.

SANGAREE

(n.) This close descendant of punch uses a formula of an alcoholic base (usually a fortified wine such as port or Madeira), sugar, and cracked ice, all shaken together and poured unstrained into a serving glass, with a grating of nutmeg on top. Like sangria, sangaree likely gets its name from the Spanish word *sangre*, meaning "blood," for the drink's rich red color when made with port or another fortified red wine. But unlike sangria,

which was brought to the United States in 1964 with the World's Fair in New York, the sangaree has a much longer history, dating to the early 1700s, when it was a popular drink for the English and the residents of its colonial outposts.

SANGRIA

(n.) A sweet wine-based punch made with a rotating cast of ingredients, commonly chopped fruit, a sweetener, liquor, and sometimes soda water or juices. Named for its blood-red color (when made with red wine), the drink can trace its origins to spiced wine drinks from European countries such as Spain, which has had vineyards planted since the Roman era two thousand years ago. Perhaps a relative of the sangaree, an eighteenth-century mixed drink with a base spirit and beer or wine combined with sugar, water, and nutmeg, sangria is thought to have been introduced to Americans with the 1964 World's Fair in New York. Though the drink has a poor reputation as a way to doctor bad wines, many bars

SAZERAC

BORN in New Orleans in the mid-1800s at the Sazerac Coffee House, the Sazerac originally featured French Cognac. But in the late nineteenth century, the phylloxera outbreak caused a shortage of grapes, and therefore of Cognac. In the absence of the drink's original spirit, rye whiskey became the de facto base. The Sazerac morphed again when absinthe became illegal in the United States in 1912 and a local New Orleans pastis made from botanicals meant to approximate the taste of absinthe, Herbsaint, was subbed in. In 2007, a reformulated absinthe became legal again in the United States—just in time for the rising tide of the classic cocktail movement, and most bartenders have reverted back. The drink's super-bold flavors—anise, spicy rye, and herbal absinthe—make this a favorite among the cocktail cognoscenti.

Serves 1

1 splash absinthe
1 sugar cube (see note)
1 splash soda water
2 ounces rye
2 dashes Peychaud's bitters

Garnish: lemon peel

Glassware: rocks

In a rocks glass, add a dash of absinthe and swirl to coat. Discard. In another rocks or mixing glass, muddle sugar cube or sugar with soda water. Once dissolved, add rye, bitters, and ice and stir well. Strain rye and bitters mixture into the prepared rocks glass. Garnish with a lemon peel.

Note: *If you don't have sugar cubes on hand, a teaspoon of sugar or a generous ¼ ounce of simple syrup will do the trick.*

S

and restaurants are experimenting with making high-quality versions from good ingredients.

SCHNAPPS

1. *(n.)* From the German *Schnaps*, this generally refers to an eau de vie produced in Austria and other Alpine locals. The spirit is usually bottled without sugar at an alcohol level of around 40 percent and comes in flavors such as raspberry, pear, quince, apple, or mint.

2. *(n.)* In the United States the term generally refers to sweet flavored liqueurs that are sometimes thickened with glycerin. These come in many flavors, the most famous of which is probably peppermint schnapps.

SCOTCH ALE

(n.) A strong ale, often dark brown in color, with a full body and sweet, malty caramel flavor. Sometimes labeled as "wee heavy," beers made in this style are often high in alcohol, coming in between 6 and 11 percent ABV. Some brewers add smoked or peated malt for a smoky character or age their beers in barrels. Though the style originally comes from Scotland, Scotch ales may be made around the world.

SCOTCH WHISKY

(n.) Scotch, a type of Scottish whisky made from malted barley, must be distilled below 190 proof and aged for three years in oak barrels. Basic production works like this: A low-alcohol product is made from fermenting malted barley, which is then distilled twice in pot stills for a more artisanal bent, or in column stills for industrial production. Variations come from the quality of the barley (which can be imported from elsewhere), the water source, the yeast, the stills, and, in particular, the type of malting that the barley undergoes.

Though it's possible to buy malted barley, many houses malt their own, which entails soaking the grain until it sprouts, then drying it out with either hot air or a peat fire.

SCOFFLAW

THE proliferation of hyperstylized speakeasies in the first decade of the 2000s resulted in a fetishization of the Prohibition era that wouldn't necessarily hold up to historical scrutiny. But to be fair, even during dark dry days of the ban, this predilection for all things Prohibition was already happening. Take this cocktail for instance, named for a word invented in a 1924 contest to describe those who still imbibed alcohol illegally but created at Harry's Bar in Paris, a whole ocean and then some away from where the illicit action was taking place. The drink, a mix of whiskey and vermouth with citrus accents courtesy of bitters and lemons, is thought to be too complicated to compare with what was actually being served in speakeasies, but nevertheless, it was a worthy toast to the times, both then and now.

Serves 1

1½ ounces rye whiskey
1 ounce dry vermouth
¾ ounce fresh lemon juice
¾ ounce grenadine
1 dash orange bitters

Garnish: orange peel

Glassware: coupe

Add all ingredients to a shaker, add ice, and shake. Strain into a chilled coupe glass. Garnish with an orange peel.

Peat, which is made up of decomposed vegetation, is common in the bogs of Scotland, particularly on the island of Islay. When burned, peat imparts a particularly smoky note to the barley, which correlates to smoky notes in the whisky.

Different areas of production are known for certain styles. Islay scotches tend to have a particularly smoky character. Scotch from the Speyside region, which has more distilleries than any other region, skews fruitier. Other areas of production include the Highlands, the Lowlands, and Campbeltown, and styles vary widely among individual producers.

Scotch may be made either in a single-malt style, which comes from one particular distillery, or a blended style, which mixes two or more single malts from different distilleries. If made with grains besides malted barley, it is labeled "grain whisky," which can be sold in either single-grain or blended styles. Any type of cereal grain is permitted (such as corn, wheat, or unmalted barley), though malted barley must also be used.

The popularity of single-malt Scotch is a relatively recent phenomenon. Blended whiskies were considered a better bet during the nineteenth and early twentieth centuries, giving rise to the big Johnnie Walker, Chivas Regal, and Cutty Sark brands. In 1963, however, William Grant began promoting the Glenfiddich single malt worldwide, which sparked a rise in the perception of quality of single malts, and almost every other distillery has followed suit.

Without a vintage date, Scotch must be aged for three years in wooden barrels before being sold. The barrels are typically used bourbon barrels, which impart notes of vanilla and caramel. Sherry and port barrels, which are used to a lesser extent, leave notes of fruit, nuts, and spice. If a Scotch bears a vintage date, it is the youngest vintage used in the bottle.

SCREW CAP

(n.) A metal cap used to seal bottles of alcohol employed by some wine producers as an alternative to the

SCORPION PUNCH

THERE is nothing halfway about this emblem of tiki culture. Legend has it that a bar in Honolulu called the Hut came up with the original recipe in the 1930s. Trader Vic's, the iconic tiki bar, picked it up sometime after, popularizing it for the masses that would embrace tikidom after World War II. There's no one official recipe (Trader Vic printed no fewer than three versions in his cocktail books), but it is generally agreed that it should include rum, brandy, citrus juice, and orgeat, all blended with ice and served unstrained.

Serves 1

2 ounces light rum
1 ounce brandy
2 ounces orange juice
1 ounce orgeat

Garnish: citrus wheels

Glassware: tiki mug or Collins

Add all ingredients to a blender with 8 ounces of crushed ice and blend for three secounds. Pour into tiki mug or Collins glass unstrained. Garnish with citrus wheels.

more traditional cork. The cap twists onto the opening of a bottle, making a seal by compressing a layer of plastic or rubber over the mouth. The screw cap has been well received by some wine makers and consumers, as it reduces potential exposure to cork taint or unintended oxidation, and it may be opened without a corkscrew. Detractors say caps have poor aesthetics and minimize oxygen transfer, which is important for the aging process.

SECONDARY FERMENTATION

(n.) A wine- and beer-making technique; after a wine or beer undergoes its first fermentation, in which yeast converts sugar to alcohol and carbon dioxide, a producer might allow the product to undergo a second or third fermentation to achieve the desired flavor and body characteristics. These subsequent fermentations can take place in the cask or vat, or in the bottle, which will cause the liquid to become carbonated.

In beer making, certain styles of beer benefit from longer fermentation and conditioning times and are moved into another vessel after the first fermentation is completed to continue fermenting and resting. This allows the beer to further settle and clarify without developing any off flavors from the sediment (lees) that develops during the first fermentation, as well as continue to ferment any remaining sugars. Secondary fermentation can also refer to bottle conditioning, when the producer bottles flat beer with extra sugar in order to encourage a new fermentation, which will release carbon dioxide, carbonating the beer.

In wine making, secondary fermentation most often refers to the *méthode champenoise*, when wine is bottled with a dose of extra sugar and yeast, sparking a new fermentation in the bottle, which will release carbon dioxide and carbonate the wine for a sparkling wine. It can also refer to a second stage in the fermentation process when the fermented wine is racked or transferred into a new container and a slower, anaerobic

SEELBACH

THE Mint Julep may dominate the sphere of Kentucky cocktails, especially around Derby time, but the Seelbach, the other iconic cocktail from the bluegrass state, is also a worthy contender. Born in 1917 at Louisville's Seelbach Hotel, this drink also builds off a base of bourbon, the state's native spirit, but it quickly establishes a more festive profile, with a splash of Cointreau and a dose of sparkling wine. A generous amount of bitters—both Angostura and Peychaud's—helps balance the sweetness for a complex finish.

Serves 1

1 ounce bourbon
½ ounce Cointreau
7 dashes Angostura bitters
7 dashes Peychaud's bitters
Champagne
   (or a dry sparkling wine)

Garnish: orange peel

Glassware: flute or coupe

Add bourbon, Cointreau, and both bitters to a mixing glass. Add ice and stir until chilled. Strain into a chilled flute or coupe glass. Top with Champagne or sparkling wine. Garnish with an orange peel.

S

fermentation is allowed to continue. Some also use the term to refer to malolactic fermentation, in which sharper malic acid is converted to rounder-tasting lactic acid.

SEKT

(n.) The German term for sparkling wine.

SERCIAL

(n.) The driest style of classified Madeira wine, made from the Sercial grape. The wine will have up to 1.5 percent residual sugar and is often served as an apéritif.

SESSION BEER

(n.) A lower-alcohol beer so named for being a beer that one could conceivably drink throughout a "session" of drinking without becoming intoxicated. Though the term is not precisely defined, it is generally accepted that session beers are lower than 5 percent ABV, have balanced flavors, and display a crisp finish.

SHAKE

(v.) A cocktail-making technique in which the ingredients are rapidly shaken by hand in a shaker before being strained into the service glass. Cocktails that include "cloudy" ingredients, such as juice, cream, or egg whites, are good candidates for being shaken, while all-spirit cocktails are best stirred. There are different schools of thought about the perfect technique, but the goal is always the same: to fully integrate the ingredients and cool the drink rapidly by maximizing the exposure to ice while not letting the ice dilute the drink excessively. Shaking the ingredients should also change the texture of the drink, adding a slight froth and air bubbles.

To shake a cocktail, add the ingredients to the shaker, then fill halfway with ice. Seal the shaker, then shake rapidly for 15 to 30 seconds until frost coats the shaker, or to the recipe's specifications. Strain the shaken cocktail into a glass.

S

SHAKER

(n.) This tool used to shake ingredients for a cocktail comes in two main styles: the traditional, or cobbler, shaker and the Boston shaker. Both work equally well for personal use. The traditional is comprised of three pieces: a mixing tin, a built-in strainer, and a lid that can also be used as a jigger. This style is prized for its simplicity—simply pour the ingredients in, add ice, cover, shake, and strain—but it is considered impractical for heavy usage, as it is more challenging to clean, and sometimes dislodging the lid after shaking it can be difficult.

The Boston shaker, preferred by most professional bartenders, is just two pieces: a pint-sized metal or glass mixing glass and a shaker tin, which usually holds 28 ounces. To use the Boston shaker, pour the ingredients directly into the mixing glass, then add ice to the glass. Top the mixing glass with the shaker tin at a slight angle so that it forms a seal. Turn the sealed shaker over, so the bottom of the mixing glass is facing up, and,

holding one end of the shaker in each hand, raise the shaker to ear level and shake hard for ten to fifteen seconds, or until a frost has covered the mixing tin. (The time depends on both the ingredients and the quality of the ice; the high-quality ice used by many professional bartenders requires a longer shake, while low-quality ice needs only a shorter one.) To dislodge the tin from the glass, hit the tin lightly where the glass and the tin begin to separate. Strain the cocktail into the glass using a Hawthorne strainer.

SHANDY

(n.) A beer cocktail made from mixing beer with juice or soda, traditionally lemonade or lemon soda. The descendant of a mixture of beer and Champagne popular with the British in the nineteenth century, the shandy evolved to include the more affordable ginger beer or lemonade rather than sparkling wine. Many other countries and cultures have their own version of the beer and soda or lemonade combination,

SHERRY COBBLER

THIS simple mix of sherry, sugar, and fruit shaken with crushed ice represented the height of drinking fashion in mid-nineteenth-century America and is thought to be the first drink to be served with a straw. Now, with the dovetailing of the cocktail revival and a renewed interest in sherry, this mixed drink is primed for the spotlight again. A note: The type of sherry you use will affect the finished drink; if using a sweeter style, dial down the sugar by half.

Serves 1

2–3 orange slices
1 tablespoon sugar
3½ ounces sherry (preferably amontillado)

Garnish: seasonal berries, mint, and a straw

Glassware: Collins

Add oranges and sugar to a mixing glass and muddle. Add sherry and ice and shake. Strain into a Collins glass filled with crushed ice. Garnish with seasonal berries, mint, and a straw.

Note: *The Sherry Cobbler is incredibly easy to riff on and is highly adaptable to the seasonal fruit at hand. High summer might call for raspberries muddled with lemon, while fall is for cranberries and orange. Furthermore, crushed ice is preferred for this drink, but you can get away with a pile of smaller ice cubes as well. Switch up the sherry and adjust the simple syrup to your taste. Demerara simple syrup is not always a necessary detail, but it tends to play nice with oloroso and amontillado.*

including Germany's *Radler* and Switzerland's *panaché*.

SHERRY

(n.) A fortified wine of 15 to 22 percent ABV made in the Jerez region of southern Spain, sherry comes in a range of styles, from lean and light in weight to sweet and viscous plus a bit of everything in between. Prized by sommeliers and bartenders for its versatility in both food pairing and cocktail making, sherry has recently roared back from afterthought to cornerstone of forward-thinking bar programs. But don't call it a fad: sherry has been around for more than a thousand years.

The process of making sherry begins with adding a mixture of grape brandy and young wine (called *mitad y mitad*) to a light wine. If the wine is fortified to around 15 percent alcohol, a layer of yeast called flor will form over the liquid as it ages in the barrels, protecting it from oxidation. This process is called biological aging. Styles of sherry that age almost exclusively under the layer of flor are called fino or manzanilla; they are generally light and crisp, sometimes with notes of salinity.

If the wine is fortified to 17 percent alcohol or more, the flor cannot develop and the wines oxidize as they age in barrels, forming oloroso sherry, which, though still dry, has a rich, nutty, and caramelized character. Amontillado and palo cortado sherries begin with a layer of flor that dissipates during aging, forming a hybrid between the biological and oxidative styles.

Sweet sherries fall into two categories: naturally sweet and blended. The two naturally sweet wines of the Jerez region are Pedro Ximénez, often abbreviated as PX, and Moscatel, both made from fermented, dried grapes.

Blended sherries are generally a mixture of a sherry—oloroso for cream or medium blends, and fino for pale cream—and either PX or concentrated grape must.

A key component of sherry production is the solera system, in which older and newer vintages are blended and aged according to a complex system.

SHERRY FLIP

EGGNOG may be the best-known contemporary example of the flip family of cocktails, which consist of alcohol, sugar, and an egg, shaken with ice, strained, and served up with a dusting of grated nutmeg, but this sherry-based iteration makes for an elegant alternative. It comes with a distinguished historical pedigree too, as it was described in cocktail writer Jerry Thomas's 1887 edition of *How to Mix Drinks*. For the best results, use dry oloroso sherry, which has a rich, nutty flavor and velvety texture that complements the egg and sugar.

Although a number of spirits make for a fine flip, the deep walnut-like character of dry oloroso sherry combined with the creaminess of an entire egg results in what Jerry Thomas aptly describes as a "very delicious drink" that "gives strength to delicate people." The Sherry Flip does well during the holidays as a less polarizing—and less boozy—stand-in for eggnog.

Serves 1

2 ounces oloroso sherry
½ ounce simple syrup
(1:1, sugar:water)
1 egg

Garnish: freshly grated nutmeg

Glassware: copita or small wineglass

Add all ingredients to a shaker without ice. Shake vigorously for 30 seconds. Add ice and shake for another 30 seconds. Strain into a copita or small wineglass. Grate fresh nutmeg over the top.

S

The newer vintages are used to top off the barrels holding medium-age vintages, which are used to top off the old vintage barrels as sherry is withdrawn for bottling. Major bodegas (sherry houses) use multiple solera systems, many of which total thousands of barrels each.

As of 2000, sherries may be classified as either VOS (Vinum Optimum Signatum or Very Old Sherry), for wines more than twenty years old or VORS (Vinum Optimum Rare Signatum or Very Old Rare Sherry), for wines more than thirty years of age.

Though vintage-dated, or "añada," sherries are far less common than they were in the nineteenth century, some houses still bottle wines from a single vintage.

Dry sherries are typically consumed as an apéritif alongside salty snacks, but they are also making further inroads with sommeliers who appreciate their versatility with food. The return of sherry to the bartender's repertoire has also furthered its growth in the United States. A few producers worth seeking out: Valdespino, El Maestro Sierra, Gutiérrez

Colosia, La Guita, Equipo Navazos, Fernando de Castilla, Hidalgo–La Gitana, and Lustau.

SHOOTER

(*n.*) A diminutive mixed drink comprised of 1 to 2 ounces of liquid, generally served in a shot or pony glass. These wide-ranging cocktails, invented in the late twentieth century, are usually consumed quickly and among a group of people. The names tend to either be militaristic (B-52, Bomb, Kamikaze) or suggest soft-core naughtiness (Sex on the Beach, Slippery Nipple).

SHOT

(*n.*) A serving of 1 ounce of a spirit, either used in building a mixed drink, consumed quickly, or served alongside another order. This term is often used interchangeably with "shooter," which more accurately describes a category of small mixed drinks served in a shooter or shot glass.

S

SHOT GLASS

(n.) A small glass that holds between 1 and 2 ounces and is most commonly used to serve shooters or shots of liquor. Because the volume of shot glasses varies—especially among novelty souvenir glasses—they are not recommended for measuring when making cocktails; choose a jigger instead.

SHRUB

1. (n.) A vinegar-based syrup used as a mixer. From the Arabic word *sharab*, meaning "to drink," these acidic concoctions have roots in the eighteenth century, when colonialists in the United States would preserve seasonal fruits and berries in a vinegar-sugar solution. Commonly mixed with soda water or alcohol, the ingredient gained in popularity in the nineteenth century but soon faded from the collective consciousness until their recent revival via the cocktail renaissance. Today bartenders across the United States are experimenting with unique infusions, both sweet and savory, to make cocktails, palate cleansers, and non-alcoholic sodas.

2. (n.) A fruit-infused liquor. Both the ancestor to the vinegar-based shrub and the descendant of the cordial, this ingredient, which evolved out of the seventeenth-century English tradition of soaking fruits and berries in liquor, usually rum or brandy, was a popular ingredient in the punches of the era.

SHU

(n.) "Alcohol" in Japanese; sometimes used as a suffix to a sake style, such as "junmai-shu."

SILVER FIZZ

(n.) This variation on the fizz made with gin, lemon juice, sugar, egg white, and seltzer over shaved ice was one of the more popular drink orders of the 1880s in Chicago. The traditional version of the drink calls for Old Tom gin, a sweeter variation of the spirit.

SIDECAR

COMPETING theories about this cocktail's origins locate its birthplace in either London or Paris at the end of World War I, but the inspiration for the recipe comes from much earlier: the Brandy Crusta, a Cognac-based twist on the Old Fashioned created in New Orleans in the mid-nineteenth century. If you study the proportions, you'll see the Sidecar is basically a Cognac Sour with Cointreau in place of simple syrup. The sugared rim? Most likely a borrowed trick from the crusta, but it only started showing up in written Sidecar recipes in the 1930s, and it stuck.

Serves 1

2 ounces Cognac
¾ ounce Cointreau
¾ ounce lemon juice

Garnish: sugar for rimming and an orange peel

Glassware: cocktail or coupe

Prepare a cocktail or coupe glass ahead of time with a sugar rim. Add all ingredients to a cocktail shaker. Add ice and shake until chilled. Strain into prepared cocktail or coupe glass. Garnish with an orange peel.

Note: *For best results, prepare and chill cocktail glasses at least a couple of hours prior to making cocktails. This will ensure a perfect candy-like coating.*

SINGAPORE SLING

PRECURSORS to the Old Fashioned, the slings of the eighteenth century were nearly interchangeable with toddies and could be served either hot or cold. Essentially a spirit mixed with water, a little sugar, and perhaps a dash of ground nutmeg, the drink most likely acquired its name because of how easy it was to "sling back." By the 1830s, the sling was almost uniformly served cold, nutmeg optional. And a funny historical sidenote: The most famous drink to bear the name, the Singapore Sling, is not technically a sling, but rather a tiki-fied punch.

Serves 1

1 ounce gin
1 ounce Cherry Heering
1 ounce Bénédictine
1 ounce lime juice
2 ounces soda water
2 dashes Angostura bitters

Garnish: orange slice and brandied cherry

Glassware: Collins

Add first four ingredients to a shaker, add ice, and shake well. Strain over ice into a Collins glass. Top with soda and bitters. Garnish with an orange slice and a brandied cherry.

S

SIMPLE SYRUP

(n.) A cocktail ingredient made from granulated white sugar and water, most often in a ratio of 1:1, cooked until the sugar is dissolved. Because the sugar is already completely dissolved in the water, simple syrup sweetens drinks without causing any grittiness.

SINGLE BARREL

(n.) A spirit that is aged in one barrel and then bottled, usually used in reference to bourbon or whiskey. These are generally considered to be of higher quality (with a matching high price tag) and are usually released in limited-edition quantities.

SINGLE MALT

(n.) A whiskey made from malted grains at one distillery. If it is from Scotland, it must be made from malted barley in a pot still and aged for three years in oak casks.

SIROP DE CASSIS

(n.) A commercially made sweetened black currant syrup used in mixed drinks. Note: Sirop de cassis is nonalcoholic syrup, while crème de cassis is an alcoholic liqueur.

SIROP DE CITRON

(n.) A commercially made sweetened lemon syrup used in mixed drinks.

SIROP DE GROSEILLES

(n.) A commercially made sweetened red currant syrup used in mixed drinks.

SKUNKY

(adj.) A descriptor for beer that has spoiled from exposure to light; also known as "lightstruck." When exposed to natural or artificial light, alpha acids, a component of hops, combine with other ingredients in beer to form a sulfuric compound that can make beer smell like skunk spray. This chemical reaction can

S

happen within a matter of hours. Many manufacturers protect beer by bottling it in cans or dark-brown or green bottles. Beers that are bottled in clear glass often don't contain hops but tetra hops, a hop-like substance.

SLICE

(*n.*) A cocktail garnish, usually made from citrus fruits. To make a slice, first make a wheel from the fruit, then cut the wheel in half. Make a notch in the flesh to insert it on a glass, or float the slice whole in the cocktail.

SLING

(*n.*) Born from the primordial soup of American mixed drinks that pre-dated the cocktail's emergence in the early 1800s, the sling often over-lapped with toddies and juleps and could be served either hot or cold. The definition gradually evolved to refer to a base liquor mixed with sugar and water and served over ice. Jerry Thomas's *How to Mix Drinks* of 1862 makes the distinction that a sling should be served with grated nutmeg. Note that the most recognizable drink to bear the sling name—the Singapore Sling—skews closer to punch than it does to a traditional sling.

SLOE GIN

(*n.*) Not a true gin, but a tart-sweet liqueur flavored with sloe plums and made with a gin base. Brownish–ruby red in color, this English spirit is made by infusing gin with the astringent fruit, then adding sugar. In England and Ireland, it is most often made at home, though commercial brands do exist. In 2008, Plymouth, famous for producing real gin, released a version based on an 1883 recipe to great acclaim. The liqueur may be served neat, over ice, or in cocktails, most famously the Sloe Gin Fizz.

S

SMASH

(n.) A julep in miniature, a smash is a mix of a base spirit, sugar, and water served over crushed ice in a small bar glass. Cocktail expert David Wondrich says the category reached the zenith of its popularity between 1840 and the Civil War, after which it got folded back into the julep category until its rather recent revival. The formula is ripe for embellishment, with modern bartenders mixing in fruit, berries, herbs, spices, and even vegetables with an array of base spirits. Popular versions include the brandy, whiskey, and gin iterations, which are mixed with sugar and mint and served over crushed ice with a fruit garnish.

SNIFTER

(n.) A type of glassware with a large bowl and short stem holding anywhere from 5 to 25 ounces; most often associated with the consumption of brandy.

SODA GUN

(n.) A piece of bar equipment that dispenses carbonated and noncarbonated beverages.

SODA SIPHON

(n.) A piece of equipment, available for home use, that can carbonate liquids. Most versions have a chamber for liquid and a screw-on lid that holds a carbon dioxide cartridge that will force carbon dioxide into the liquid.

SOFT DRINK

(n.) A nonalcoholic carbonated sweetened beverage, such as cola or lemon-lime soda; the name contrasts the beverages with "hard" drinks, which contain alcohol. These can be served chilled or over ice or used as mixers in alcoholic drinks.

S

SOJU

(n.) A Korean spirit distilled from rice, wheat, barley, sweet potatoes, or other starches. Though not popular in the United States, the product has found footing elsewhere in the world; *Drinks International* ranked Jinro's soju as the top-selling spirit in the world in 2013. Clear and colorless, the spirit is usually served chilled and consumed neat, but some bartenders are experimenting with using it in mixed drinks.

SOLERA

(n.) A complex aging system for wines in which vintages are blended together; sometimes called fractional blending. In the solera system, wines are aged in multiple barrels. A portion of wine is removed from the oldest barrels to be bottled, with the next oldest wine used to top off what has been removed and so forth. This technique is most often used in sherry production, where some systems have more than a hundred vintages in the blend.

SOMMELIER

(n.) A wine-focused restaurant professional in charge of anything from creating the wine list, maintaining wine inventory, recommending wine to customers, and training the staff about wine. Additionally, as beverage programs at restaurants expand beyond wine, a sommelier may be required to know about and maintain an inventory of beer, spirits, and cocktails. The exact duties of a sommelier vary across restaurants. In establishments with a small staff, the position is often filled by someone who is also a waiter or manager; at larger establishments with an emphasis on fine dining, there might be several sommeliers of varying rank. Though there are no official requirements to call oneself a sommelier, there are several certification programs that offer rigorous training.

SOUR

(n.) A direct descendant of punch, the basic sour forms the template for a host of modern drinks. First men-

tions of the sour, made from a base spirit, citrus, sugar, and water and served neat in a small bar glass, can be traced to the mid-nineteenth century. The name—a reference to the citrus component—is a bit misleading, as the drink can be quite sweet, depending on the ratio of citrus to sweetener, as well as any additional cream, eggs, fruit, or other liquors included in the mix. The Whiskey Sour may be the most recognizable version of this drink, though the Daiquiri (rum) and the Southside (gin) also belong in the category. A common embellishment in the late nineteenth century for the whiskey version was floating a cap of red wine on the drink.

SOUR BEER

(n.) A style of beer that has been intentionally inoculated with bacteria by exposing fermenting beer to strains of wild yeasts and bacteria. After consuming the available sugar in fermenting beer, the bacteria leave a desired acidic character, as well as introduce a complex array of flavors and aromas that can range from fruity to leathery. The category originated in Belgium, where sour styles, such as lambic and Flanders ales have been produced for centuries, but the discovery of pasteurization steered many brewers toward making non-sour beers. In the 2000s, experimental American craft brewers began to have commercial success with the sour style, and now the category is growing in popularity.

SOUR MASH

(n.) Some bourbon and Tennessee whiskey producers hold back a portion of the fermented mash (the water-soaked grain mix that will be distilled) from each batch and add it to the next, much like sourdough starter is used for baking some breads. The recycled mash is thought to both inoculate the next batch from harmful bacteria and add a distinct character to the alcohol.

SOUTHSIDE

DEPENDING on how you look at it, this summer-perfect cocktail lands somewhere between a gin Mojito sans soda water and a Gimlet with mint. Though New York's 21 Club lays claim to the recipe as part of its Prohibition-era menu, some cocktail historians place the drink's conception some forty years earlier at the South Side Sportsmen's Club in Long Island, a private establishment where tony Manhattanites went to hunt, fish, and drink Mint Juleps, the drink that probably evolved into this one. The clubby association stuck, and the drink became standard-issue for the pearl and nine-iron set, but one would be remiss in passing this over on principle. It is simple and delicious.

Serves 1

6–8 mint leaves
¾ ounce simple syrup (1:1, sugar:water)
2 ounces gin
¾ ounce lime juice
1 dash orange bitters

Garnish: mint sprig

Glassware: cocktail or coupe

In a cocktail shaker, gently muddle mint leaves with simple syrup. Add all other ingredients, add ice, and shake until chilled. Double strain into a chilled cocktail or coupe glass. Spank a mint sprig against your hand to release the oils and garnish.

Note: *London-style dry gin plays nice in Southsides, especially this version. If you've got it, use it.*

S

SOUR MIX

(n.) A premixed blend of citrus juice and sweetener used by bartenders as a shortcut for making cocktails such as the Whiskey Sour or Margarita. Though commercial versions, sometimes sold as "sweet and sour mix," are convenient, they tend to be of low quality; many contain high-fructose corn syrup and dyes. Because of this, making your own homemade version is highly recommended as an alternative.

SOUTHERN COMFORT

(n.) Originally conceived as a spiced bourbon blend in 1874 by New Orleans bartender Martin Wilkes Heron, this product is now formulated as a fruit-, spice-, and whiskey-flavored liqueur based on a neutral spirit. The "reserve" version, which is sold on the international market, blends Southern Comfort and actual bourbon. Flavored versions featuring lime and black cherry are also available.

Usually mixed with sweet tea, lemonade, or cola, Southern Comfort is also featured in many cocktails, including the Alabama Slammer and Scarlett O'Hara.

SPARGE

(v.) A beer-making technique in which hot water is poured over strained cooked grains (from the mash) to extract leftover sugar and flavor. This liquid is then collected and added to the wort (the sugary water strained from the mash) that will be fermented.

SPARKLING

(n.) A term that describes an effervescent beverage. Although water from certain springs develops carbonation naturally, all other fizzy beverages (including soda water, soda, sparkling wines, and beer) are carbonated artificially for stylistic reasons.

There are a number of ways to induce carbonation. In the production of alcoholic beverages, a common method is to use yeast; the by-products of fermentation (when yeast cells consume sugar) are carbon dioxide and

S

alcohol. If the carbon dioxide is not allowed to escape, it will dissolve into the liquid. The carbon dioxide will remain suspended in the liquid, turning into a fizz only when the container is opened. The *méthode champenoise* and Charmat process of making sparkling wine use this method of carbonation, as does bottle or cask conditioning for making beer.

Another common method of achieving effervescence is force carbonation, in which a liquid is put in a sealed container such as a keg or a can and carbon dioxide is injected into the container. The carbon dioxide then dissolves into the liquid until the seal is broken.

SPÄTLESE

(n.) A German classification for wines made from grapes harvested after the normal harvest; literally, "late harvest" in German. Richer in style and higher in alcohol than Kabinett wines, these wines may be dry, medium-dry, or sweet. Dry wines will bear the label "trocken."

SPEAKEASY

(n.) During Prohibition in the United States, a speakeasy was an establishment that illegally sold alcohol. During the cocktail revival of the 2000s, the term was repurposed to describe bars that adopted a Prohibition aesthetic, including hidden entrances, secret passwords for entry, bartenders in retro apparel, and menus featuring classic cocktails.

SPEED RAIL

(n.) A piece of equipment used in commercial bars to shelve the most frequently used spirits and mixers. Usually rectangular in shape, this open box can be mounted to the front of the bartender's station.

SPEYSIDE

(n.) A region in Scotland that houses more whisky distilleries than any other. Although it is difficult to generalize about overarching styles across the many distilleries, some say

that Speyside Scotches tend to be fruitier than others.

SPHERIFICATION

(n.) A technique for encasing liquids in spheres with thin edible membranes that burst easily. Originally popularized by chefs in the molecular gastronomy movement, this time-intensive yet theatrical process has since been adopted by those making high-tech cocktails.

SPICED AND FLAVORED RUM

(n.) This nebulous category of rums, which may be bottled at a lower ABV than regular rum (30 percent), is doctored with spices and flavorings. The flavorings can be anything from coconut to vanilla, spices, and bananas. According to the Distilled Spirits Council of the United States, flavored rums represented 52 percent of all rums sold in the United States in 2012. Recommended brands try include Sailor Jerry and Hum.

SPLASH

(n.) A measurement indicating a small but imprecise amount of liquid slightly larger than a dash. The term is most often used in conjunction with syrups, mixers, or water.

SPLIT

(n.) A wine bottle containing 187.5 milliliters, or one-quarter the standard bottle size; most commonly used for Champagne or sparkling wines.

SPRIG

(n.) A semi-imprecise unit of measurement used to indicate a single stem of an herb, such as mint, rosemary, or thyme.

SPRITZER

(n.) A chilled cocktail made from white wine and seltzer or club soda, usually poured in a ratio of 1:1 and served over ice.

S

SPUMANTE

(n.) An Italian term that describes wine with some amount of carbonation. "Spumante" refers to wines that have a more aggressive carbonation, while the carbonation in frizzante wines is gentler.

STANGE

(n.) A tall, narrow glass holding between 100 and 200 milliliters, traditionally used to serve certain German beers such as Kölsch.

STEMS

(n.) A slang term for wine glassware consisting of a bowl atop a spindle or stem.

STIRRED

(n.) A method of mixing cocktails. Although shaking ingredients with ice works best for drinks containing juices, eggs, and dairy, as it helps to emulsify the different liquids and create a frothy texture, stirring is a better method for drinks such as the Martini or Manhattan that call for spirits only, so the drink retains its clarity. Some argue that shaking spirits can "bruise" the alcohol, though that idea has been thoroughly debunked.

To properly stir a cocktail, chill a mixing glass and a serving glass by either storing them in a freezer or adding ice water to the vessels and then dumping it out. Pour the cocktail ingredients into the mixing glass, then add ice. Insert a barspoon until it touches the bottom of the glass. Stir carefully in one direction for around 60 seconds (take more time when using solid blocks of ice or Kold-Draft, less for poor-quality ice), taking care not to aerate the drink. Some bartenders maintain that this step should be done as silently as possible, with no clinking or rattling. Strain the cocktail into the chilled serving glass.

STOUT

(n.) A strong, dark, malty style of beer, usually with a roasted flavor.

STINGER

THIS iconic pre-Prohibition cocktail—an unlikely combo of white crème de menthe and brandy shaken and served up—stormed bar menus in the 1920s, becoming a favorite among high society (the mint flavor supposedly helped disguise alcohol on one's breath). It has pop culture credentials too, tallying up screen time in the 1957 Cary Grant vehicle *Kiss Them for Me*, as well as in 1956's *High Society*, featuring Bing Crosby and Frank Sinatra.

Serves 1

1 sprig mint
¾ ounce white crème de menthe
1 dash orange bitters
2¼ ounces Cognac

Garnish: mint

Glassware: rocks or coupe

In a mixing glass, muddle mint with crème de menthe and orange bitters. Add Cognac and ice, and shake until chilled. Strain over ice into a rocks glass or strain into a chilled coupe. Garnish with a small sprig of mint.

STORK CLUB

THIS gin-based cocktail was christened at the Stork Club, a tony Manhattan nightclub and restaurant popular with the glitterati of the 1930s. The bar program led by Nathan "Cookie" Cook was legendary, and in 1946 it inspired *The Stork Club Bar Book*, written by journalist and man-about-town Lucius Beebe. Once the club's namesake cocktail, this orange-hued drink is a study of citrus, with a heavy pour of orange juice augmented by lime juice and Cointreau. As a result, sweet Old Tom gin makes a better base than herbal or peppery London dry examples.

Serves 1

1½ ounces gin
1 ounce orange juice
¼ Cointreau
¼ ounce fresh lime juice
1 dash Angostura bitters

Garnish: orange peel

Glassware: coupe glass

Add all ingredients to a shaker, add ice, and shake. Strain into a chilled coupe glass. Garnish with an orange peel.

S

The term originally referred to any type of strong British ale, and in the 1700s it was commonly paired with other descriptors of beer styles, as in "brown stout," which referred to a more alcoholic brown ale. The opposite was a "slender ale," which indicated a weak beer. Over time stout came to refer to a strong version of porter, though the terms have become somewhat interchangeable.

There are a number of substyles within the category. Milk or sweet stout, made with added lactic sugar, is sweeter. Made with up to 30 percent oats, oatmeal stout, a smooth and slightly sweet style that appeared in the late nineteenth century, was thought to have healthful properties. Irish stout (the most famous example being Guinness) tends to be dark in color but lighter in alcohol and body; sometimes it is carbonated with nitrogen for a creamy effect. Chocolate stouts usually have a roasted chocolaty flavor, either from the use of heavily roasted malts or the addition of chocolate flavoring.

STRAIGHT UP

(phrase) This ambiguous drink order requests either that a spirit be served neat (without ice) or a cocktail be served up (shaken or stirred with ice and then strained). To avoid confusion when ordering, it is best to use either "neat" or "up" instead.

STRAINER

(n.) This bartending tool, usually made of metal, is used to strain a chilled cocktail into the service glass. It comes in two main types: the Hawthorne strainer, a flat perforated disk with a wire coil that encircles the disk, and the julep strainer, a shallow perforated bowl with a handle. Traditionally, the Hawthorne is used to strain shaken drinks, while the julep is used for stirred drinks. In a pinch, however, either will work.

STREGA

(n.) A slightly sweet Italian herbal liqueur. Produced in Campania, Italy, by S.A. Distilleria Liquore

S

Strega since 1860, this digestif with a yellow-green tinge takes its color from saffron and is rumored to have around seventy botanical ingredients in its proprietary recipe. Usually consumed chilled after meals, it also works well as an ingredient in cocktails.

SUPERFINE SUGAR (CASTER SUGAR)

(n.) Granulated white sugar that has been ground to a very fine consistency. The small grain size allows the sugar to dissolve in liquids more easily than regular granulated sugar, making it a good choice for mixed drinks that call for sugar rather than simple syrup. Superfine sugar is available in most grocery stores, but it can also be made at home by pulverizing granulated sugar in a food processor until fine, which usually takes one to two minutes. In the U.K., superfine sugar is known as "caster sugar," and sometimes is called "bar sugar" or "baker's sugar." Note that superfine sugar is different than powdered sugar, which is a finer grade of sugar

that sometimes has additives to keep it from caking together.

SWEET MASH

(n.) An unregulated marketing term for bourbon made without sour mash.

SWIZZLE

(n.) A category of drinks, usually rum-based, likely invented in the West Indies in the nineteenth century. The defining characteristic of the drink is the method of preparation, in which ingredients are added to a cup with crushed ice, then mixed with a swizzle stick (a long stick with skewed prongs at the end). The correct way to use the stick is to insert the end with the prongs into the drink, then hold the stem between your palms and roll it back and forth rapidly until a frost has formed on the glass. If no swizzle stick is available, a bar spoon makes a suitable replacement.

S

SWIZZLE STICK

1. *(n.)* A bartending tool used to make swizzle drinks, this thin wand comes with short, skewed prongs on one end. Although traditionally made of wood from the Caribbean swizzlestick tree (*Quararibea turbinata*), modern versions can be manufactured from metal, plastic, or other woods. A barspoon can be used as a substitute.

2. *(n.)* The term is occasionally used to refer to what can better be described as a stirrer, straw, or skewer.

SYRUP

(n.) Commonly used in nineteenth-century cocktails in the United States, these sugar-sweetened solutions provide viscosity as well as intense flavor and color to cocktails. Early gum (gomme) syrups were made from gum arabic, a resin of the acacia tree, but these fell out of favor after Prohibition, when cost and ease favored plain simple syrup (a mix of sugar and water) instead. Other enduring syrups include Falernum (almond, ginger, and cloves), grenadine (pomegranate), and orgeat (almond).

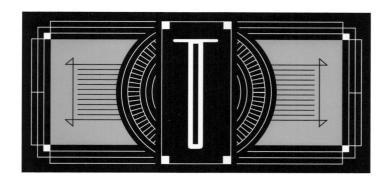

TAILS

(n.) The final amount of ethanol produced by distilling after the "heads" and "hearts" comes off the still, marked by a number of toxic compounds. The tails are discarded and not bottled.

TALL

(adj.) A catchall category for cocktails that include a nonalcoholic mixer, usually juice or soda, and are served over ice in a tall glass, such as a Collins glass. These drinks usually contain the same amount of alcohol as their more diminutive compatriots but are diluted by the mixer. Fizzes, highballs, and Collins cocktails can be grouped into this family.

TARTUFO

(n.) An uncommon style of Italian amaro flavored with truffles, usually served chilled as a digestif. Most versions come from the Italy's Umbria region.

TAWNY PORT

(n.) A style of port made from blending vintages that have been aged in oak casks between ten and forty

years. The aging process exposes the wines to oxidation, which results in a nutty flavor and brownish-red color, from which the style takes its name. As it is made from a blend of aged wines, tawny ports are ready to drink upon sale.

TEMPRANILLO

(n.) A red wine grape native to Spain but now grown in outposts around the world, including Australia, Mexico, and Washington State. An early ripening variety, Tempranillo plays a key role in the wines of two of Spain's top regions, Rioja and Ribera del Duero. When made in a traditional Rioja style, the wine tends to express notes of leather and cherries on a medium-bodied frame with a brick red color. Modern and New World styles exhibit more tannins and fruit flavors, including plum and berries, and are generally darker and more purple in color. Though many Tempranillo wines are intended to be consumed soon after the vintage date, those from the best vineyards and producers can age for decades.

TENNESSEE WHISKEY

(n.) This straight bourbon whiskey made in Tennessee must be distilled from a mash of at least 51 percent corn plus a mix of barley, rye, and wheat and aged for two years in oak barrels.

Some Tennessee whiskeys undergo a charcoal filtration before being aged in barrel, called the Lincoln County Process, which helps to either mellow and smooth the liquor or strip the flavor away, depending on whom you ask. Although many of the big producers employ this step to distinguish their product from plain bourbon, it is not a requirement.

Though production of Tennessee whiskey had been limited to a handful of producers, including Jack Daniel's and George Dickel, for a long time thanks to a longstanding statewide prohibition on new distilleries, change is on the horizon. In 2009, Tennessee's legislature changed a state law that brought the number of counties in which liquor could be made from three up to forty-one, prompting an expansion in the number of boutique distilleries.

I

TEQUILA

(n.) One of Mexico's most famous exports, tequila is made from the heart of the blue agave plants grown in Jalisco and a handful of other states, which is harvested and steamed to release fermentable sugars. The juice is then extracted from the plants and fermented before being distilled. The final product must be double distilled at a minimum and is subject to a number of aging regulations.

Believed to be one of the first distilled products of the Americas, tequila is a descendant of pulque, fermented agave juice, which was made by the Aztecs. When Spanish conquistadors and Filipino sailors brought distillation know-how to the Americas in the sixteenth century, pulque went higher proof. By the early 1600s, a rustic version of mezcal, tequila's direct parent, was being mass-produced in Jalisco. The spirit became further refined to what we would recognize as tequila in the nineteenth century, when producers narrowed on the blue agave plant from Jalisco as the favored source.

Many Americans were introduced to the spirit during Prohibition, as Mexico, the closest neighbor to the dry United States, never stopped producing alcohol. The tequila-based Margarita, invented during or soon after Prohibition, has hardly flagged in popularity stateside since.

Although tequila has long had a reputation as being down-market, suitable only for shots and mixed drinks, evidence suggests that Americans are recognizing higher-quality versions of the spirit. The Distilled Spirits Council of the United States reports that imports of super-premium tequila grew over 400 percent from 2002 to 2012.

The best tequilas are distilled from 100 percent blue agave; all others bear the mixto label, which permits anything made with more than 51 percent blue agave to be named tequila. There are five categories based on time spent aging barrels, which range from bright and clean in flavor to smooth and almost Cognac-like: blanco or plata (less than two months in neutral barrels), reposado (two months to a year),

TI PUNCH

MARTINIQUE'S answer to Cuba's Daiquiri, Brazil's Caipirinha, and the Rum Sour, the Ti Punch pushes rhum agricole, the island nation's artisanal spin on rum, to center stage. Traditionally the drink (pronounced "tee paunch" in the Caribbean) is rounded out with lime juice and cane syrup, a special sweetener made from raw sugar-cane juice, though simple syrup will do perfectly well in a pinch.

Serves 1

½ teaspoon cane syrup
Lime wedge
2 ounces rhum agricole

Garnish: lime peel

Glassware: rocks

Add cane syrup, a squeeze of lime, and rhum agricole to a rocks glass. Add a large chunk of ice and stir. Garnish with a lime peel.

joven (a mix of blanco and aged), añejo (one to three years), and extra añejo (a minimum of three years). The blanco and reposado types make the best mixed drinks.

TÊTE DE CUVÉE

(n.) The top wines made in a single vintage by a Champagne producer or grower; also known as prestige cuvée. These are generally more expensive than the rest of the producer's line of wines. Examples include Louis Roederer's Cristal and Taittinger's Comtes de Champagne.

TIA MARIA

(n.) A brand of coffee-flavored liqueur thought to have originated in Jamaica. The ingredients include vanilla, coffee, Jamaican rum, sugar, and other spices. The dark-brown spirit can be consumed neat or on the rocks as a digestif or mixed into cocktails, sometimes with cream.

TINTO DE VERANO

(n.) A simpler version of sangria, this red wine spritzer, whose name mean "red wine of summer," is made with lemon-lime soda and served over ice. It is popular as an apéritif in Spain.

TODDY

(n.) A precursor to the original cocktail of the early 1800s, the toddy—a mix of liquor, water, and sugar—could be served either hot or cold, with some distinguishing the toddy from the sling by the fact the former had no garnish of nutmeg. The modern toddy, however, is recognized as a hot beverage: a mix of liquor, hot water, sugar, and an optional grating of nutmeg.

TONIC WATER

(n.) This soda flavored with quinine became popular as a malaria-prevention tonic in the eighteenth century. In the seventeenth century, by way of the Peruvian Incas, it became known that

TODDY (HOT)

THOUGH today the word "toddy" almost always refers to any alcoholic beverage served hot, this wasn't always so. One of the ancestral drinks of the cocktail world, the toddy likely originated from a number of different traditions, but it loosely meant a base spirit (usually rum or whiskey) plus a sweetener, served either hot or cold. Such a combination was often considered medicinal, especially when it included citrus. Today the word can be used to refer to a wide swath of drinks, from the most basic recipe of a base spirit plus sugar to more complex iterations with cream, egg, fruit, liqueurs, spices, and garnishes aplenty.

Serves 1

1½ ounces bourbon or rye
   (or any dark spirit including
   aged rum or Cognac)
¾ ounces honey or maple syrup
4–5 ounces hot water

Garnish: lemon wheel and
cinnamon stick

Glassware: mug or rocks

Add spirit and honey or maple syrup to a mug or rocks glass. Top with hot water and stir gently to dissolve honey or maple syrup. Garnish with a lemon wheel and a cinnamon stick.

malaria symptoms could be treated by ingesting the bark of the cinchona tree. British colonialists in India figured out a way to make quinine, the bitter extract of the bark, tolerable: by mixing it with sugar, gin, and (newly invented) soda water. In 1771 the Schweppes Company devised a recipe for the first commercial tonic water, a mix of sugar, quinine, and soda water, with the name a reference to the health benefits. As other cures for malaria have arisen over time, the ingredients have been cheapened by using synthetic quinine and corn syrup. Boutique tonic waters that have recently come to market, however, mark a vast improvement over the supermarket brands. Try examples from Fever-Tree, Fentimans, Q Tonic, or Tomr's. Some restaurants are also making the product in-house, and it is possible to make your own version at home.

TOP OFF

(v.) Filling a glass to the top with a liquid, usually used in reference to adding soda water or ginger ale as the final ingredient of a cocktail.

TOP SHELF

(adj.) A slangy phrase that has come to mean high-end alcohol; a reference to where bartenders store the priciest bottles of alcohol because they are ordered less frequently.

TRAPPIST BEER

(n.) A beer, most often an ale, brewed by Trappist monks. Monastic breweries were common throughout Europe in the Middle Ages, and although many were destroyed or dismantled during the French Revolution at the end of the eighteenth century and World Wars I and II, some continue the practice. Today's Trappist breweries, which are mostly located in Belgium, must be run without an eye toward profit and the revenues used to fund the monastery and charity work. The most famous examples include Chimay and Orval.

Though classifications differ among breweries, the most common

TOM & JERRY

THIS descendant of eggnog is a pain in the ass to mix, but it's well worth the effort for the rosy noses it will produce. Professor Jerry Thomas claims he invented it in 1847, saying he named it after himself and "two small white mice" he kept as pets called, of course, Tom and Jerry. However, the warm nog has been reported in America since the 1820s, and sometimes it is even credited to English author Pierce Egan, who penned a play of the same name in 1821. According to Dave Wondrich, the name does come from Egan, at least indirectly: "To go Tom & Jerrying was to go out on the town, and a Tom & Jerry was also a low dive. And, in this case, a festive but lethal sort of drink." Though Thomas's tale of ownership is a tall one, he became the drink's greatest ambassador, and, according to Dave Wondrich's *Imbibe!*, bowls across America were filled with the batter for the drink each winter until its popularity died down near the turn of the twentieth century.

Serves 25

12 eggs
1 stick butter, at room
    temperature
1 cup superfine sugar
1 teaspoon ground allspice
1 teaspoon ground cinnamon
1 teaspoon ground cloves
1 teaspoon vanilla extract
Whole milk, hot water, or a
    mixture (1:1, milk:hot water)
1 bottle (750 ml) brandy
1 bottle (750 ml) aged rum

Garnish: freshly grated nutmeg

Glassware: mug or small
rocks glass

Separate egg whites from yolks into two large bowls. Add butter and sugar to egg yolks and beat with an electric mixer. Mix will be slightly chunky. Using clean beaters, beat egg whites to stiff peaks.

Using a spatula, gently fold egg whites into yolk mixture until color and consistency is the same. To finish the batter, stir in allspice, cinnamon, cloves, and vanilla.

If desired, the batter can be made ahead of time and kept in the refrigerator, covered, for a few hours before assembly. To assemble Tom & Jerrys, gently heat milk in a saucepan over low heat (amount depends on how many drinks you plan to serve).

Add 1 tablespoon of batter to a mug or small rocks glass. While constantly stirring batter, add 1 ounce brandy and 1 ounce rum. Fill to the top with milk (or hot water, or a 1:1 ratio), and stir until foamy. Grate fresh nutmeg over top to garnish.

TOM COLLINS

TAKE the American side: that this drink evolved from the Great Tom Collins Hoax of 1874, in which pranksters would tell a friend that one Tom Collins had said some slanderous things about said friend, then left to go to a bar around the corner, sparking a goose chase of perhaps not-so-epic proportions in search of Mr. Collins (what passed for entertainment!). Or choose the British: that London bartender John Collins dreamed up an eponymous gin punch in the latter half of the nineteenth century that, when made with Old Tom gin, became the Tom Collins. By either route (or perhaps a combination of the two), you've got a spritzy summer-ready drink made of lemon, sugar, soda water, and gin—the original hard lemonade. Here's a tip: the super-simple Collins template is the basis for a host of easy variations.

Serves 1

1½ ounces gin
¾ ounce lemon juice
¾ ounce simple syrup
    (1:1, sugar:water)
Soda water

Garnish: brandied cherry and an orange wheel

Glassware: Collins

Add gin, lemon juice, and simple syrup to a cocktail shaker. Add ice and shake until chilled. Strain over ice into a Collins glass. Top with soda water. Garnish with a brandied cherry and an orange wheel.

TRIDENT

WHEN Seattle bartender Robert Hess created this Negroni look-alike in 2000, he chose a trifecta of ingredients that are less common than the familiar Negroni components though still somewhat analogous: aquavit for gin, Cynar for Campari, and sherry for sweet vermouth (plus a dash of peach bitters to tie it all together). The cocktail renaissance in the decade that followed may have rendered these alcohols slightly more mainstream, but that doesn't dampen the enjoyment factor of this drink, which has become a staple in its birth town.

Serves 1

---

1 ounce aquavit (preferably Linie)
1 ounce Cynar
1 ounce fino sherry (preferably La Ina)
2 dashes peach bitters

Garnish: lemon peel

Glassware: cocktail or coupe

Add all ingredients to a mixing glass. Add ice and stir well. Strain into a chilled cocktail or coupe glass. Garnish with a lemon peel.

substyles are the dubbel (double), a dark-brown ale with a fruity mocha character, and the tripel (triple), which is lighter in color but stronger in alcohol content, often notching in the range of 8 to 10 percent ABV. Many of these beers are bottle-conditioned, which means flat beer is bottled with an extra dose of sugar, which feeds the yeast cells, inducing carbonation.

Trappist ales are highly regarded in the beer-drinking community, and some nonreligious breweries offer comparative offerings, often termed "Belgian-style" or "abbey-style" ales.

TRIPLE SEC

(n.) One of the two main styles of sweetened orange liqueur, triple sec is thought to have been invented by the French in the nineteenth century as a drier alternative to the curaçao style, the Dutch liqueur made from pot-distilled brandy and orange peels. There is some debate about the name, which translates to "triple dry," but most believe it's a reference to either the number of times the original liqueur was distilled or its comparative level of dryness to curaçao. Today's triple secs, made from neutral spirit flavored with orange peels and sugar, are most often clear. Cointreau may be the best-known brand in this category. Triple secs are usually consumed in mixed drinks, such as the Margarita, Southside, and the Bee's Knees.

TROCKEN

(adj.) A German term that means "dry" and describes a still wine that has little to no residual sugar. For German sparkling wines, however, the term indicates a medium amount of sweetness. The term is occasionally used for Austrian wines.

TROCKENBEERENAUSLESE

(n.) A German classification for wines made from hand selecting individual berries that have shriveled on the vine after harvest; literally, "dry berries select picking" in German. These grapes have highly concentrated sugars and produce intense

TUXEDO

MANY late nineteenth-century variations on the Martini skew sweet, but not this one, which swaps vermouth for dry sherry, which results in a nutty profile rather than a herbal one, with a hint of citrus from the orange bitters. The drink takes its name from Tuxedo Park, built in New Jersey in 1886 as the first planned living community, complete with sewers, recreational sports facilities, and, yes, balls at which the residents sported short dress coats, an outfit that would come to be known as the tuxedo. The story goes that the Tuxedo Park suburbanites who commuted to Manhattan would frequent the bar at the Waldorf-Astoria bar before heading home, where this drink was created.

Serves 1

2 ounces gin (preferably Plymouth or Beefeater 24)
1 ounce fino sherry (preferably La Ina)
2 dashes Regans' orange bitters

Garnish: orange peel

Glassware: cocktail or coupe

Add all ingredients to a mixing glass. Add ice and stir well. Strain into a chilled cocktail or coupe glass. Garnish with an orange peel.

Note: *If you read this and wonder where the absinthe and maraschino are, there are many drinks that bear the Tuxedo name, but according to cocktail historian David Wondrich, this appears to be the first.*

dessert wines with honeyed flavors, considered to be the sweetest of German wines. Though the wines are high in sugar, they often have a corresponding high acidity level, which helps to create balance and reduce the impression of overall sweetness.

TROPHY WINE

(n.) A rare or expensive wine that is challenging to acquire, either because allocations are small or it is prohibitively expensive. It is often purchased or consumed as a status symbol.

TUACA

(n.) A brandy-based liqueur flavored with orange and vanilla. First produced by Gaetano Tuoni and Giorgio Canepa in 1938 in Livorno, Italy, the sweet, viscous golden-brown alcohol is now made in Kentucky by the Tuaca liquor company. Tuaca is most often served as a shooter, but it may also be added to coffee or hot cider and is used in some cocktails.

TUMBLER

(n.) A drinking glass of any size without a stem, handle, or foot.

TWIST

(n.) A thin slice of fresh citrus peel used as a cocktail garnish. When squeezed or flamed over the surface of a cocktail, it contributes citrus aroma and flavor. Note: Avoid the pith of the citrus, as it adds bitterness.

TYPICITY

(n.) A wine-tasting term that indicates how closely the wine in question exhibits characteristics that conform to the archetypical examples of its grape or region. For example, one might say, "This Nebbiolo has great typicity because it tastes like cherries, roses, and tar."

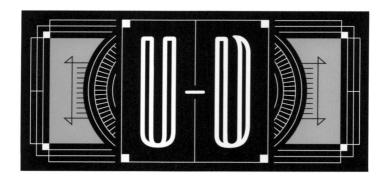

ULLAGE

1. *(n.)* The headspace between the top of the bottle and the liquid in it, most commonly used in reference to wine bottles. An older bottle will have a larger ullage, as some of the liquid will have evaporated over time. Wine experts can make general estimates about the quality of an aged wine based on the ullage.

2. *(n.)* In the United Kingdom, the term can refer to the leftover unsalable beer left at the bottom of a keg or cask, or to beer spilled at the tap.

UP

(adj.) A drink order requesting that a cocktail or spirit be shaken or stirred with ice, then strained and served chilled without ice.

VACUUM ROTARY DISTILLATION

(n.) The process of using a rotovap (rotary evaporator) to flavor alcohols.

VARIETAL

(n.) A wine made from a single grape variety. "Varietal" is often mistakenly used when the speaker intends to

mean "variety," referring to the grape or vine. For example, blends from Bordeaux are not varietal wines, but the single-grape Pinot Noir and Chardonnay wines from Burgundy are.

VARIETY

(n.) A single cultivar of wine grape (for example, Chardonnay or Cabernet Sauvignon). The term is frequently confused with the adjective "varietal," which refers to wines made with a single grape variety.

VERDELHO

(n.) A medium-dry style of classified Madeira wine made from the Verdelho grape. The wine, which will have up to 2.5 percent residual sugar, if often served as an apéritif or digestif.

VERMOUTH

(n.) A fortified aromatized wine, vermouth is made by adding a neutral spirit to a low-alcohol wine, then infusing it with spices, roots, and herbs before bottling. It generally comes in two styles, sweet (red) and dry, though there are other versions that are less common, such as white, rosé, or golden. Manufacturers tend to keep their herb and spice blend a proprietary secret, but common additions include citrus peel, coriander, juniper, ginger, cloves, and cinnamon, among others. The finished product is bottled at 16 to 18 percent ABV.

What we recognize as vermouth likely originated in Italy in the late eighteenth century as a medicinal tonic. The name comes from the German word for wormwood, *Wermut*, which was a common ingredient before the banning of absinthe. Sweet vermouth came first, from Antonio Benedetto Carpano in Turin, Italy, in 1786. Less than twenty years later, Joseph Noilly would introduce the dry version in France.

Commonly used as a mixer for many famous cocktails (the Martini, the Manhattan), it is also consumed as an apéritif in European cultures. Once dominated by big brands such as Martini & Rossi and Noilly Prat, vermouth has been getting the artisanal treatment

VESPER

THE Vesper was first mentioned by writer Ian Fleming in his 1953 novel *Casino Royale*, in which James Bond places a detailed order for the drink, specifying the use of Kina Lillet, a white apéritif wine flavored with quinine that was the forerunner of today's Lillet Blanc. Considering that the Lillet company used to produce not only Kina Lillet but also a Lillet-brand vermouth, some beverage historians have speculated that Bond simply slipped up when specifying the Kina Lillet, intending for the drink to be made with vermouth all along. Others note that modern Lillet Blanc is lighter and less sweet than Kina Lillet once was and suggest increasing the quantity of Lillet in the drink to keep it from being drowned out by the flavor of the gin. And though Bond asked for the drink shaken, it's better stirred.

Serves 1

3 ounces vodka
1 ounce gin
½–¾ ounce Lillet Blanc (or
  ½ ounce Cocchi Americano)

Garnish: lemon peel

Glassware: cocktail or coupe

Add all ingredients to a mixing glass. Add ice and stir well. Strain into a chilled cocktail or coupe glass. Garnish with a lemon peel.

Note: *The Vesper is an extremely dry (and heady) cocktail despite Bond's addition of Lillet. He may have recommended shaking it, but please, do stir. It will maintain the silky texture of an all-spirits drink.*

VIEUX CARRÉ

NEW Orleans does strong and stirred better than most American cities. From the Hurricane to the Sazerac, from Pat O'Brien's to the Napoleon House, much of the Big Easy's cocktail history insists on specific coordinates of conception. Stanley Clisby Arthur, author of *Famous New Orleans Drinks and How to Mix 'Em,* attributed this drink's original recipe to the Hotel Monteleone, located in the New Orleans's Vieux Carré (French Quarter). Today the cocktail remains a New Orleans classic, and it can be experienced at its original post at the Monteleone's Carousel Bar, which turns slowly around as life in the peculiar precinct passes by on Royal Street.

Serves 1

1 ounce rye
1 ounce Cognac
1 ounce sweet vermouth
¼ ounce Bénédictine
2 dashes Peychaud's bitters
2 dashes Angostura bitters

Garnish: orange or lemon peel

Glassware: rocks

Add all ingredients to a mixing glass. Add ice and stir until chilled. Strain over ice into a rocks glass. Garnish with an orange or lemon peel.

of late too, with many smaller labels, such as Carpano Antica and Mauro Vergano, and new craft producers, such as Uncouth Vermouth, more common on bar shelves.

VERTICAL TASTING

(n.) A wine-tasting event in which a producer's wines are compared across vintages. The progression can be used to show how the wine fares with bottle age or how the producer has evolved as a wine maker. The tasting may be performed from oldest to youngest or vice versa.

VIN CHAUD

(n.) A French style of mulled wine that typically consists of red wine heated with sugar, citrus, and spices. The name means "hot wine" in French.

VIN DOUX NATUREL

(n.) Fortified sweet wine from southern France. Less well known than their fortified counterparts, port and Madeira, this class of dessert wines can offer good value. These wines are generally made by adding neutral grape spirit to kill the yeast before fermentation can complete, leaving behind a sweet wine with a higher alcohol content. Common types of *vin doux naturels* include Muscat de Beaumes de Venise, Banyuls, and Maury Doux.

VIN JAUNE

(n.) A wine made from Savagnin grapes in the Jura region of France. Meaning "yellow wine" in French, vin jaune is unusual in that it is aged for at least six years in almost full oak casks, with a layer of yeast (*voile*) allowed to form on the top of the liquid to partially protect it from oxidation. The wine develops a deep yellow color, akin to dessert wines, but it remains dry, with flavors of nuts, resin, and saline.

VINICULTURE

(n.) The study and science of growing grapes specifically for wine.

VINTAGE

1. **(n.)** The year in which the grapes for a wine were harvested.

2. **(n.)** A term to describe aged spirits. If a spirit is made from a blend of vintages, the bottle is allowed to count only from the most recent year of the blend.

VINTAGE PORT

(n.) A style of port made only in the best vintages. It must be aged for two years in oak casks and bottled with little exposure to oxidation. The style is intended to be aged for many years.

VIOGNIER

(n.) A white grape variety most commonly associated with the Rhône Valley in France, where it is the sole grape variety allowed in the Condrieu appellation, it is also used in white blends throughout the region. Noted for its rich texture and fragrant qualities, Viognier will produce wines with aromas of flowers, peaches, and tropical fruit. Wine makers often use oak barrels to vinify the grape.

Though Rhône plantings of the grape dwindled during the twentieth century, a revival of sorts has been ongoing, and now good examples of Viognier can be found in California (particularly around the Central Coast), Australia, and South Africa, which in turn has boosted Condrieu's profile as well. Though Viognier is most often used to make still table wines, a number of producers also make a sweet dessert-style wine from the grape.

VIRGIN

(adj.) A cocktail made without alcohol, a term most frequently applied to frozen drinks, such as Daiquiris.

VITICULTURE

(n.) The study and science of grape growing.

VODKA

(n.) A close relative to neutral grain spirit, vodka is made by distilling almost anything—potatoes, grains, fruits, sugar—to above 190 proof, filtering the distillate, and then bottling at more than 80 proof. Flavored vodkas are usually made by adding extracts. By legal definition vodka must be odorless and colorless.

Details on its birth are muddied, but most believe vodka originated somewhere in eastern Europe or Russia in the twelfth century. Americans had little taste for vodka until clever marketing in the mid-twentieth century rebranded the product first as "white whiskey," then as the backbone to the Moscow Mule cocktail, which got a boost from endorsement by Hollywood heavyweights such as Woody Allen. It surpassed gin in total sales in 1967, then whiskey in 1976, and has held on to its rank as the most popular spirit in the United States ever since.

The success of super-premium vodka brands especially is the stuff that business school studies are made of. With few regulations on production, some producers simply rebottle a filtered neutral spirit and affix a brand label, pouring their funds into high-budget marketing programs rather than into manufacture. Recently, however, craft distillers have found success by trying an opposite tack, making a selling point of using local potatoes, grains, or sugar.

Long shunned by the craft cocktail movement for its lack of flavor and its popularity among the masses, vodka is being reconsidered by some bartenders for its ability to amplify delicate fruit, herb, and vegetable flavors that might be outgunned by a more robust spirit.

VOLATILE ACIDITY

(n.) The presence of acetic acid (a component of vinegar) in wine, often abbreviated to "VA." All wines contain some acetic acid. In small amounts it can contribute positively to the flavor profile, although in larger amounts it is viewed as a flaw.

WALNUT LIQUEUR

(n.) Also known as nocino, this walnut liqueur is made from infusing a neutral base spirit with green walnuts and a mix of spices, commonly cinnamon, vanilla, cloves, sugar, and citrus peels. The sweet, slightly bitter liqueur is common in France and Italy, where it is typically served chilled as an after-dinner drink or used in desserts.

WASSAIL

(n.) A sweetened hot alcoholic punch usually served around Christmas. It originated in England around the thirteenth century, when revelers would dip bread into a "wassail bowl," a heated mixture of fortified wine and ale. The name comes from an Old English greeting that bestowed a wish of health on the recipient. The tradition of "wassailing" as a celebration continued throughout the centuries, arriving on American shores with the Puritans, and it remained popular through the nineteenth century. The contents of the bowl evolved, and now the term denotes a combination of wine, beer, or cider mulled with spices and sugar.

WARD EIGHT

THIS grenadine-sweetened twist on the Whiskey Sour most likely dates to the turn of the twentieth century, with the most popular origin myth crediting bartender Tom Hussion of Boston's Locke-Ober restaurant for the recipe. Some historians say he dedicated the drink to Martin M. Lomasney, a leader of Boston's West End (which housed Ward Eight), who survived an assassination attempt. Others say the drink was a celebratory nod to JFK's grandfather's election as mayor of Boston. The important take-away is that this brick-orange cocktail is fairly easy to make with basic bar ingredients—and even easier to drink.

Serves 1

1½ ounce rye whiskey
¾ ounce fresh lemon juice
¾ ounce fresh orange juice
1 teaspoon grenadine
Soda water, if using Collins glass

Glassware: coupe or Collins

Add first four ingredients to a shaker, add ice, and shake. Strain into a chilled coupe or Collins glass. If using a Collins glass, add ice, and top with soda water.

W

WEDGE

(n.) A cocktail garnish, usually made from a small citrus fruit such as a lemon or lime. To make a citrus wedge, slice the fruit in half from top to bottom (through the stem end). Depending on the size of the fruit, slice each half again into halves, thirds, or quarters from top to bottom, for a total of four, six, or eight wedges. Slice off the pithy ends, remove any seeds, and make a slit in the flesh. If the wedges look too large for the serving glass, consider cutting them in half or thirds widthwise. To serve, perch the wedge on the rim of the glass by bisecting the flesh of the fruit at the slit. The drinker may squeeze the wedge into drink if they desire.

WELL

(n.) The area behind the bar that comprises the bartender's station, usually holding a cache of house liquor, ice, and glasses all within easy reach.

WELL DRINK

(n.) A cocktail made from house liquor, which is usually a cheaper and less prestigious label; the opposite of a call drink (an order in which the brand of alcohol is specified). The term takes its name from the bartender's station behind the bar, sometimes called the well, which holds the ingredients most frequently used for cocktail making.

WET

1. *(adj.)* A drink order, usually to refer to the amount of vermouth used in a contemporary Martini, usually at a ratio of one part vermouth to three parts gin.

2. *(adj.)* A description for a bounded geographic area in which it is legal to sell alcohol; the opposite of dry.

WHEAT BEER

(n.) A beer that is made with a good portion of wheat in addition to malted barley. Wheat doesn't add

much flavor, making these beers generally subtle in taste, but it does contribute to a higher level of carbonation and usually some level of haziness. This category encompasses a number of styles coming out of the Belgian and German brewing traditions, including hefeweizens, white (wit) beers, dunkelweizens, weisse beers, sours, and lambics.

WHEATER

(n.) A style of bourbon made with a high percentage of wheat in the grain bill, sometimes entirely replacing rye in the traditional mix of corn, barley, and rye. Wheat can bring a softer, sweeter profile to the spirit as it allows the character of the corn to dominate. Examples of this style are Maker's Mark, Weller, and Rebel Yell. Note that these are all still technically bourbon, not wheat whiskey, as they are made with more than 51 percent corn in the grain bill.

WHEEL

(n.) A cocktail garnish, usually made from medium-size citrus fruits, such as oranges. To make a wheel, slice the top and bottom off an orange until the flesh is just exposed. Then continue slicing narrow cross sections of the fruit in the same direction. Remove the seeds, and if the wheel is to be placed on the rim of glass, make one radial slice through the flesh to the center. Otherwise wheels may simply be floated on the surface of the cocktail.

WHISKEY

(n.) A large umbrella category covering spirits distilled from a fermented mash of grains. In the United States, all whiskeys must be distilled under 190 proof and bottled at more than 80 proof. The slate of acceptable grains includes corn, rye, wheat, sorghum, malted barley, and any combination thereof. The precise mix of grains and aging methods determines the subtype of the spirit, such as bourbon, rye, Scotch, malt

WHISKEY SMASH

THE layman's Mint Julep, the Whiskey Smash comes with all the flavor of its more famous relative but without the associated frippery (tin cups, Derby hats). A splash of lemon juice helps lift and brighten the flavors, making this potent number dangerously easy to toss back.

Serves 1

1 large mint sprig (8 leaves)
½ lemon, cut into 4 wedges
½ ounce simple syrup
   (1:1, sugar:water)
2 ounces bourbon or rye

Garnish: mint sprig

Glassware: rocks

In a rocks glass, muddle mint, lemon wedges, and simple syrup. Top with crushed ice and add bourbon. Swizzle to mix. Top with more ice. Garnish with a mint sprig.

WHISKEY SOUR

PERHAPS the most famous beverage in the sour family, this iconic drink—whiskey, lemon juice, sugar, and water stirred over ice—is the building block for many a cocktail, but it is also worth a look itself for its simplicity. Add an egg white and it becomes a Boston sour. The New York Sour or Continental sour variation popped up in the late 1800s, calling for red wine ("claret" in the parlance of the times) to be floated on the top of a finished Whiskey Sour.

Serves 1

2 ounces bourbon
¾ ounce lemon juice
¾ ounce simple syrup
   (1:1, sugar:water)
½ ounce or 1 small egg white

Glassware: cocktail, coupe, or rocks

Add all ingredients to a cocktail shaker and dry shake. Add ice to the shaker and shake well. Strain into a chilled cocktail or coupe glass or over ice into a rocks glass.

WHITE LADY

A **SMOOTHED-OUT** Gin Sour, the White Lady was made famous by two different Harrys. Its creator, Harry MacElhone of Harry's New York Bar in Paris, noted several different versions (including one with unsavory proportions of crème de menthe), but he settled on this pared-down mix of gin, Cointreau, and lemon juice with an optional egg white. Harry Craddock included it in his 1930 *Savoy Cocktail Book*, and to this day you can still order a White Lady at the Savoy Hotel's American Bar.

Serves 1

1½ ounces London dry gin
¾ ounce Cointreau
¾ ounce lemon juice
1 small egg white

Garnish: lemon peel

Glassware: cocktail or coupe

Add all ingredients to a cocktail shaker and shake without ice. Add ice and shake until chilled. Strain into a chilled cocktail or coupe glass. Garnish with a lemon peel.

Note: *This version of the White Lady calls for an egg white (for its foaming power), and because this is a rather dry cocktail, a dash of simple syrup will round out any edges for those that prefer a slightly less dry drink.*

whiskey, and the trio of place-named whiskeys (Irish, Tennessee, and Canadian). Grammarians take note: When made in the United States and Ireland, whiskey is spelled with an "ey," but when made in the United Kingdom and Canada, it is spelled only with a "y."

WHISKEY STONES

(n.) Soapstone rocks of various sizes that are chilled and then used in place of ice in a cocktail. They are most often used in whiskey-based cocktails or in straight whiskey because the stones will slightly chill the drink without diluting it.

WHITE WHISKEY

(n.) Also known as "white dog," or "white lightning," this clear, often harsh-tasting spirit is essentially unaged whiskey that hasn't seen any barrel time. Because it has not been infused with color of flavor from wooden barrels, the liquor often carries the flavor of the grains from which it was distilled. Selling white

whiskey is widely considered a financial coup for producers, as they don't have to invest in the expensive aging process.

WINE

(n.) An alcoholic beverage made from fermented grapes or, less traditionally, other fruits such as strawberries or pineapples. In the United States the term is generally understood to mean an alcoholic product made from fermented grape juice with an ABV of 7 to 14 percent. Wines with ABVs up to 24 percent are classified as "dessert wines" and taxed at a higher rate.

WINE COOLER

(n.) The term originally referred to a mixed drink made from wine, fruit juice, and, optionally, a carbonated beverage, making it similar to a spritzer. Commercially, however, the term now refers to a low-alcohol sweetened malt beverage. Bottled wine coolers, which became popular in the 1980s with brands such as Bartles & Jaymes,

switched their formulation in the early 1990s to avoid new taxes on wine, and they now use malt beverage as a base.

WINE KEY

(n.) Also known as a waiter's friend or sommelier's knife, this corkscrew consists of a lever, a handle, and a metal spiral corkscrew, all of which fold up as a pocketknife would. Professional wine servers tend to appreciate the tool because it can slip into one's pockets for easy carrying.

WINE LABEL TERMS

A wine label will often include the following information: a brand name, the grape variety (not required in France), the region in which the grapes were grown, the vintage, the alcohol content (in percent by volume with a 1.5 percent margin of error), the name and address of the producer or importer, the amount of liquid in the bottle (expressed in milliliters). If sulfites (either naturally occurring or added as a preservative) are present in the wine at more than ten parts per million, the producer is required to add "contains sulfites" to the label if it is to be sold out of state.

Labels also commonly include information about where the wine was bottled or produced and frequently use the following terms:

"Estate bottled" or "château bottled": The grapes came from vineyards owned or controlled by a long-term lease by the producer, and the wine was made and bottled on site at the winery.

"Cellared and bottled by": The brand or company on the bottle purchased finished or nearly finished wine from someone else and bottled it themselves.

"Produced (or made) and bottled by": At least 75 percent of the wine was made by the company or brand on the bottle.

"Imported by": A legal requirement for wines coming from outside

the United States to disclose the importer.

WINEGLASS

(n.) Wineglasses vary greatly, from decorative etched or colored goblets to models said to enhance the flavor of wines made from certain grape varieties. In general, however, the category can be broken into two primary groups: those for white wine and those for red. The bowls of glasses for white wine tend to be smaller and narrower than those for red. A good wineglass has enough room to swirl the wine, and the opening of the glass is narrower than the bowl in order to concentrate the aromas of the wine as it is drunk. Serious wineglasses come with a stem so that the warmth of one's hand does not alter the temperature of the wine when holding the glass, but stemless tumblers are gaining in popularity.

WORCESTERSHIRE SAUCE

(n.) A sweet, salty, and savory condiment, usually made from fermented anchovies, vinegar, and a number of spices. Commonly used to flavor meat or fish dishes, this condiment is also used in cocktails such as the Bloody Mary and Michelada.

WORT

(n.) A beer-making term that describes the sugary liquid strained from heating malted grains and water together. The wort will go on to be boiled with hops for flavoring, and then fermented with yeast to make beer.

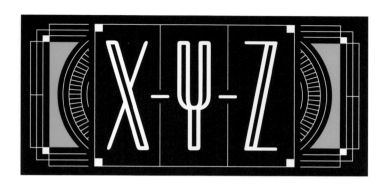

XANTHAN GUM

(n.): A derivative of a bacterium, xanthan gum is commonly used commercially as a thickener, and it can also be used to enhance and stabilize the foam in egg white cocktails.

YARD GLASS

(n.) A novelty beer glass that measures a yard and holds 1.4 liters of beer. It is long and narrow, usually with a bulb at the bottom, and is commonly used during drinking games in England. The shape has no effect on the taste of the beer.

ZYMURGY

(n.) The science of fermentation.

ZOMBIE

THE exact recipe for the Zombie, one of the 1930s-era rum-based creations of Don the Beachcomber, could have been lost for good, as the oft-credited founder of tiki was notoriously secretive about his drink formulas. As a result, many versions of this classic umbrella drink proliferated, most of them bad, but almost all potent enough to justify the brain-sucking reference in the title. Enter cocktail historian Jeff "Beachbum" Berry, who in 2005, after years spent doing archival research, uncovered what he believes to be the original recipe, a complex and balanced mix that includes no less than three types of rum and three types of fruit juice.

Serves 1

1½ ounces golden rum
1½ ounces aged Jamaican rum
1 ounce 151 rum
¾ ounce fresh lime juice
½ ounce fresh grapefruit juice
¼ ounce cinnamon syrup
½ ounce velvet falernum
1 teaspoon grenadine
1 dash absinthe
1 dash Angostura bitters
¾ cups crushed ice

Garnish: mint sprig

Glassware: zombie mug or large glass mug

Add all ingredients to a blender and blend until combined. Pour contents into a zombie mug or a large glass mug. Garnish with a sprig of spanked mint.

About the Author

Jennifer Fiedler is a contributing editor at *Wine Spectator* magazine and co-author of *Brooklyn Brew Shop's Beer Making Book*. Born and raised in Honolulu, Hawaii, she got her start in the food and wine world while working harvest at a winery in New Zealand. A graduate of Yale University and the French Culinary Institute, she has notched time in the fields on an organic farm in Virginia, in New York City kitchens as a personal chef and caterer, and behind the desk as a researcher and writer for books and magazines. She lives on the North Shore of Oahu.

Library of Congress Cataloging-in-Publication Data

Fiedler, Jennifer.
The essential bar book : an A-to-Z guide to spirits, cocktails, and wine, with 115 recipes for the world's great drinks / Jennifer Fiedler.
pages cm
1. Bartending—Handbooks, manuals, etc. 2. Cocktails—Dictionaries. I. Title.
TX951.F484 2014
641.87'4—dc23
2014011854

Hardcover ISBN: 9781607746539
eBook ISBN: 9781607746546

Printed in China

Design by Headcase Design
www.headcasedesign.com

10 9 8 7 6 5 4 3

First Edition

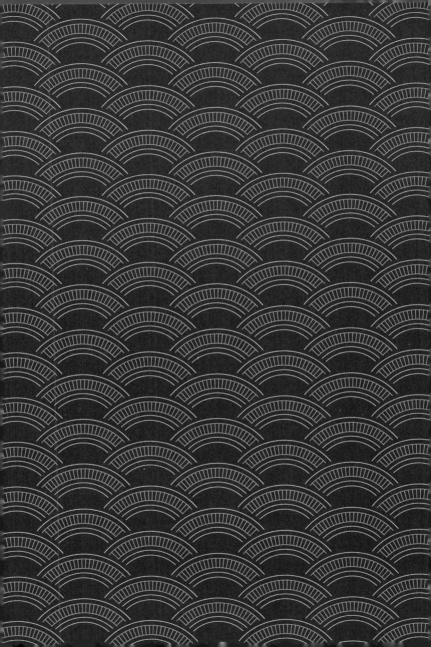